M.V. Rama Sarma
His Mind and Art

In the same series

Major Indian Novelists
K. Venkata Reddy

Studies in Indian Writing in English
P. Bayapa Reddy

Comparative Perspectives on Indian Literature
A. Ramakrishna Rao, ed.

Five Indian Novelists
V.V.N. Rajendra Prasad

Fiction of the Nineties
Veena Noble Dass and R.K. Dhawan, ed.

Recent Indian Fiction
R.S. Pathak, ed.

Style in Indian English Fiction
Z.N. Patil

M.V. Rama Sarma
His Mind and Art

Essays presented to Professor M.V. Rama Sarma,
Formerly Vice-Chancellor, S.V. University, Tirupati,
on his 75th Birthday, 6 September 1995

Edited by

K. Venkata Reddy

PRESTIGE

Published by
Prestige Books
New Delhi 110 008

1995

ISBN: 81-85218-37-4

Laser Typesetting by
Media Ventures
New Delhi 110 058

Printed at
Mehra Offset Press
New Delhi 110 002

Contents

Drama

Section C: 'Mellow Fruitfulness'
Rama Sarma, the Critic

Contributors

1. Professor John T. Shawcross, University of Kentucky, Lexington, USA.
2. Professor William B. Hunter, 9031 Kapri Lane, Houston, Texas, USA.
3. Professor Albert C. Labriola, Duqaesne University, Pittsburg, USA.
4. Professor Anniah Gowda, Director, Centre for Commonwealth and American Literature, Mysore.
5. Dr. M. Padma, R.D.O., Kovvur, A.P.
6. Professor Ronald G. Shafer, Indiana University of Pennsylvania, Indiana, USA.
7. Mrs. Daisy Gunaseeli, Methodist Girls Hr. Sec. School, Tiruchi.
8. Dr. Asoka Rani, S.P. Mahila University, Tirupati.
9. N. Ganesh, Hr. Sec. School, Madras.
10. Dr. Syed Mukharam, Jawahar Bharati, Kavali, A.P.
11. Dr. V.V.N. Rajendra Prasad, S.K. University, Anantapur.
12. Dr. H.G.S. Arulandram, Director, Curriculum Development Cell, Bharatidasan University, Tiruchi.
13. Deva Rajendra, Govt. Degree College, Puttur, A.P.
14. Dr. K. Santhanam, Jamal Mohamed College, Tiruchi.
15. Dr. P. Somnath, Govt. Junior College, Penukonda, A.P.
16. S. Hari Babu, Bishop Heber College, Tiruchi.
17. Professor G. Nageswara Rao, S.V. University, Tirpuati.
18. Mrs. A. Vijaya Rani, Avinisalingam College of Home Sc., Coimbatore.
19. Dr. Obula Reddy, S.K. University, Anantapur.
20. Dr. S.A. Khayyoom, S.K. University, Anantapur.
21. Dr. Basavaraj S. Naikar, Karnataka University, Dharwad.
22. Dr. M.S. Nagarajan, Formerly Professor of English, Madras Univ.
23. Professor K. Chellappan, Bharatidasan University, Tiruchi.
24. Professor C.R. Visweswara Rao, S.K. University, Anantapur.
25. Dr. M. Rama Devi, S.K. University, Anantapur.
26. Dr. P. Hannah Padma, S.K. University, Anantapur.

Editor: Professor K. Venkata Reddy, S.K. University, Anantapur.

(Names of the contributors figure as per articles appearing in the volume)

PREFACE

Although Professor M.V. Rama Sarma, who is well known as an erudite Milton scholar, has produced so far (i) six novels—*The Stream* (1956), *The Farewell Party* (1971), *Look Homeward* (1978), *The Bliss of Life* (1979), *Pastures New* (1985) and *Height of Noon* (1994)—dealing with a variety of themes and techniques, (ii) eleven plays, written over nearly four decades and brought out in a single volume, *Collected Plays* (1982), revealing as they do a tremendous influence of Shaw in exposition of social evils, and (iii) seven seminal works of criticism, five on Milton—*Paradise Lost: A Study* (1951), *The Heroic Argument* (1971), *The Eagle and the Phoenix* (1976), *Things Unattempted* (1982) and *Milton and the Prophetic Strain* (1991), one on Heywood, *Heywood: A Prose Shakespeare* (1962), and the other on Shakespeare, *Harmony Restored* (1991)—surprisingly enough, he has not received the critical attention he deserves. Barring a few articles published in journals by critics like G. Nageswara Rao and H.G.S. Arulandram there has been no full length study of his novels or plays or books of criticism, assessing him as a novelist, playwright and critic.

It is the fulfilment of this long-felt need that the present work addresses itself to. Conceived and executed as a festschrift volume of critical essays in honour of Professor Rama Sarma to mark the completion of 75 years of his purposeful life, the book reveals not only his creative fecundity but also his critical acumen. It is a modest attempt on the part of some persons associated with this task towards expressing their gratitude for what their academic lives owe to Professor Rama Sarma, while on the part of others it is a way of expressing their appreciation of a very distinguished career of academic, creative, and critical pursuit.

Divided into three distinct sections, the book aims at making an in-depth study of the creative and critical corpus of Professor Rama Sarma, besides giving a taste of the areas of profound interest to him. Section A, "Happy Boughs," seeks to present a critical analysis of some 'happy boughs' of the luxuriant tree of the seventeenth century English literature, an area that is dearest to Professor Rama Sarma. Significantly enough, some of these critical studies, fresh from eminent critics from the West, stem from the critical writings of Professor Rama Sarma himself.

Section B, "Ivy and Laurel," is devoted to a critical study of the creative writing of Professor Rama Sarma in which the predilections of a scholar in his search for authentic selfhood and quest for fulfilment are touched upon. It is shown how, stemming from the "inescapable Odyssey of the self," the novels reflect the rich fabric of Indian life, presenting the evolution of life from passion to liberation and its realization through the very act of living. The thematic concerns and the technical virtuosities of the novelist are driven home to the reader. The critical essays on the plays project the evolution of the playwright from the stage of protest to the maturity of enlightened acceptance while being alive to the social realism ingrained in the plays.

Section C, "Mellow Fruitfulness," is concerned with Rama Sarma as a critic. The six essays seek to establish him as a critic with a Johnsonian expansiveness of literary concern. It is revealed that his Milton criticism, spread over a period of four decades, is distinguished by his moralistic slant and, more importantly, the Indian sensibility he brings to bear on his study. His refreshing critical assessment of Shakespeare and Heywood is rightly shown as rooted in the Elizabethan world order and Jacobean dramatic traditions.

It is hoped that this first book on Professor Rama Sarma would serve the purpose of placing him in a proper perspective in the growth and development of Indian writing in English as well as Indian criticism in English, by assessing his strengths and limitations as a novelist, playwright, and critic. It is believed that the book, with all its limitations, would go a long way in establishing Rama Sarma as a major writer in Indian English literature and as a critic of considerable significance. From these critical essays one can profitably glean insights into some of the major trends in criticism through the ages. It is also expected that this maiden venture would be of considerable interest to both teachers and students of English studies in India. It can also serve as a source book for research scholars who like to make a deeper study of Professor Rama Sarma's novels, plays, and criticism.

It is now my pleasure and duty to thank all those who have been responsible for bringing out this festschrift as a Platinum Jubilee Tribute to Professor Rama Sarma. I am grateful to all distinguished scholars from India and abroad who have taken keen interest and spared no pains in contributing their articles. I am deeply indebted to Prestige Publishers, New Delhi, for their prompt and quick action in bringing out the book in a record time. I am thankful to my colleagues for their unstinted cooperation and help in this regard. Words fail me to express my deep sense of gratitude to Professor Rama Sarma himself for extending his full cooperation and guiding me at every stage with affectionate care in carrying the work through.

Sri Krishnadevaraya University **KV**
Anantapur 515 003

Platinum Jubilee Tribute to Professor M.V. Rama Sarma

K. VENKATA REDDY

Eminent Milton scholar and recipient of the honour of the Milton Society of America and a veteran teacher who pursued the exacting demands of the profession with a Miltonic sense of vocation, Professor M.V. Rama Sarma will be completing his 75th year on September 6, 1995. A "pilgrim resolute" who laboured diligently to exert sweet and wholesome influence on his students, Professor Rama Sarma made a deep and abiding impact on the course of English studies in India by both precept and practice. Furthermore, the Vice-Chancellorship of Sri Venkaṭeswara University, which he adorned with distinction and in "wreathed smiles," all through demonstrates how this man who thought but globally invested the position with an aura of disinterested pursuit of academic excellence.

Professor Rama Sarma is fondly remembered by his students for his scrupulous promptness, "slim-feasting smile," vast erudition and, above all, for his life-long fellowship with "unreproved pleasures." His accent has always been on enriching the mind of his students and tempering their lives with a sense of discipline and refined sensibility. The object, unstated and unobtrusively sought, is to let the student discover, as the protagonists of his fiction do, the "hidden soul of harmony."

The quest for this "bliss of life" led Professor Rama Sarma to recover values from literature, for he considered, like Leavis, that literature helps one reach after the picked experience of the ages. In a relentless quest for this, he advocated, when he was at the helm of affairs and when the language-literature debate arose, that the study of language divorced from literary content would be dry, sterile and counter-productive in terms of human values and their generation. He revealed his sagacity and wisdom in refusing to succumb to the ill-conceived but specious cogitations on the methodology of teaching English. Standing as a bulwark against the propagation and domination of this school of thought, Professor Rama Sarma carved out for himself a nichê in the history of the growth of English teaching in India.

Rama Sarma, the man, is no less important. Born into a cultured family with national outlook, he imbibed a patriotic spirit and catholicity of approach to persons and problems in life right from the beginning. His three-year stay in England and a five-year stint in Delhi University, before he came to Tirupati in 1954, must have helped him cultivate a broad-minded and large-hearted disposition that characterized his life throughout. A votary of the Renaissance humanism, he has abundant faith in man and his potentialities. He believes that man is the architect of his own destiny. With his firm conviction that life is worth living, with all its vicissitudes, he is out and out an affirmationist.

Professor Rama Sarma has so far produced six novels, ten plays and six books of Milton criticism. Now in his peaceful hermitage where old age does attain to something of a prophetic strain, Professor Rama Sarma has reached yet another milestone in his relentless academic journey by completing the writing of his book, *Milton and the Indian Epic Tradition*, which has been released recently.

Professor Rama Sarma, who refuses to retire from teaching and research, has been actively engaged in the literary field, since he laid down his office in 1984, delivering extension lectures at different universities and vigorously continuing his creative and critical work. It is, therefore, a moment of joy for all of us—his students and admirers—to join together and felicitate Professor Rama Sarma on the occasion of the completion of his 75th year by way of releasing his latest book, *Milton and the Indian Epic Tradition*, and bringing out a festschrift volume, *Rama Sarma: His Mind and Art* in his honour. Wide as Professor Rama Sarma's literary interests are, they would be adequately reflected in this volume. Several distinguished scholars from India and abroad have contributed articles on Shakespeare and Milton to this volume, the areas of interest of Professor Rama Sarma, apart from touching upon his creative writings.

Both in his creative and critical writings, Professor Rama Sarma touches upon the predilections of a scholar in his search for authentic selfhood and quest for fulfilment. The book devoted to these significant areas deals with Rama Sarma, the man, Rama Sarma, the novelist, Rama Sarma, the playwright and Rama Sarma, the critic. This volume presents a comprehensive picture of Professor Rama Sarma's contribution to Indian writing in English and to Milton studies.

Fruitful Region, Splendorous Vegetation: Some Remarks on *Rasa* and Sir William Jones, and the Influence of John Milton

JOHN T. SHAWCROSS

It would seem that only a few students of the life and works of John Milton have examined the varied interconnections that exist between them and India. While interconnections will not provide the overwhelming presence of classical literature and thought or his influential presence in German literature and American thought, there are significant points of tangency that do provide further awareness of his own broad reading and thinking and mythic sensitivity and of his impress on poets, thinkers, and political beings. Some of this has been sorted out over the years, of course, but one area only slightly touched has been the way in which Milton has emerged in the work and activities or Sir William Jones, who spent the last twelve years of his life in India as judge of the high court at Calcutta. In this essay I offer some remarks on this matter, but fuller study would yield even deeper connections between Milton and this "fruitful region noted for its splendorous vegetation."

My title and the preceding quotation come from an examination of "Milton and the Orient" by M.V. Rama Sarma, Chapter IX of his critical book on *The Heroic Argument: A Study of Milton's Heroic Poetry* (Madras: MacMillan, 1971). Detailed are Milton's employment in his works, particularly *Paradise Lost,* of images — both geographic and aesthetic — legends and history, and concepts drawn from India and its literature and its lore. And importantly we recognize that *The Mahabharata* and *Paradise Lost* have affinities in thematic content and in concepts of heroism, idealism and faith in God, which make them one in essence. An overview drawn from this chapter will also be found, written by Dr. Rama Sarma, in *A Milton Encyclopedia,* gen. ed. William B. Hunter (Lewisburg: Bucknell University Press, 1978), II; 185-90, under the entry "East, Milton and the." Further extensive discussions of these "Epics of Righteousness and Justice" (dharma) appear as Chapter 9 of *Things Unattempted: A Study of Milton* (Vikas, 1982) and as Chapter 9 "Revelation as Epic Narrative" of *Milton and the*

Prophetic Strain (Sterling, 1991). It is clear that Milton knew much about India and that his view of the paradisal harmonized with both its concepts and its typography. It will, thus, not seem unusual that Sir William Jones, a rather intense student of Milton's works, saw the same kind of paradisal harmony and reflected it in his translations of works like *Sakuntala* and in his own Miltonic poetry.

Yet another aspect of Milton's relationship with India lies in translation of his major poems into Urdu. The popular and faithful translations of *Paradise Lost* as *Firdaus Gumshudah* (Lucknow, 1914), of *Paradise Regained* as *Firdaus Baziyaftah* (Lucknow, 1921) and *Samson Agonistes* as *Shansum Mahzun* (Lucknow, 1927) by Isa Charan Sada (1870-1957) have enabled many in the twentieth century to read Milton, and, one trusts, to recognize the affinities which his writing has with India. Sada's life and work are lovingly examined in *Magnificient Quest. Isa Charan Sada: Urdu Poet and Milton Scholar* (Delhi: I.S.P.C.K., 1986) by his grand-daughter, herself a Milton scholar of note, Dr. Shahla Anand. Dr Anand cites Mohammad Abdulhalim Sharar, "Mr. Sada has contrived to make the *Masnavi's* 'turns of speech and incidents' available to Urdu-knowing individuals; a courageous enterprise. He is to be congratulated on this excellent cultural achievement," and adds that the poet-scholar followed "all the conventions of Urdu poetry, even to the use of couplets (hemistichs with their internal rhyme) instead of the Milton blank verse. . . . [But] he maintained the *Wazan* or rhythm and metre necessary in Urdu poetry, yet is close to Milton in expressions." (309)[1]

In the late eighteenth and early nineteenth centuries in England reverse translation was occurring as Indic literature found its way into English. Charles Wilkins published *The Bhagvat-geeta, or Dialogues of Kreeshna and Arjoon; in Eighteen Lectures; with Notes* (London: Printed for C. Nourse) in 1785, for example, and he reasonably suggests that the source of the discovery of gunpowder sequence in the War in Heaven in *Paradise Lost* (VI, 469-534) was the story in the "Bhagavad-gita" of searching the ocean for the fourteen mystic jewels.[2] Of him Jones's biographer writes that Wilkins was "the first Englishman who acquired a critical knowledge of the language of the Brahmins, and who by the application of rare talents and industry, by his own personal exertions, invented and cast types of the Debnagree, Persic, and Bengalese characters, in such perfection, that no succeeding attempts have exhibited any improvement upon his labours."[3]

Jones, for further examples, produced a prose extract of the "Bhushanda Ramayan," among his many writings, as well as extracts from the Vedas.[4] Even prior to his move to India in 1783, Jones was deeply interested in the land and its people. In a letter dated April 1772 to Robert Orme (1728-1801), author of the often-reprinted *A History of the Military Transactions of the British Nation in Indostan, from the Year MDCCXLV. To which is prefixed, a Dissertation on the Establishment made by Mahomedan Conquerors in Indostan* (London, 1763-78, two volumes with maps), Jones wrote: "It is impossible for me to describe the delight and admiration I have felt, from the perusal of your History of the War in India. The plans, circumstances, and events of it, are so clearly described by you, that I felt an interest in them rather as an actor than a reader. . . . [N]or was I less delighted with the elegance of your topographical descriptions, that of the Ganges particularly pleased me; it is absolutely a picture. [And in regard to the forthcoming second volume] Indeed it is not just, that the Coromandel coast only should receive the ornament of your pen, to the neglect of Bengal, which an Indian monarch pronounced *the delight of the world.*" (*Works*, I, 184-86) His own work also engages knowledge of India before he left England as "The Palace of Fortune, An Indian Tale" (1769) and *Poeseos Asiaticae Commentariorum Libri Sex* (1774) attest. The later critical study, which was begun in 1766 and finished in 1769, also includes analyses of Persian, Turkish, and other Asian literature, and was praised by Oriental scholars in Europe as the first on Eastern literature to be both elegant and erudite.

To be remarked also are the issues of *The Indian Observer* which Hugh Boyd edited in Calcutta in 1793-94 and which reflect not only Boyd's enthusiasms for Milton but the receptivity of Milton by an audience in India. No. 14, 10 December 1973, for instance, adapts *PL*, IX, 1058-59, to make an observation that greatest adornment exists in unadornment; No. 15, 17 December 1793, alludes to Milton; No. 20, 21 January 1794, comments on music, poetry and sacred song, and quotes from "L'Allegro" and *Paradise Lost;* No. 21, 28 January 1794, employs *PL*, II, 556, as epigraph and there are further references to Milton; No. 25, 25 February 1794, which discusses marriage and divorce, and Milton's ideas thereon, has as its epigraph *PL*, IV, 750-57, and later cites IV, 758-64; No. 29, 25 March 1794, and No. 39, 3 June 1794, both make allusions to Milton and the epic; and No. 34, 29 April 1794, presents a poem in blank verse (with *Paradise Regained* in the background) while being influenced by "Il Penseroso."[5] Thomas Maurice was another Englishman involved in study of India. His *Indian Antiquities: or, Dissertations* (London: Printed for the Author, and sold by W. Richardson) is in three parts in four volumes, published in 1793 and 1794. In Volume II appear quotations of *PL*, IV, 219-20 (p. 181*), and IV, 33-34 (pp. 195-96), speaking of the sun; in Volume III, *PL*, IX, 1099-1110 (p. 496); and in Volume IV, *PL*, II, 600-1 (p. 650). These all evoke the "fruitful region" and "splendorous vegetation" of Milton's poem, but also, appropriately, of India. The quotation in Volume III, it will be remembered, specifically relates Eden and India:

> So counsel'd hee, and both together went Into the thickest Wood, there soon hey chose The Figtree, not that kind for Fruit renown'd, But such as at this day to *Indians* known In *Malabar* or *Decan* spreds her Armes Braunching so broad and long, that in the ground The bended Twigs take root, and Daughters grow About the Mother Tree, a Pillard shade High overarch't, and echoing Walks between; There oft the *Indian* Herdsman shunning heat Shelters in cool, and tends his pasturing Herds At Loopholles cut through thickest shade.

Jones was sought out by Edmund Burke in June 1781, we learn from a letter of that date, for opinion and advice on the conduct of the Bengal Bill, for "The natives of the East, to whose literature you have done so much justice, are particularly under your protection for their rights."[6] Two years later Jones sailed to his post in Calcutta; he held the Puisne Judgeship in Bengal Supreme Court of Judicature until his death on 27 April 1794. He founded the Asiatic Society of Bengal in 1784 and worked on a digest of Indian contract and succession laws from 1786 on, which he had hoped to compete in 1795 or 96. His studies in India, aside from his translations and own poetic endeavours, examined botany, geography, religion and most significantly Sanskrit and Persian. There is a monument erected to his memory in the anti-chamber of the Chapel of Uni versity College, Oxford (his alma meter), through subscription by those residing in Bengal who had received their education at Oxford or at Cambridge, the inscription having been executed by Thomas Flaxman. The Duchess of Devonshire in 1795 wrote an ode "On the Death of Sir William Jone," the third stanza of which reads:

> Admir'd and valued in a distant land,
> His gentle manners all affection won;
> The prostrate Hindu own'd his fostering hand,
> And science mark'd him for her fav'rite son.

The pervasiveness of Milton's poetry and life upon Sir William Jones is obvious from his personal letters that have survived.[7] The only citations to such material in studies of Milton, it seems, although some mention is made by writers on Jones, is John Good's quotation from a letter to Lady Spencer, dated 7 September 1769, and his summary of Charles D. Cleveland's comments in *Compendium of English Literature*.[8] Good may have been directed to the letter to Lady Spencer by two notes that appear in the *Monthly Review* 45 (1804): 338-39 and the *Edinburgh Review* 5 (1805): 329-46, both reviews of Lord Teignmouth's 1804 edition of *Memoirs* (mentioned here in n3). In his letter (*Works*, I, 119; *Letters*, I, 37-39) Jones makes much of Milton's stay at Forest Hill in Ox ford. In reality it seems to have been shortlived, and apparently made to collect a debt for his father from Richard Powell, but from which he returned to London married to the young daughter Mary Powell. Here, according to Jones, "in all probability, he composed several of his earliest productions," connecting it with (and quoting from) "L'Allegro" and noting that "the groves near this village are famous for nightingales, which are so elegantly described in the Penseroso." He tells us, "I am informed that several papers in Milton's own hand, were found by the gentleman who was last in possession of the estate. The tradition of his having lived there is current among the villagers." We recognize that Jones wanted to believe all of this convenient memory of "Milton, the most perfect scholar, as well as the sublimest poet, that our country ever produced." The reviewers of the *Memoirs* also wanted to believe, and Good exhibits the same kind of romantic adulation, wrong though the biographical imaginings are, except that Milton did go to Forest Hill.[9]

A similar kind of speculation based on partial truth, often appearing and reappearing in popular pieces of literature during the eighteenth century, is reviewed in a letter to Viscount Althorp, dated 14 April 1775. Jones, visiting Shrewsbury and Ludlow Castle of the Lords Presidents of Marches, recalls that "in this very castle . . . Milton, in his youth, was upon a visit to Lord Bridgewater, when he wrote his beautiful poem of Comus, on the accident of the young lady and her two brothers losing themselves in the wood. The mask was acted in the castle by the young people of the family, and must have been a glorious time when Milton and Henry Lawes, the best poet and musician of their age, were entertained in the same house, while the one composed such exquisite strains and the other set them to musick." There is, of course, no proof that Milton went to Ludlow, and certainly the implications that the text and the music were written rather quickly during the alleged sojourn are far-fetched. Perhaps most significant for us today, however, is that the poem was being read at this time quite literally, as built upon an actual occurrence, without any suggestion of its allegorical or tropological nature. Another attitude expressed by numerous literary figures in the last part of the century is the negative reaction to Samuel Johnson's "Life of Milton," published in *Prefaces to the Works of the English Poets* in 1779. In a letter to Viscount Althorp of 6 December 1779 Jones shows some restraint when he writes, "Johnson and I are very cool to one another. Can I be *cordial* with the libeller of Milton, whom of all men I most admire? He is displeased with me for not praising his lives. Believe me, I cannot praise him; nor do I wish to have the good word of a man, who abuses all the friends of Liberty, because they are so: his abuse on that ground is true praise, and his praise is defamation." The comment of Edmund Burke concerning the Indian people cited before makes clear that Jones would abhor Johnson's politics and social prejudices.

Milton, perhaps even more than Shakespeare, supplied quotations for writers during the period, quotations given exactly as the author recalled them in relation to an idea or an emotion, or revised deliberately to fit a context, or just as a remembered phrase (perhaps even subconsciously).

Jones's letters are replete with such quotations from various works, although *PL* and Sonnet 22 seem to dominate. In his letter to Samuel Parr of 29 November 1781 Jones enclosed a Pindaric ode which he wrote on Lord Althorp's marriage; it brings to mind for him "The translation of the Ode to Phrrha . . . merely a whimsical contest with Milton," and he later in this same letter gives his own translation followed by Milton's "for the sake of comparison." And Milton's poetic influence is acknowledged in a letter written from Calcutta, 13 April 1784, to an unknown recipient: "I enclose however a hymn to the Indian cupid, which is here said to be the only correct specimen of Hindu mythology that has appeared; it is certainly new and quite original, except the form of the stanza, which is Milton's." This was, of course, "A Hymn to Camdeo," with its discussion of the Hindu God and the mythology surrounding him; the stanza is that of Milton's "Song: On *May* Morning," and its language and images ("Vales and groves," "dresses," "Brighter . . . morning," etc.) reflect that poem as well. Jones's immersion in Indian lore and geography is clear from lines such as

> Strong Chumpa, rich in od'rous gold
> Warm Amer, nurs'd in heavenly mould
> Dry Nagkeser in silver smiling,
> Hot Kiticum our sense beguiling,
> And last, to kindle fierce the scorching flame,
> Loveshaft, which gods bright Bela name.
>
> Can men resist thy pow'r, when Krishen yields,
> Krishen, who sill in Matras hold fields
> Tunes harps immortal, and to strains divine
> Dances by moonlight with the Gopis nine?

This fusion of English and Indian worlds and its expression in Miltonic measures characterize Jones's poetry and his translations from Eastern literature.

The letters that Jones wrote after his arrival in India frequently discuss the land, the "divine" Ganges, "Bengal the paradise or regions," for example, his letter to the second Earl Spencer, begun on 4 August 1787 and continued for many more days until ended on 30 August, written from Crishna-nagar. On 12 August he reported, "I am reading, (and, as I read, I always translate" a noble Sanscrit work on Hindu Law, which is believed to have been written by Manu, the first created Man, and to be many millions of years old. . . . I had made a *Sanscrit* stanza, signifying that 'as I *thirsted* for all kinds of knowledge, which was sweet as nectar.' This verse has given me a place among the Hindu poets: the Raja copied it; his son got it by heart & his Brahmans entered it among their records; but one of the Brahmans objected to the word *thirsty* in the 2nd line, and said it was applicable to *water literally*, but *not literally* to *learning*. My *Pandit*, who has just told me the story, urged that I, as a poet & consequently inspired, could not err, & he produced an authority to prove, that my word *trishna* means not only *thirst*, but any *ardent desire*. The Raja, & his Brahmans acquiesced, and they call me a Hindu of the *Military* tribe, which is next in rank to the Brahmanical. "This country," he says, writing to Samuel Devis on 2 March 1786 from Jaferabad, "is delightful, and, in parts, mountainous and sublime enough to be worthy of your pencil. The proper name of the district is *Chatigram*, and I cannot help deriving it from the *Chatig*, a bird which is said to haunt these woods, and is famed in the Indian poetry." "The province of Chatigan (vulgarly Chitigong)," he tells Patrick Russell on 28 September 1786, "is a noble field for a naturalist." It is so called, I believe, from the *Chatag*, which is the most beautiful little bird I ever saw. The hills and woods about with uncommon plants and animals; indeed the whole Eastern peninsula would be a new world to a philosopher." In all, we see in Sir William Jones a knowledgeable observer of India, a student of its culture and conduit of its literary heritage, and a lover of Milton's works. These combine in his poetry and translations, as we have said, and to those works we can now give some attention.

The only examination of the relationship between Milton's work and Jones's poems is "'Harmonious Jones' and Milton's Invocations" by Ann Gossman, in *Notes & Queries* N.S. 1 (1954): 527-29 [O.S. 199], and Raymond Dexter Havens cites a few works in his *Influence of Milton on English Poetry* (Cambridge: Harvard University Press, 1922; rpt., New York: Russell & Russell, 1961) *The Heroic Argument* "Britain Discovered, an Heroic Poem in Twelve Books" (1770) is included under poems influenced by *Paradise Lost* (see p. 651); "The Muse Recalled, an Ode" (1781), under poems influenced by the octosyllabics (see p. 675); and a Petrarchan sonnet (c. 1777?), under Sonnets. The latter poem is addressed to George Hardinge and was printed in *Works*, II, 78. "Caissa, or the Game at Chess" is also noted as a "Rimed Technical Treatise," and a few additional remarks concern the abortive heroic poem and its prosody. Professor Gossman is not very commendatory towards Jones's work, but she does parallel many phrases and images shared by the poets, showing us that "Many of the landscapes of Jones's poems—Agra's flowery plains, lofty Mandar, bless'd Cailasa, Tibet's musky shades, and the rest—are also decked with borrowings from Milton." (527) Echoes and appropriation are cited for such poems as "The Seven Fountains," "A Hymn to Sereswaty," "The Hymn to Bhavani," "The Palace of Fortune," "A Hymn to Indra," "A Hymn to Lacshmi," "A Hymn to Camdeo," and most notably "A Hymn to Narayana." It is interesting that "Solima, an Arabian Eclogue" is not singled out by either Havens or Gossman although it has echoes from "L'Allegro," "Il Penseroso," "Comus," "Lycidas," and *Paradise Lost*.[10] The proposed heroic poem that has been remarked seems to have been envisioned as "The Idea of an Epic Poem, at Spa, July 1770, anno aetat. 23"; "Britain Discovered: a Poem. In Twelve Books" refers in "The Design" to Milton and his youthful thought of writing a poem with Arthur as hero (both in "Mansus" and "Epitaphium Damonis") and to the figure "machinery." The few fragmentary parts that are extant make reference to Asian places and Eastern images. "The Palace of Fortune, An Indian Tale," written in 1769, shows much less knowledge of things Indian, though in Miltonic style throughout, than "The Enchanted Fruit; or, The Hindu Wife," which was written in the Province of Bihar and is replete with Hindu story, characters, religious ideas, and images, even though they seem rather superficially employed. The poem is in octosyllabics but records language and pictures that come from *Paradise Lost.* Fusion of the Indian and British worlds is seen in "Plassey-Plain, A Ballad, Addressed to Lady Jones, by her Husband, Aug. 3, 1784," since it works on Indian themes to celebrate Lord Clive's victory over Serajuddou la, Subahdar of Bengal.

Many of the poems (translation, largely, or loose renditions) after Jones came to live in India unite his two studies of India and Milton. One example, among many, lies in "A Hymn to Surya," the Sun god with numerous names or epithets in the Sanskrit language, as he notes. In unpatterned rhyme and various metric feet (not unlike Milton's prosodic experiment in "Lycidas," the hymn begins: "Fountain of living light, / That o'erall nature streams"; suggests the "Nativitiy Ode" in lines like "Ere long he shall emblaze th'bounded sky: / The fiends of darkness yelling fly; / While birds of liveliest note and lightest wing / The rising day-star sing, / Who skirts th'horizon with a blazing line"; reveals in the world of *Paradise Lost:*

> Yes, though the Sanscrit song
> Be strown with fancy's wreaths,
> And emblems rich, beyond low thoughts refin'd,
> Yet heav'nly truth it breathes
> With attestation strong, —
> That, loftier than thy sphere, the Eternal Mind,
> Unmov'd unrival'd undefil'd,
> Reigns with providence benign:
> He still's the rude abyss, and bade it shine.

And as Jones's headnote to this poem tells the reader, "the following description of the demon Rahu, decapitated by Narayan, [should] be compared with similar passages in Hesiod and Milton."

The importance of John Milton to Sir William Jones can be seen in various other ways than we have mentioned. His calling card with his printed name, for instance, set forth a basic religious principle in its two-line quotation of *Paradise Lost*, XII, 133-34: "Not wand'ring poor, but trusting all his wealth / With God, who call'd him to a land unknown." In *Introduction to the History of the Life of Nader Shah,* Part I, "A Description of Asia," the epigraph is *Paradise Regain'd*, III, 314-21; in Part II, "A Short History of Persia," the epigraph is drawn from *Paradise Regain'd*, III, 269-302, with its geographic catalogue. In this same work Jones remarks that Milton pronounced the word "*Basra* very improperly, and makes also a considerable mistake, in putting into the mouth of *the Tempter* the name of a city, which *was not built till six hundred years after the temptation*." (*Works*, XII, 365-66) The name of this port (now in Iraq) is variously given as Basrah, Busra, Busrah, and is called Basorah in the *Arabian Nights' Entertainments;* the form Balsara, if indeed it was Milton's spelling and represented his pronunciation, is not that unusual. Jones has not read very precisely, of course, for it is the narrative voice that instances Balsara as denoting the southern limit of the view available from the mountain to which Satan has brought the Son. And in the Preface to *The Life of Nader Shah* (XII, 331) he anticipates many twentieth-century critics who have found the military action of Book VI of Milton's epic that of tin-soldiers: for Jones the "impertinence of his jokes in his battle of the angels" is inexcusable.

Sir William Jones, while not a particularly noteworthy poet, exhibiting rather the ordinary poetic of the lesser eighteenth century "Miltonic" poet, is worthy of being known by Miltonists and by those interested in Indian literature. His language studies, his renditions of items like "Gitagovinda, or the Song of Jayadeva" and the "Hitopadesa" of Vishnusarman, his understanding of Indian geography and vegetation which emerges in "A Hymn to Lacshmi" (Sri, the goddess of the power of nature) and the religious underpinnings that the mythology surrounding her have epitomized for the people—all embolden that statement. We see these things coming together in the latter poem, devoted to the "fruitful region, splendorous vegetation," and acknowledge the pervasive presence of John Milton, yet once again:

A Brahman young, who, when the heav'nly boy
In Vraja green and scented Gocul play'd,
Partook each transient care, each flitting joy,
And hand in hand through dale or thicket stray'd,
By fortune sever'd from the blissful seat,
Had sought a lone retreat.

NOTES

1. Biographical connection also exists, largely one suspects, as a result of the international affairs of the government of England in the eighteenth century with the Indian states. William R. Parker has told us what little has been discovered about Milton's daughter Deborah Clarke's children, one of whom Caleb, was living in Madras, at Fort St. George, in 1702 and later, with his wife Mary and children Abraham, Mary, and Isaac. He dies in 1719 and there is no

contact known between the English Clarkes and those in India after 1738. See *Milton: A Biography* (Oxford: Clarendon Press, 1968), I, 652-55; records from the parish of St. George's Cathedral, Madras are cited by Parker, II, 1163-64.

2. See p. 145, note.
3. *The Works of Sir William Jones. With the Life of the Author, by Lord Teignmouth. In Thirteen Volumes* (London: Printed for John Stockdale; and John Walker, 1807), II, 25. The "Life" was first published by John Shore, First Baron Teignmouth in 1804. It should also be noted that Wilkins produced a catalogue, dated 28 June 1798, of works from the Eastern world, including fifty-nine items from Hindic literatures. There is also *A Catalogue of Sanscrit, and other Oriental Manuscripts, Presented to the Royal Society by Sir William and Lady Jones,* with a letter of transmittal dated 29 January 1792; see *Works,* XIII, 399 ff.
4. These are published in *Works,* XIII.
5. The periodical is reprinted as *The Indian Observer. By the Late Hugh Boyd, Esq. With the Life of the Author, and Some Miscellaneous Poems, by Lawrence Dundas Campbell* (London: Printed by T. Burton, For T. Cadell, Jun. and W. Davis, 1798). See pp. 133, 138, 164- 70, 171, 174, 199, 200-02, 205, 222, 255-56, 284. "A Monody on the Death of Hugh Boyd," by Campbell, has *PL,* XI, 61-63, as epigraph.
6. *Works,* I, 360.
7. A listing of letters in which Milton figures is given here as an appendix. The texts will be found in *The Letters of Sir William Jones,* ed. Garland Cannon (Oxford: Clarendon Press, 1970), 2 vols.
8. John Walter Good, *Studies in the Milton Tradition* (Urbana: University of Illinois, 1915), pp. 210-11. This study was first published as Volume I, Nos. 3 and 4, in the University of Illinois Studies in Language and Literature, and was reprinted by Johnson Reprint Corporation in 1967. Cleveland, who published an 1867 concordance to the English poetry and a critical edition of the poetical works in 1853 (reissued 1865?), has not been cited otherwise in Milton bibliography. *Compendium of English Literature* was first published in 1847, followed by numerous further editions. Good cites the 1869 reprint, pp. 698-700. He also quotes from Thomas Campbell's *Specimen of the British Poets* (London, 1819), VII, 205, on Milton's importance for Jones's educational theories. *Specimens of the British Poets. A New Edition* (London: John Murray, 1844) has an additional title page dated 1841. In this edition (the life and two poems being given on pp. 633-38) Campbell writes of Jones (p. 634): "He pursued in theory, and even exceeded in practice the plan of education projected by Milton; and boasted, that with the fortune of a peasant, he could give himself the education of a prince." Campbell is reflecting remarks in letters to the first Earl Spencer, 22 October 1770 and 1 November 1770.

   Harris F. Fletcher in *Contributions to a Milton Bibliography 1800-1930 Being a List of Addenda to Steven's Reference Guide to Milton* (Urbana: University of Illinois Press, 1931), p. 34, cites Campbell's inclusion of Milton (pp. 257-65) in the edition of 1844, but not for such remarks as those about Jones. Parker (II, 950) makes reference to Campbell in discussing Milton's residences during 1649-52, because "Peter Cunningham" in *London* (London, 1927), p. 203, says that Milton lived at 10 Duke Street, St. James's on the basis of Campbell's statement, although this is in error. Uncharacteristically Parker does not otherwise identify Campbell or his work, but this is symptomatic of errors in his remarks. Fletcher (p. 120) lists Cunningham's book, correctly assigned to George H[amilton] Cunningham, *London, Being a Comprehensive Survey of the History* (London: J.M. Dent, 1927). [Fletcher does not give the subtitle.] Peter Cunningham had published *London As it is* (London: J. Murray), with no date but it is mid-nineteenth century. Henry B. Wheatley published *London Past and Present: Its History, Associations, and Traditions. Based upon the Handbook of London by the Late Peter Cunningham* (London: John Murray, 1891). Incidentally Wheatley makes mention of Jones's statue (I, 48), his wife's death (I, 80), and his having had chambers in Lamb's Buildings, Temple (II, 354), but not of Milton.

9. Another letter of the same date to Viscount Althorp also mentions his "account of Milton's House" in Oxford.
10. The poem (written in 1768) was published in the first collection of *Poems Consisting Chiefly of Translations from the Asiatick Languages* (Oxford: Clarendon Press, 1772), pp. 1-7. We might compare "Ye maids of Aden! hear a lofties tale / Than e'er was sung in meadow, bor'r or dale" (1-2) with "I will tell you now / What never yet was heard in tale or song / From old or modern Bard in hall, or bow'r" ("Comus," 43-45); "And bade all Eden spring before our eyes" (34) with "And bring all Heav'n before mine eyes" ("Il Penseroso, 166); "While fresh-blown violets drink the pearly dew" (88) with "And fresh-blown Roses washt in dew") ("L'Allegro," 22) "Now hastes the swain to tune his rapturous tales / In other meadows, and in other vales" (103-4) with "At last he rose and twitcht his mantle blew: / Tomorrow to fresh woods and pastures new." ("Lycidas," 192-93)

APPENDIX

List of Letters with References to Milton

To Viscount Althorp, 7 September 1769, I, 36-37
To Lady Spencer, 7 September 1769, I, 37-39
To the first Earl Spencer, 22 October, 1770, I, 70-73
To the first Earl Spencer, 1 November 1770, I, 73-75
To Samuel Parr, 22 March [1773], I, 123-25
To Viscount Althorp, 1 January 1774, I, 138-40
To John Alleyne, 13 March 1774, I, 146-49
To Viscount Althorp, 14 April 1775, I, 185-92
To Viscount Althorp, 20 September 1775, I, 196-205
To Viscount Althorp, 12 January 1776, I, 209-12
To Viscount Althorp, 28-29 December 1777, I, 251-55
To Viscount Althorp, 19 October 1779, I, 324-27
To Viscount Althorp, 6 December 1779, I, 335
To Lady Spencer, 18 May 1780, I, 347-48
To Samuel Parr, 20 May 1780, I, 382-83

To Lady Spencer, 24 May 1780, I, 383-85
To Francis Milman, 30 May 1780, I, 394-95
To Lady Spencer, 9 June 1780, I, 404-07
To Lady Spencer, 9 June 1780, I, 413
To Samuel Parr, 21 July 1780, I, 422-24
To Viscount Althorp, 28 September 1781, II, 497-501
To Samuel Parr, 19 November 1781, II, 505-07
To an unknown recipient, 13 April 1784, II, 641-42
To Sir John MacPherson, 22 May 1785, II, 673-74
To the Second East Spencer, 4-30 August 1787, II, 742-61
To the Second East Spencer, 22 October 1787 - 2 March 1788, II, 792-94
To the Second East Spencer, 25 September - 24 November 1793, II, 920-25
Professor John T Shawcross, Professor of English, University of Kentucky, Lexington, U.S.A.

The Incest Motif in *Hamlet*

WILLIAM B. HUNTER

In the fine discussion of *Hamlet* included in his recent group of studies in Shakespeare, *Harmony Restored,* M.V. Rama Sarma raises a question that I have not come across before in criticism of this most discussed work of English literature. He asks why the Ghost directs his son "to murder Claudius but leave his mother alone to her own guilt. Her incestuous relationship with her brother-in-law is the first rude shock of Hamlet."[1] That is, Hamlet first learns from his father that his mother's recent marriage to her brother-in-law Claudius is incestuous. Most modern readers and viewers of the play would reject this idea as biologically preposterous in any case: there is clearly no blood relationship between such-in-laws and so incest is impossible. But as Rama Sarma asks, why "leave her to heaven" rather than include her in the plans for vengeance?

Both Hamlets accept the designation of incest; the younger in his first soliloquy mourns his mother's having posted "With such dexterity to incestuous sheets." (I, ii, 157)[2] Note that he has not yet seen the ghost of his father but already is quite well aware of the charge of incest. The father will then repeat it but lay the blame on Claudius, "that incestuous, that adulterate beast" (I, v, 42) and call the royal bed "a couch for luxury and damned incest." (line 83) Later, he hesitates to kill the King at prayer but wants instead to catch him in "th'incestuous pleasure" of his bed. (III, iii, 90) Shakespeare evidently judged that no evidence was necessary to support so serious a judgment as incest and assumed that it would be immediately evident to his audience, strange though it seems today. Indeed, Claudius himself brings the topic to attention in his first speech when he alludes to "our sometime sister, now our queen." (I, ii, 8) Let us look again at the evidence, which has been recognized for some time

One need go no further than Old Testament law. Leviticus flatly asserts, "Thou shalt not uncover the nakedness of thy brother's wife: it is thy brother's nakedness" and again, "If a man shall take his brother's wife it is an unclean thing: he hath uncovered his brother's nakedness: they shall be childless." (xviii, 16; xx, 21) The context of both of these verses is a list of various incestuous acts.

Clearly Claudius and Gertrude are guilty of having violated this law, and the judgment brought against them by both Hamlets is fully justified. At the same time, however, another Old Testament law would seem to provide them with a loophole through the so-called levirate marriage. "If brethren dwell together," directs Deuteronomy xxv, 5, "and one of them die, and have no child, the wife of the dead shall not marry without unto a stranger: her husband's brother shall go in unto her, and take her to him to wife, and perform the duty of a husband's brother unto her" — the purpose being, as the next verse explains, to keep alive the name of the deceased. We must recognize, however, that the excuse offered in Deuteronomy cannot apply to the Hamlets: the son is a living testimony to the family name. The Claudius-Gertrude union must stand as condemned by the law of Leviticus.

Would an Elizabethan audience have viewed these laws as the musty old curiosities that they are for us? By no means, for the very legal standing of the Queen rested upon the political and religious applications of these principles to her parents, Henry VIII and Anne Boleyn. He was assumed to have been married for many years to Catherine of Aragon. The marriage had produced several children of whom only one, Mary, lived to maturity. When Anne came to Henry's attention he wanted to beget a son on her. Because of the succession there would have to be a legitimate marriage. But Catherine stood in the way.

Accordingly scholarly supporters of Henry discovered in the verses of Leviticus authority for declaring that his marriage to Catherine violated this law and so was null and void. For she had been married to Henry's older brother Arthur in 1501, but he had died in a few months — the marriage unconsummated according to his widow. As a practical matter of state, Henry then married her in 1505 when he became 15. The Pope issued a special dispensation permitting this union with his sister-in-law. All this had to be undone with enormous effort to effect the divorce in 1533 that would legalize by marriage the child of then-pregnant Anne. With this act the English Reformation was under way—and the legitimacy of the new baby Elizabeth derived directly from the authority of Leviticus.[3]

We may thus conclude that Elizabethans certainly knew and (unless they were Recusants) accepted the law forbidding such a marriage as Claudius and Gertrude had contracted because the legitimacy of their Queen rested on it. It was also part of the current canon law defining the forbidden degrees of marriage (which remained effective in some jurisdictions into our own century). An audience of the play then would certainly bring to the performance an immediately hostile judgment of the royal couple that no modern audience can experience. A minor problem is that Gertrude does not seem to be aware of any guilt in this respect: she sees her marriage in a negative sense only as "o'er hasty." (II, ii, 57) As Rama Sarma has first pointed out, the elder Hamlet directs that his son's vengeance not be visited upon her too.

It seems that the guilt must rest on Claudius alone because the Levitical prohibition is specifically addressed only to the man who "uncovers" his sister-in-law, not to her.

On a few other occasions in the play Hamlet recurs to the idea of incest, often without actually naming it as such. In his opening line, replying to the King's naming him as "son," he responds, "A little more than kin and less than kind." (I, ii, 65) The "unkindness" that he has in mind seems to be the "unnaturalness" or incest of his mother's marriage to her brother-in-law. Later, when the King identifies himself as Hamlet's father, Hamlet calls him mother: "Father and mother is man and wife, man and wife is one flesh; so my mother." (IV, iii, 54-55) This well-known idea, originating in Genesis ii, 24 and repeated several times in the New Testament, e.g. Matthew xix, 6, represents the same thinking as that underlying the law in Leviticus. As he stabs Claudius at the conclusion he calls him an "incestuous, murd'rous damned Dane" and forces him to "Drink off this potion. Is thy union here?" (V, ii, 330- 31), where "union" is both the poisoned "pearl" of the drink and the poisoned illegal marital union.

In conclusion, Shakespeare's audience would have seen the marriage of Claudius and Gertrude as inherently a far more evil one than we do now. Recognition of this fact gives us a deeper appreciation for Hamlet's horror over his mother's guilt and for his detestation of Claudius.

NOTES

1. M.V. Rama Sarma, *Harmony Restored* (New Delhi: Classical, 1991), p. 23.
2. Harold Jenkins (New Arden Shakespeare, 1982).
3. For full details see any biography of Henry — *e.g.* J.J. Scarisbrick, *Henry VIII* (London: Methuen, 1968), Chapters VII and VIII.

Environmentalist Shakespeare

ALBERT C. LABRIOLA

In the 1992 presidential campaign in the USA, the environment gained the attention that it surely deserves. That attention, in fact, reflected what has been happening in the past few years not only in America but across the globe. People everywhere have focused on environmental issues: air pollution, toxic waste from industry, the dangers of pesticides to animals and humankind alike, nuclear pollutants, and the contamination of natural resources by oil spills and other disasters. These concerns are often translated into action, so that we have special celebrations, notably Earth Day; virtual crusades against all forms of pollution; and campaigns to restore the "greening" of America, including projects of reforestation.

Underlying such endeavors, surprisingly, is a limited outlook on the significance of the environment, which we tend to view only as our immediate surrounding. This outlook falls far short of Shakespeare's understanding. For Shakespeare, the natural environment is the setting in which the speeches, actions, and inner conflicts of characters acquire more profound significance. Shakespeare's use of the seasons, moreover, highlights, not only the descriptive details of spring and winter but also the symbolic value associated with the respective settings in which emergent life is celebrated and imminent death is anticipated. In addition, the principal natural settings in Shakespeare's plays (the forest, the island, the heath, and the garden) develop implications for understanding the perennial questions confronting humankind. Such questions include one's changing self-perception and the psychological coloration of inner conflicts; interactions with one's family, with political authority and institutions, and with the larger cultural community; one's relationship with the deity; and especially one's profound involvement in the paradoxes and problems that beset the human condition. These perennial questions resonate with psychological, moral, political, and philosophical overtones.

The most renowned speech in all of Shakespeare's plays—Hamlet's "To be, or not to be" soliloquy—is the starting point for my presentation. In the course of the speech, Hamlet manifests intense inner conflict, a dilemma: whether or not to commit suicide. In Shakespeare's era, such a dilemma was called a "case of conscience" because of its moral overtones. Indeed, Hamlet himself uses the word "conscience" toward the end of the soliloquy:

> To be, or not to be, that is the question:
> Whether 'tis nobler in the mind to suffer
> The slings and arrows of outrageous fortune,
> Or to take arms against a sea of troubles,
> And by opposing end them. To die, to sleep—
> No more—and by a sleep to say we end
> The heartache and the thousand natural shocks
> That flesh is heir to! 'Tis a consummation
> Devoutly to be wished. To die, to sleep—
> To sleep—perchance to dream: ay, there's the rub,
> For in that sleep of death what dreams may come
> When we have shuffled off this mortal coil,
> Must give us pause. There's the respect
> That makes calamity of so long life:
> For who would bear the whips and scorns of time,
> Th'oppressor's wrong, the proud man's contumely,
> The pangs of despised love, the law's delay,
> The insolence of office, and the spurns
> That patient merit of th'unworthy takes,
> When he himself might his quietus make
> With a bare bodkin? Who would fardels bear,
> To grunt and sweat under a weary life,
> But that the dread of something after death,
> The undiscovered country, form whose bourn
> No traveller returns, puzzles the will,
> And makes us rather bear those ills we have,
> Than to fly to others that we know not of?
> Thus conscience doth make cowards of us all,
> And thus the native hue of resolution
> In sicklied o'er with the pale cast of thought,
> And enterprises of great pitch and moment,
> With this regard their currents turn awry,
> And lose the name of action.

As often as this speech has been analyzed by critical commentators, usually as an example of Hamlet's so-called procrastinating or dilatory nature, three crucial elements in it are almost always overlooked: "pale cast," "great pitch and moment," and "currents." It was not until Sir Laurence Olivier's film version of the play in 1948 that the three crucial elements were not only emphasized but interrelated. Olivier, who both directed the film and played the title role, delivers the soliloquy from the ramparts of the castle at Elsinore, which is on the sea. Atop the castle and buffeted by winds in which swirls of white fog envelop him, Olivier is literally and psychologically immersed in "pale thought." Periodically, the camera angles toward the heavens, in which intense upheaval is evident, with the clouds in rapid, helter-skelter motion. When the camera angles downward, the breakers are pounding against the base of the castle, their white spume erupting in all directions. The waves are of "great pitch"—a reference to the up-and-down motion of the sea and anything on it. The waves are also of great "moment," a reference to the tendency to produce motion especially around a point or an axis.

What Olivier has done is to translate Shakespeare's language to the medium of film, using both sky and sea as environmental backdrops for Hamlet's troubled mind. At one point, the camera, its eye situated in the heavens, zooms down onto the very top of Hamlet's head, the blond hair appearing white. In other words, the white swirls of intense activity in the sky and on the sea are projections of Hamlet's inner state of mind, the point of axis where motion is most intense. Whereas "pale cast" is traditionally interpreted as inactivity or non-action, this film renders the whiteness of the clouds and waves as evidence of swirling activity, during which Hamlet is buffeted by "great pitch and moment" and "currents." In fact, Olivier's Hamlet, who in the initial stages of intended suicide has drawn his dagger or "bare bodkin," drops it onto the rocks at the base of the castle. In the course of the soliloquy, Olivier's Hamlet reclines at the top of the castle, perilously close to the edge. He and the castle are sensationally enveloped by a veritable cinematic montage—the tempestuous clouds, pounding waves, and mist—so that the sky and the sea combine in the images of "pale cast," "great pitch and moment," and "currents."

It was a film version of Hamlet that drove home the relationship between humankind and the environment in that play, if only by using the natural environment (the wind, the sky, the fog, and the sea) to contextualize a speech that is usually presented indoors with the actor in a state of lassitude—whether in a room of the castle, an oratory, or in another place where Hamlet's solitary thinking takes place in silent surroundings. Olivier's film begins to redress an imbalance, not simply in relation to Hamlet but with reference to our understanding of Shakespeare's plays. Today's presentation will pursue the concept of "environmentalist Shakespeare" to a degree, as John Milton would have it, "unattempted yet in prose of rhyme."

As we shift our attention from the castle at Elsinore to the Forest of Arden in *As You Like It,* we witness Duke Senior and his fellow noblemen in exile as they brave the winter winds. At the outset of Act II, the Duke speaks:

> Now, my co-mates and brothers in exile,
> Hath not old custom made this life more sweet
> Than that of painted pomp? Are not these woods
> More free from peril than the envious court?
> Here feel we but the penalty of Adam,
> The seasons' difference, as the icy fang
> And churlish chiding of the winter's wind,
> Which, when it bites and blows upon my body
> Even till I shrink with cold, I smile and say,
> "This is no flattery; these are counselors
> That feelingly persuade me what I am."
> Sweet are the uses of adversity,
> Which, like the toad, ugly and venomous,
> Wears yet a precious jewel in his head;
> And this our life, exempt from public haunt,
> Finds tongues in trees, books in the running brooks,
> Sermons in stones, and good in everything.

A fellow nobleman, Amiens, comments on the Duke's speech:

> I would not change it; happy is your grace
> That can translate the stubbornness of fortune
> Into so quiet and so sweet a style.

In his speech, Duke Senior contrasts the court and the country. The court is "envious" because its noblemen are covetous of power and lucre. Indeed, Duke Senior, having been overthrown by his "envious" brother, enjoys refuge in the forest. Both treachery among one's disloyal followers and flattery from obsequious courtiers are perils to be feared at court. The natural adversity of the "winter's wind" is preferable to treachery and flattery for other reasons. For example, the natural environment is distant from the temptations of power and lucre, the very temptations to which characters such as Duke Frederick and Olivier yield. Olivier, of course, had usurped the patrimony of his younger brother, Orlando. The natural environment—where one "Finds tongues in trees, books in the running brooks, / Sermons in stones, and good in everything"—affords wholesome instruction unmediated by the corrupting influence, actual or potential, of human institutions and human vices. In the natural environment of the Forest of Arden, humankind tends to be generous and magnanimous, not envious and avaricious; benevolent, not hateful; compassionate and merciful, not callous and treacherous. Despite the misfortune of having been deposed by his brother, revenge does not impel Duke Senior and his cohorts. Instead, as Amiens comments, the Duke, a virtual role model, exemplifies not simply a philosophical stoicism or "quiet" manner but also a philosophical optimism or "sweet style" With such a nature and disposition, Duke Senior attracts many of the noblemen from the court, so that eventually his malicious younger brother, Duke Frederick, enters Arden to slay his older brother. Frederick, however, having encountered "an old religious man," presumably a hermit, undergoes conversion, restores the dukedom to his older brother, and chooses to remain behind Arden as a contemplative. The consequence is that the political environment of the court will receive an enlightened ruler whose experiences in the natural environment have informed his perspective, his values, and his virtue.

Having dwelled on *As You Like It* and its "green world" distant from the court, we might cite numerous other plays, including *The Two Gentlemen of Verona, A Midsummer Night's Dream*, and *Twelfth Night*, as examples where court and country are contrasted. But one play not often perceived in this light is *The Merchant of Venice*, in which the last act takes place in Belmont, particularly in a garden outside Portia's home. This "green world" contrasts with the locations in Venice—the Rialto, the court of justice, Shylock's home, and elsewhere. Under the moonlight, Lorenzo and Jessica, who have eloped in order to be married glance heavenward. Lorenzo speaks:

> How sweet the moonlight sleeps upon this bank!
> Here will we sit and let the sounds of music
> Creep in our ears; soft stillness and the night
> Become the touches of sweet harmony.
> Sit Jessica. Look how the floor of heaven
> Is thick inlaid with patens of bright gold.
> There's not the smallest orb which thou behold'st
> But in his motion like an angel sings,
> Still quiring to the young-eyed cherubins;
> Such harmony is in immortal souls,
> But whilst this muddy vesture of decay
> Doth grossly close it in, we cannot hear it.

Gold or lucre in the play has distracted not only Shylock but also the typical suitors of Portia, who were misled by the caskets of precious metals (gold and silver). In Lorenzo's speech, the reference to "patens of bright gold" recalls the biblical injunction to lay up one's treasure in Heaven, not on earth. In Luke's Gospel, Christ, having inveighed against earthly treasures, concludes that "where your treasure is, there also will your heart be." Significantly, in Lorenzo's speech the ceiling of the firmament becomes the floor of Heaven, so that humankind oriented heavenward, not downward toward materialism, can bring to hear the music of the spheres, emanating from the choirs of angels whose presence and singing suggest the immanence of God in the human condition. Lorenzo and Jessica sublimate themselves, using the silence and solitude of the "green world" as a contemplative environment in which a heightened awareness of things heavenly overtakes them. Not to be overlooked is the images of "patens of bright gold," a reference presumably to the dish or thin metal plate of precious metal used for the bread or host during a Eucharistic service. Sacramental and liturgical symbolism becomes associated with the heavenly banquet awaiting the faithful in the hereafter. Humankind's access to such an intuition, if not vision, emerges from the natural environment distant from the vices of materialism and the taint of hate and revenge.

While Shakespeare's plays are rich with examples of the philosophical and religious profundities associated with the natural environment, we must not forget that this brilliant dramatist was a spokesman to and for the common folk, who associated particular experiences with the seasons of the year. At the very end of *Love's Labour Lost*, companion songs, often recited as poems, aptly and simply titled "Spring" and "Winter" recount the experiences of the common folk:

Spring

When daisies pied and violets blue
And lady-smocks all silver-white
And cuckoo-buds of yellow hue
Do paint the meadows with delight,
The cuckoo then, on every tree,
Mocks married men; for thus sings he,
"Cuckoo!
Cuckoo!, Cuckoo!" O word of fear,
Unpleasing to the married ear!
When shepherds pipe on oaten straws,
And merry larks are ploughmen's clocks,
When turtles tread, and rooks, and daws,
And maidens bleach their summer smocks,
The cuckoo then, on every tree,
Mocks married men; for thus sings he,
"Cuckoo!
Cuckoo!, Cuckoo!" O word of fear,
Unpleasing to a married ear!

Most prominent is the cry of the cuckoo, which induces fear in husbands who suspect that their wives have been unfaithful. The word "Cuckold," which is derived from cuckoo, designates a husband whose wife has been unfaithful to the extent that she has conceived a child by liaison with another man. Like the cuckoo bird—whose habit it is to lay eggs in the nest of another bird, which cares for the fledglings as if they were its own—a woman who conceives outside of her marital relationship and presents the newly born infant as her spousal offspring has "cuckolded" her husband.

The companion song or poem, "Winter," presents an opposite picture seasonally:

Winter

When icicles hang by the wall,
And Dick the shephered blows his nail,
And Tom bears logs into the hall,
And milk comes frozen home in pail,
When blood is nipped, and ways be foul,
Then nightly sings the staring owl, "Tu-whit,
Tu-who!" a merry note,
While greasy Joan doth keel the pot.

When all aloud the wind doth blow,
And coughing drowns the parson's saw,
And birds sit brooding in the snow,
And Marian's nose looks red and raw,
When roasted crabs hiss in the bowl,
Then nightly sings the staring owl, "Tu-whit,
Tu-who!" a merry note,
While greasy Joan doth keel the pot.

The first of the two songs, "Spring," furnishes a context for understanding the natural environment in two plays not typically associated with *Love's Labour Lost*: the one is *Romeo and Juliet*, the other *A Midsummer Night's Dream*. Early in the play Romeo retreats into the natural environment, a "green world" where he pines as a victim of lover's melancholy. Benvolio tells the Lord and Lady Montague of Romeo's action:

Madam, an hour before the worshipped sun
Peered forth the golden window of the East,
A troubled mind drove me to walk abroad;
Where, underneath the grove of sycamore
That westward rooteth from this city side,
So early waking did I see your son.
Towards him I made, but he was wary of me
And stole into the covert of the wood.

Romeo's father, the Lord Montague, adds:

Many a morning hath he there been seen,
With tears augmenting the fresh morning's dew,
Adding to clouds more clouds with his deep sighs;
But all so soon as the all-cheering sun
Should in the farthest East begin to draw
The shady curtains from Aurora's bed,

> Away from light steals home my heavy son
> And private in his chamber pens himself,
> Shuts up his windows, locks fair daylight out,
> And makes himself an artificial night.
> Black and portentous must this humor prove
> Unless good counsel may the cause remove.

Of course, when Benvolio engages Romeo, who is returning from the meadow at dawn to sequester himself in the darkness of his chamber, the young lover is infatuated with Rosaline, on whom he dotes before his encounter with Juliet. In Franco Zeffirelli's brilliant film of the play, Romeo emerges from the "green world" with flowers in his hand, a bouquet Then and thereafter, flowers and their symbolism of short-lived beauty are related in numerous ways to the love of Romeo and Juliet, starting with the song at the Capulets' masquerade feast. Indeed, the song ("What is a Youth?") by the soloist, who casts a rose onto the floor at the maskers' ball, answers the very question by reference to flower symbolism: "A rose will bloom, then it will fade, so does a youth, so does the fairest maid." The melody, which recurs in the film, becomes the "theme song" of the young lovers.

Another instance in *Romeo and Juliet* of the natural environment at springtime occurs in Act II, when Friar Laurence, a botanist and herbalist, witnesses the coming of dawn, precisely the time when Romeo typically returns from the "green world" to sequester himself in his chamber. In Shakespeare's play, the friar gives the speech before he goes outside; in the Zeffirelli film he is culling flowers in the meadow outside the walls of Verona, where he is eventually joined by Romeo. The friar's speech, like the "theme song" of the young lovers, ominously foreshadows early death by reference to the natural environment:

> The gray-eyed morn smiles on the frowning night,
> Check'ring the eastern clouds with streaks of light;
> And flecked darkness like a drunkard reels
> From forth day's path and Titan's burning wheels.
> Now, ere the sun advance his burning eye
> The day to cheer and night's dank dew to dry,
> I must upfill this osier cage of ours
> With baleful weeds and precious-juiced flowers,
> The earth that's Nature's mother is her tomb.
> What is her burying grave, that is her womb;
> And from her womb children of divers kind
> We sucking on her natural bosom find,
> Many for many virtues excellent,
> None but for some, and yet all different.
> O mickle is the powerful grace that lies

In plants, herbs, stones, and their true qualities;
For naught so vile that on the earth doth live
But to the earth some special good doth give;
Nor aught so good but, strained from that fair use,
Revolts from true birth, stumbling on abuse.
Virtue itself turns vice, being misapplied,
And vice sometime by action dignified.

In *Romeo and Juliet*, the natural environment enhances our understanding of the premature deaths of the young lovers.

In Shakespearean comedy, on the other hand, the natural environment, including its flowers and herbs, will share some features with the comparable setting in the tragedies, such as *Romeo and Juliet*. The infatuation or lover's melancholy that afflicts Romeo is also evident in a *A Midsummer Night's Dream*, when, for instance, Oberon instructs Puck to acquire the love potion that will induce, as he puts it, "love-in-idleness":

The very time I saw, but thou couldst not,
Flying between the cold moon and the earth,
Cupid all armed. A certain aim he took
At a fair vestal throned by the west,
And loosed his love shaft smartly from his bow,
As it should pierce a hundred thousand hearts.
But I might see young Cupid's fiery shaft
Quenched in the chaste beams of the wat'ry moon,
And the imperial vot'ress passed on,
In maiden meditation, fancy-free,
Yet marked I where the bolt of Cupid fell,
It fell upon a little western flower,
Before milk-white, now purple with love's wound,
And maidens call it love-in-idleness.
Patch me that flow'r; the herb I showed thee once;
The juice of it on sleeping eyelids laid
Will make or man or woman madly dote
Upon the next live creature that it sees.
Fetch me this herb, and be thou here again
Ere the leviathan can swim a league.

Traditionally, the "fair vestal" or "imperial vot'ress" is interpreted as Queen Elizabeth I, who by her rational control was immune to the instability of infatuation and lover's melancholy.

Having focused on how the song "Spring" in *Love's Labour Lost* may be related to the plays *Romeo and Juliet* and *A Midsummer Night's Dream*, we should pursue, if only briefly, the applicability of the song "Winter" to, of all plays, *The Taming of the Shrew*. The song, particularly the line "and ways be foul," comments on the travels and travails of Kate in *The Taming of the Shrew*, when she and Petruchio encounter the harsh natural environment enroute to his country estate. Petruchio's servant, Grumion, in prose not verse, recounts the story to a fellow-servant:

> . . . thou shouldst have heard how her horse fell, and she under her horse. Thou shouldst have heard in how miry a place, how she was bemoiled, how he left her with the horse upon her, how he beat me because her horse stumbled, how she waded through the dirt to pluck him off me; how he swore, how she prayed that never prayed before; how I cried, how the horses ran away, how her bridle was burst, how I lost my crupper.

The "green world," as we have thus far described it, has been a forest, meadow, or other such natural setting, even the landscape over which Kate and Petruchio travel as they depart Padua. Another natural environment fraught with significance in certain plays is the island setting, notably Illyria in *Twelfth Night* and Prospero's island in *The Tempest*. Prospero's island and the actions that take place there present allegorically a host of relationships and interactions; between father and daughter, husband and wife, ruler and realm, nature and art, order and disorder in human society, and most, important, the matter and spirit of human nature never fully harmonized but conjoined in a state of tension. Whereas Ariel, the sprite who serves Prospero, is identified with the more rarefied elements of fire and air, Caliban, the savage and deformed slave, is associated with the coarser elements, earth and water. When Ariel gives Prospero an account of the tempest and shipwreck, images of air and fire predominate:

> . . . Now on the beak, Now in the waist, the deck, in every cabin,
> I flamed amazement. Sometime I divide
> And burn in many places; on the topmast,
> The yards, and boresprit would I flame distinctly,
> Them meet and join. Jove's lightnings, the precursors,
> O'th'dreadful thunderclaps, more momentary
> And sight-outrunning were not. The fire and cracks
> Of sulfurous roaring the most mighty Neptune
> Seem to besiege, and make his bold waves tremble;
> Yea, his dread trident shake.

The most renowned speech in the play, of course, is Prospero's so-called farewell to his magical art. This speech strives to harmonize the numerous opposites that have signified human nature in a state of tension, to stabilize the interpersonal and political relationships in the play and to achieve in Prospero himself the psychological equanimity that would engender contentment. The supreme irony is that this speech, breathtaking in its macrocosmic imagination, really treats the makeup and mix-up of the tensions and turmoils in human nature. Played out against the grand scale of the natural environment, the paradoxes and problems of human nature acquire transcendent significance:

> Ye elves of hills, brooks, standing lakes, and groves,
> And ye that on the sands with printless foot
> Do chase the ebbing Neptune, and do fly him
> When he comes back; you demi-puppets that
> By moonshine do the green sour ringlets make,
> Whereof the ewe not bites; and you whose pastime
> Is to make midnight mushrumps, that rejoice
> To hear the solemn curfew; by whose aid
> (Weak masters though ye be) I have bedimmed
> The noontide sun, called forth the mutinous winds,
> And 'twixt the green sea and azured vault
> Set roaring war; to the dread rattling thunder
> Have I given fire and rifted Jove's stout oak
> With his own bolt; the strong-based promontory
> Have I made shake and by the spurs plucked up
> The pine and cedar; graves at my command
> Have waked their sleepers, open and let'em forth
> By my so potent art. But this rough magic
> I here abjure; and when I have required
> Some heavenly music (which even now I do)
> To work mine end upon their senses that
> This airy charm is for, I'll break my staff,
> Bury it certain fathoms in the earth,
> And deeper than did ever plummet sound
> I'll drown my book.

If Prospero's island is the apt setting for such a macrocosmic vision, then the heath in *King Lear* provides another example in which humankind is measured against the natural environment. Lear, having relinquished his monarchy, and been rejected, in turn, by his ungrateful daughters, suffers madness. The upheaval in the political state, the disruption in his family, and the anguish in his mind are all interrelated by Lear in his speeches on the heath:

> Rumble thy bellyful. Spit, fire, Spout rain!
> Nor rain, wind, thunder, fire are my daughters
> I tax not you, you elements with unkindness.
> I never gave you kingdom, called you children,
> You owe me no subscription. Then let fall
> Your horrible pleasure. Here I stand your slave,
> A poor, infirm, weak, and despised old man.

> But yet I call you servile ministers,
> That will with two pernicious daughters join
> Your high-engendered battles 'gainst a head
> So old and white as this. O, ho! 'tis foul.

Despite the torment, Lear acknowledges the onset of wisdom through suffering, a heightened self-perception and self-knowledge, not to mention an understanding of human nature generally, all of which he previously lacked.

Of all of the environmental features in Shakespeare's plays, the most significant is the garden, which is fraught with political significance. The most dramatic use of the garden as an image of the kingdom occurs in *Richard II*, when the gardener comments to one of his helpers on the reign of the dissolute king and its unwholesome effects on the realm:

> . . . O, what a pity is it
> That we had not so trimmed and dressed his land
> As we this garden! We at time of year
> Do wound the bark, the skin of our fruit trees,
> Lest being overproud in sap and blood
> With too much riches it confound itself;
> Had he done so to great and growing men,
> They might have lived to bear, and he to taste
> Their fruits of duty. Superfluous branches
> We lop away, that bearing boughs may live;
> Had he done so, himself had borne the crown,
> Which waste of idle hours hath quite thrown down.

Virtually the same image of the garden recurs in *Henry V*, when Burgundy describes the decadence of France. Speaking to the kings of both England and France, he inquires why Peace, personified as a woman:

> Should not, in this best garden of the world,
> Our fertile France, put up her lovely visage.
> Alas, she hath from France too long been chased!
> And all her husbandry doth lie on heaps,
> Corrupting in its own fertility.
> Her vine, the merry cheerer of the heart,
> Unpruned dies; her hedges even-pleached,
> Put forth disordered twigs; her fallow leas
> The darnel, hemlock and rank fumitory
> Doth root upon, while that the coulter rusts
> That should deracinate such savagery;
> The even mead, that erst brought sweetly forth
> The freckled cowslip, burnet, and green clover,
> Wanting the scythe, all uncorrected, rank,
> Conceives by idleness, and nothing teems

But hateful docks, rough thistles, kecksies, burrs,
Losing both beauty and utility.
And all our vineyards, fallows, meads, and hedges,
Defective in their natures, grow to wildness.

Other examples of decadence in nature as manifestations of corruption in the realm occur in *Macbeth* and *Hamlet*. When Macbeth, the tyrannical king of Scotland, feels beleaguered by the onset of the English forces against him, his utterances become disjointed and irascible:

Seyton!—I am sick at heart,
When I behold—Seyton, I say!—This push
Will cheer me ever, or disseat me now.
I have lived long enough. May way of life
Is fall'n into the sear, the yellow leaf.

Soon thereafter, having learned of the madness of Lady Macbeth, the beleaguered tyrant requests that the ministering doctor diagnose the malady of the realm:

. . . cast the water of my land, find her disease
And purge it to a sound and pristine health.

To describe the devastating effect of Macbeth's tyranny on the kingdom, Shakespeare uses such images of disease and desiccation, vividly suggested by the phenomenon of yellowing that leads inevitably to browning. In other words, the principles of vitality and fertility, evident in spring and summer, have yielded to an indefinite autumn and an imminent winter. Nothing less than a radical blood-letting, specifically the slaying of the tyrant, will restore health to the kingdom. A similar condition of disease and desiccation occurs in *Hamlet*. After all, "Something is rotten in the state of Denmark," as Marcellus senses in Act I. Even before the action of the play begins, the slaying of the king in his orchard informs the garden imagery in each and every detail. Hamlet's first soliloquy is a case in point:

O that this too too sullied flesh would melt,
Thaw, and resolve itself into a dew,
Or that the Everlasting had not fixed
His canon 'gainst self- slaughter. O God, God,
How weary, stale, flat and unprofitable
Seem to me all the uses of this world!
Fie on't, ah, fie, 'tis an unweeded garden
That grows to seed. Things rank and gross in nature
Possess it merely.

The foregoing speeches—by Burgundy, by the gardener in *Richard II*, by Macbeth, and Hamlet—imply the prescience of Shakespeare, who anticipates the present-day reality of humankind's corruption of the natural environment. For Shakespeare, humankind's vices and degeneracy produce an adverse effect in the environment. From this perspective, the environment becomes an allegorical landscape wherein humankind views the enactment and consequences of self destructive impulses. Placed along a continuum, Shakespeare foreshadows on a much grander scale the anxieties of poets such as William Blake and Gerard Manley Hopkins, to name but two examples, who lament industrialization gone awry, its abuses, and its deleterious effect on the environment. They like Shakespeare, are really decrying humankind's self-destructiveness, for which industry and technology are but the signs and symptoms and, at times, the means to magnify exponentially the ills and evils of an individual and society.

In contrast to the diseased realms in *Richard II*, *Macbeth*, and *Hamlet*, England and France in *Henry V* acquire renewed life. The vital, virile, and robust young king, especially in his relationship with Katherine of France, bonds the two kingdoms. As the epilogue to the play celebrates, England is "the world's best garden." Such an accomplishment is all the more admirable when one recognizes that from the first the young king's intent appears to be warlike. The prologue tells us:

> O for a Muse of fire that would ascend
> The brightest heaven of invention;
> A kingdom for a stage, princes to act,
> And monarchs to behold the swelling scene!
> Then should the warlike Harry, like himself,
> Assume the port of Mars, and at his heels
> (Leashed in, like hounds) should famine, sword, and fire
> Crouch for employment.

But the most resounding affirmation of the political significance of the garden as an image of the realm occurs in *Richard II*, when John of Gaunt chastises the idle King, whose profligacy has devitalized England. John of Gaunt's speech, an appropriate capstone to our presentation, ascribes both mythic and biblical significance to the environment and etches indelibly our portrayal of the dramatist as "environmentalist Shakespeare":

> This royal throne of kings, this scept'red isle,
> This earth of majesty, this seat of Mars,
> This other Eden, demi-paradise,
> This fortress built by Nature for herself
> Against infection and the hand of war,
> This happy breed of men, this little world,
> This precious stone set in the silver sea
> Which serves it in the office of a wall
> Or as a most defensive to the house,
> Against the envy of less happier lands,

This blessed plot, this earth, this realm, this England,
This nurse, this teeming womb of royal kings,
Feared by their breed, and famous by their birth,
Renowned for their deeds as far from home,
For Christian service and true chivalry,
As is the sepulcher in stubborn Jewry
Of the world's ransom, blessed Mary's son,
This land of such dear souls, this dear dear land.

Shakespeare's Relevance Forever

H.H. ANNIAH GOWDA

The fascination for Shakespeare is irresistible. Year after year his criticism grows. He is not of an age but for all times. Cassius of *Julius Caesar* was prophetic:

> How many ages hence
> Shall this our lofty scene be acted over
> In states unborn and accents yet unknown! (III.i.110-14)

The criticism varies from age to age; from character to poetry and to new criticism. The general account of the shift from the new criticism to post-modernism in Shakespeare studies considers the impact of deconstruction, of the new historicism and cultural materialism and of feminism. R.A. Foakes, a well known critic of Shakespeare, has reissued *Hamlet Versus Lear* studying the plays in terms of post-modernist aesthetics. A.C. Bradley's *Shakespearean Tragedy* discusses the "great" tragedies—*Hamlet, Othello, Lear* and *Macbeth* and their character studies. The deconstructionist would consider Bradley outdated. But his views on Shakespearean tragedy enunciated in a number of lectures and the concept of the calamity leading to the death of man of highest state, echoing Aristotle and his comments on characters and situations will not be dated. Shakespeare was not attempting to justify the ways of God to men, as show the universe as a Divine Comedy. He was writing tragedy, and "tragedy would not be tragedy if it were not a painful mystery." (*Shakespearean Tragedy*) " To proceed from the word to the image in its verse setting, and thence to trace the way in which a pattern of interdependent themes is gradually woven into the dramatic action, is the most fruitful approach—the most accurate and if properly handled, the least subject of partiality—to Shakespeare's art" (D. Traversi). But the major characteristics of contemporary post- modernist aesthetics is to see the abandonment of organic unity as an aesthetic value and to overthrow a series of formerly privileged hierarchial oppositions through a post-modernist anti-hierarchial impulse (Hugh Grady). *Shakespearean Tragedy* aims at a serious and profound consideration of the nature of tragic art. It bears a number of re-readings.

Although Shakespeare excelled in both tragedy and comedy, his tragedies are most popular and need to be reflected upon. Tragedy, with its focus on a single hero, has great intensity and intellectual clarity. Comedy, by its very nature is more closely allied to its own day and age than tragedy. Shakespeare's tragedies are closely related to his Histories. *Coriolanus* is now taken very seriously largely because it is exceptionally amenable to the two obsessions of fashionable criticism: politics and psychoanalysis. Coriolanus' dependency on his mother manifests itself in a "phallic aggressive pose" which is "a defense against collapse into the dependent oral mode of the small boy" and how he "would be inviting homosexual rape by standing naked before the crowd." (Walter Cohen) However, he melts before his mother like a ball of snow before fire. *Timon of Athens* has adherents too. Some modern critics interpret this as development thought the tragedies towards deeper and deeper social integration; and to them *Timon* represents the logical limit of this process, it "was the end of Shakespeare's career as a tragedian." G. Wilson Knight who familiarised the study of poetry instead of character in the plays saw *Timon* as the *ne plus ultra* of tragedy. In Shakespeare's dramatic art tragedy was perceived before the "big four" which cast their deep shadows backwards. It is possible to reinterpret *Hamlet* turning with relief to the immature *Romeo and Juliet* and *Titus Andronicus,* a prime achievement. Aristotle who defines tragedy as the fall of a great man due to a fatal flaw in his nature has been instrumental in keeping out of the select company of the two tragedies in which a pair of lovers are named in the title. *Antony and Cleopatra* has always been close to admission to the canon within the canon, but somehow just outside it. In this play, Zulfikar Ghose would say that it is not a great tragedy because the women don't die first: by killing Antony at the end of the fourth act, Shakespeare moved tragedy away from its martial, epic-like idiom into an erotic, romance-like one. In this Shakespeare had precedent. Ovid's re-writing of the Aeneas and Dido story from Dido's point of view, with her death as the climax of the tragedy rather than, as it was in Virgil, a distraction. It is one of the unsung triumphs of Ovid, Chaucer and Shakespeare, with their exceptional capacity to animate female tragic voices, that we now name the woman first.

Shakespeare tragedies with women in the title don't make it into the first rank. This was due to the elite and popular conceptions of Shakespeare. Probably during Shakespeare's time, those interested in stratification found it hard to countenance the idea that a play about two teenagers in love against the will of their parents what is more, was the apex of Western tragedy. *Romeo and Juliet* was the most frequently staged Shakespearian play throughout the eighteenth century. It has acquired a truly mythic status within world culture their names which stand for all secret lovers instantly recognizable. Many young people throughout the entire world, whatever may be their race, religion, social status, exchange their ardent glances and identify themselves with *Romeo and Juliet*. As a tragedy, it is not rated high as the flaw stems from accident. There is no character leading to destiny. *Hamlet* and *Lear* with no feminine names in the title are certainly great. Why consider them great? Why did Bradley concentrate on the "Big four?" These are our concerns. Foakes devotes a number of pages to confer greatness on *Hamlet* and *Lear*. But his title: *Hamlet Versus Lear* is intriguing. *Hamlet* and *King Lear* are archetypal tragedies of youth and age; Hamlet's "cursed spite"; Lear's irascibility are before us. By the end of the eighteenth century Shakespeare's status as an eminent poet and playwright was established. Naturally, critics became busy debating the high and low of the plays. The top play would come from among the tragedies. *Hamlet* was considered a great play. O.J. Campbell in his valuable *Shakespeare Encyclopedia* begins his commentary on Shakespeare's masterpiece with the words "Hamlet is undoubtedly the world's most famous play." Though convincing, the assertion is more challenging than gratifying. Foakes quotes a number of critics who follow this line of thought. Hamlet is many-sided and could take on the characteristics of the reader or play-goer; even players feel the universal validity, the typicalness, of Hamlet. "As he thought and felt, or in some like manner, have all at sometime thought and felt and acted, or rather failed to act." It was possible to focus on his nobility, his generosity, his philosophizing, his lack of resolution, his exquisite sensibility. "His strange reality is our own reality." Hamlet expresses a permanent condition of man. John Masefield has remarked that it is difficult to live anywhere in England (except in the theatre) without hearing or reading a part of *Hamlet*. Coleridge who thought that he had a "smack of Hamlet" in him saw deep feelings and exclusive sense of beauty in the play. In both soliloquy and dialogue, Shakespeare achieves a mature expression of equivocal inner feelings. This is clear from Ophelia's "O! what a noble mind is here o'erthrown." Foakes reconstructs *Hamlet* as a reflection of modern consciousness, and hence identified him with the problems of the age, and politicized as mirroring those who from weakness of will endlessly vacillate. He is abstracted from the play into an embodiment of what came to be known as Hamletism (the verb, to Hamletize, came later). Hamletism is seen in modern novels like *Pierre* or *The Ambiguities* by Herman Melville: It suggests inner turbulence in his descent into the maelstorm of self. D.H. Laurence's *Women in Love* in which Birkin says, "the life that belong to death—our kind of life." The culmination of Hamletism is in T.S. Eliot's *Prufrock:*

> No, I am not Prince Hamlet, nor was meant to be,
> Am an attendant lord, one that will do
> To swell a progress, start a scene or two

Advise the prince: no doubt, an easy tool,
Deferential, glad to be of use,
Politic, cautious and meticulous
Full of high sentence, but a bit obtuse;
At times, indeed almost, ridiculous,
Almost, at times, the Fool.

The image of Hamlet informs many modern works. John Dover Wilson's *What Happens in Hamlet* and Maynard Mack's *The World of Hamlet* are classic studies. Mack says "The World of Hamlet" in which the play in presented as concerned with Man, 'Man is his aspect of bafflement', envisaged as 'moving in darkness on a rampart between two worlds.' Hence Hamlet is our contemporary. To W.B. Yeats he represents "this filthy modern life" overwhelming all he valued. Peter Hall's production shows Hamlet relevance for the world of the H-Bomb. Hamlet is representative of the first modern man to the extent that as a subject he feels adrift his social role, in this case prince and heir to the throne of Denmark, by which the identity of men and women was established in a feudal society. For Coleridge we are all Hamlets. He has become representative of modern anxieties and has been democratised into a figure symbolising the disarray of ordinary people in the lonely crowd, at their inability to change what they see as wrong in their environment. How often have we not muttered "What a piece of work is a man, how noble in reason, how infinite in faculties; in form and moving how express and admirable, in action how like an angel, in apprehension how like a god: "the beauty of the world, the paragon of animals! and yet to me what is this quint-essence of dust?" (II, ii, 306-14) *Hamlet* is a culmination of Poetic drama. Tom Stoppard who looked at *Hamlet* from the angle of the courtiers *Rosencrantz and Guildenstern Are Dead* says, "Wheels have been set in motion, and they have their own page, to which we are condemned. Each move is dictated by the previous one—that is the meaning or order." When a king falls, a nation is affected. In *Henry V* with his death:

England ne'er lost a king of so much worth (I,i,7)

In *Hamlet* we don't really find much of this feeling. Hamlet is regretted because "he was likely, had he been put on, / To have prov'd most royal." But Fortinbras is securely in charge of Denmark. But the end of *King Lear* is a lament for Lear's death and suffering, but no hint is there that Britain's future is in danger.

If the story of the reception of *Hamlet* keeps returning to Hamletism and politics, the reception of *King Lear* is to do away with politics and property, it is a play of abdication. It is a "Heap of jewels unstrung and unpolished." Many who have written about it did not like the ending. Dr Johnson wanted a happy ending devised by Nahum Tate, on the grounds that the death of

Cordelia was "contrary to the natural ideas of justice, to the hope of the reader, and what is yet more strange, to the faith of chronicles." In the nineteenth century people were happy to see the happy ending, restoring Lear to a power he promptly hands over to Cordelia and Edgar, who are to marry. This pleased George III as there were analogues to himself. To Charles Lamb it was sublime "while we read it, we see not Lear, but we are Lear,—we are in his mind, we are sustained by a grandeur which baffles the malice of daughters and storms."

But to him it was not actable but we have a number of professional and amateur productions—all successful. Unlike *Hamlet* it has a secondary action. The story of Gloucester and his two sons leaning towards stoicism much as this attitude comes into prominence in the last scenes of *Hamlet*. But throughout there is an emphasis on compassion as the primal attitude enforced upon us by our higher nature. Hamlet's story bears witness to the basic urge of man's infinite imagination; Lear's to the need for compassion, pity and renunciation. Its leading figure is anything but a hero. He is far more acted upon than action. No serious play could diverge farther from the theory of tragedy advanced by Aristotle and his "tragic sense of life." Instead, at heart this dramatic poem, with its astonishingly eloquent expression of pity for the human lot, takes its place beside the other great documents of human compassion, such works as the *Gautama Sutras* and the *Gospel According to Saint Matthew*. The King of England becomes "A poor, infirm, weak and despised old man" who understands the poverty:

> Poor naked wretches, wheresoe'er you are,
> That bide the pelting of this pitiless storm,
> How shell your houseless heads and unfed sides,
> Your looped and windowed raggedness, defend you
> From seasons such as these? (III, iv, 28-32)

These lines make us worship Shakespeare, says Bradley.

John F. Danby in *Shakespeare's Doctrine of Nature*, a book that remained influential through the 1950s, saw the play as centrally concerned with Renaissance conceptions of nature, perceived as benignant. Bradley ended his chapters on *King Lear* by pointing to the *Tempest* as if Prospero takes over from Lear preaching to us from end to end. Fortitude is seen when Lear utters the famous lines:

> And take upon's the mystery of things
> As if we were God's spies; (V, ii, 16-17)

King Lear was adapted by Bond, a modern playwright, who called it *Lear* (1970). Bond escalated the violence in his play, in which all personal relationships break-down with no hope for the future. Bond's play is confusing and is a poor inspiration of *King Lear*. Shakespeare's great insight into mental distress and disintegration is absent. Foakes sees the plays as wholes using the process of revision and the politics to reinforce a sense of their totality and overall design.

Hamlet and *Lear* are fascinating plays, their greatness resides in our capacity to elicit feelings. Foakes defines great literature as "the value and pleasure we gain from watching or reading a play as a work of art . . . is finally determined by our sense of the design of the whole." His book accordingly ends with formalist readings of the structure of the two plays registering apocalyptic possibilities of the Cold War achieved through the new reading of *Lear* as a play of reconciliation and redemption. This is in a way close to Bradley.

However, the various forms of post-structuralist criticism of Shakespeare tragedies are manifestation of anxieties about our own age. Shakespeare's tragedies can be seen as embedded in our own culture and the preoccupation with the new methods is stimulating.

'A Sea-change / into Something Rich and Strange' Shakespeare's Late Romances

M. PADMA

Each age reads Shakespeare in the light of its own assumptions and beliefs. The various approaches to Shakespeare's plays—historical, romantic, poetic, philosophical, psychological, existential and religious—indicate the essential universality and the infinite variety of Shakespearian plays. Though these approaches have their own limitations and are subject to a lot of controversy, the religious approach has been still a tantalising subject right from the beginning. On the superficial level it would look as absurd as attributing religion to a modern, highly commercial film maker. But on a deeper understanding we come to know that Shakespeare applies to his plays the theological background of his age and brings about his personal experiences and his deeply felt convictions to the forefront.

Religious drama, in general, takes its origin from the Mystery and the Morality plays. Una Ellis Fermor defines religious drama as 'that kind of drama which takes religious experience for its main theme.'[1] Religious drama also includes in its broad outline the plays that present the religious background of the age and those that are deliberately intended to be propaganda plays. Though Shakespeare's plays cannot be called propaganda plays, they conform to the first two aspects of religious drama.

Shakespeare's tragedies mainly contain the religious and theological background of the Elizabethan age, 'whereas the tragi-comedies embody Shakespeare's religious experience . . . in which religious enthusiasm was sufficiently dormant to allow the new humanism to shape our literature.'[2] According to Elizabeth's proclamation of 1550 the stage was forbidden to meddle with religious subjects, still a number of writers chose religion as the subject. Shakespeare carefully avoids any exclusive religious messages from his plays. Moreover, for the Elizabethan audience words like heaven, hell, angel, devil, soul, grace, repentance and sin, imply suggestions that reach far beyond the play's domain.

Though Shakespeare's plays are intended for a mixed audience ranging from the aristocrats to 'the penny stinkards' the audience was familiar with the theological concepts like 'order,' 'degree,' 'chain of being,' 'conflict of good and evil,' 'free will' and 'predestination.' Shakespeare cashes on the audience's tastes and the result is a popular drama with subtle religious undertones.

In spite of close religious analogies and precise theological applications, in his plays, most critics feel disinclined to consider Shakespeare a religious thinker or that his plays are religious. Santayana bluntly states: 'Shakespeare wrote without a philosophy and without a religion.'[3] Charlton concludes, 'Shakespearian tragedy is profoundly spiritual, and yet in no real sense is it at all religious. . . . His preoccupation is moral, and not religious.'[4] Ronald Mushat Frye too argues that even if Shakespeare demonstrates an accurate knowledge of theology we cannot directly assume that he is talking in theological terms. However, R.M. Frye concedes that 'literate protestant Christians in Shakespeare's time would not have expected from literature any more explicitly Christian theology than Shakespeare patently gave in his works.'[5]

But there are critics who have been keen on allegorising Shakespeare's plays. Wilson Knight regards Shakespeare's tragic heroes as 'miniature Christs'. Paul N. Siegel too makes a repeated reference to Christ figures in Shakespeare's plays. John Vyvyan in his books *The Shakespearean Ethic* (1958), *Shakespeare and the Rose of Love* (1960), and *Platonic Beauty* (1961), confirms that Shakespeare displays a rigid orthodox Christian moral philosophy. Bryant in *Hyppolita's View* (1961) sees the plays as a story of Christ.

We can, in a way, say that Shakespearean tragedy concerns itself with what is universally human and that relates it with religion. According to Barnard, 'It is impossible to read Shakespearian tragedy without perceiving its theological implications. For Shakespearian tragedy deals with such things as sin and free will, guilt and resolution, fate and chance, good and evil, God and human suffering, God's love and man's humanity to man. These are the basic problems of man, and these are theological problems.'[6]

Shakespeare uses the Christian concepts towards a secular purpose. Tragedy sets forth a kind of experience that is familiar to everyone. Even the ethics of Shakespeare's tragedies, thought they resemble Christian ethics, they are not based on Christian eschatology and this accounts for their universality. As Frye says, 'though the plays do not furnish an evidence of Shakespeare's religious orientation, they do attest to his impressive religious knowledge to dramatic purpose.'[7]

Shakespeare's tragedies on the whole tend to reproduce the religious background of the age. It is of literary interest to see that the revival of religious drama in the twentieth century has been received with acclaim. T.S. Eliot, Dorothy Sayers, Charles Williams, Christopher Fry and Auden have responded to the need of the times. Religious drama explicitly religious in theme tries to probe man's situation in the universe.

If Shakespeare is simply interested in presenting the religious background of his age in his tragedies, in the tragi-comedies we have his rich religious experience dramatised. Harmony exists and the finer justice expresses itself in the theme of forgiveness. Shakespeare's late romances introduce us to a world of make-believe where neither realism nor time would matter. Shakespeare's innovative process of giving something new originating in *Pericles* and culminating in *The Tempest* is indeed an experiment in dramatic art. One wonders why Shakespeare should have turned to romances so late in his life. Both Sidney and Spenser are responsible for blending classical romance, epic and pastoral with the more popular tales of chivalry. What Sidney and Spenser have done in prose and verse Shakespeare does in drama. Also the new genre, the tragi-comey popularised by Beaumont and Fletcher is yet another experiment in playwriting in that age. The tragi-comedy combines the elements of tragedy and comedy. The view that is presented in the tragi-comedies is that life is a mixture of joys and sorrows, it is neither an ecstatic exuberance, nor a tragic catastrophe. This is nearer to the old traditional concept of tragi-comedy as stated by Plautus in the Prologue to his *Amphitryon.* Disguised as a slave, Mercury first refers to the play as 'comedy' then designates it 'tragedy' and tries to tease his audience, 'What? Are you frowning because I said that this would be a tragedy? I am a god, I will change it. If you wish, I will convert this tragedy into a comedy without changing a line. . . . I know your feelings in this matter.'[8] Shakespeare therefore follows the tradition in writing his late romances.

The tragi-comedies present life from a totally different perspective from that of the tragedies. It is no longer a tale 'Told by an idiot, full of sound and fury. Signifying nothing' (*Macbeth*). It is based on Christian faith that sees life as a cosmic drama. Two of Shakespeare's last plays, *Pericles* and *The Winter's Tale* might be called 'resurrection' parables. To 'the music of the spheres' (V, i, 231) Pericles finds his daughter Marina, supposed dead, like a symbol of eternity. In *The Winter's Tale* the penitent Leontes is shown by Paulina a statue of his supposedly dead queen, Hermione, and he gradually discovers that the status lives. The last plays 'represent symbolically the resurrection of that which seems to die, but is yet alive, the conquest of love over those stormy waters of temporal existence which appear to engulf it.' It is significant that tempests, 'Shakespeare's precurrent symbols of tragedy, recur. . . . But there is not only loss in the tempset: there is revival, resurrection to the sounds of music.'[9] This awareness of a just and moral world, where good triumphs, is typical of the last plays of Shakespeare. Also 'the birth theme is recurrent, and has meaning: Marina, Perdita, Posthumus—all are thrown helpless at birth into the stormy turbulence of temporal existence, but are yet guarded by heaven and, though lost, restored.'[10]

Apart from the change in the audience-response, this 'profound cleavage in Shakespeare's mental history about 1607 must have been due to some spiritual crisis the nature of which it is only possible dimly to conjecture; some such process as that which in the psychology of religion bears the name of conversion.'[11] Life as presented in the late romances is full of surprises, pleasant and unpleasant, resurrections, reunions and recognitions. They are imbued with ethical idealism, moral perception and mystic grandeur. 'The final plays reveal a spiritual rather than political salvation.'[12] A mellow fruitfulness, a transcendental vision, often reflected in these plays, differentiate them from the other writings of that age. Particularly in these plays Shakespeare's religious experience, a felt experience, is symbolised and these are often called 'myths of immortality.'[13] This drama as it emerges from the moral plays of the Middle Ages, seems to be Christian in its moral argument. In these final plays we find an expression of harmony restored.

In keeping with the blessedness of old tales Shakespeare, as an experiment, uses miracles to transform something incredible to a state of credibility. The dead queen Thaisa is found as a priestess in the temple of Diana. Jupiter appears before Posthumus as if to assure him of prosperity. The supposed statue of Hermione moves, to the surprise of everyone present, and finally Prospero strides like a superman wielding super magic. All these are woven into the fabric of these romances so effectively that we willingly suspend our disbelief and enter wholeheartedly the world of romances. It must have been a novel experience for the Elizabethan audience to behold things unapparent as apparent.

In 'the plays of the final period the characters are much less complex, less realistic than they had been in the great tragedies and comedies of Shakespeare's middle period. They are not merely simplified: they tend to be puppets, unable to control their own destinies.'[14] The well-known lines in *The Murder in the Cathedral* seem to echo the central idea of these romances,

> Neither does the agent suffer
> Nor the patient act. But both are fixed
> In an eternal action, an eternal patience,
> To which all must consent that it may be willed
> And which all must suffer that they may will it,
> That the pattern may subsist, that the wheel may turn and still
> Be forever still.[15]

No doubt there are some memorable characters in these late romances, especially women like Marina, Hermione, Imogen, Perdita and Miranda who capture our imagination. The final plays of Shakespeare can be read as parables of a profound and glorious truth. In fact it may be said that 'all great literature is about religion; it may tell us, make us experience, more than religion does.'[15]

Of literary curiosity and critical interest is the affinity that exists between the Sanskrit plays and the late romances of Shakespeare. The thematic content of all these Indian plays and Shakespeare's romances is marked by a high moral tone. They deal with recognitions, reconciliations, love and peace, imbued with religious fervour. In these plays there is a passionate return to nature and a recognition of the supernatural. Kalidasa's *Sakuntala*, Bhasa's *Swapna Vasavadatta* and Harsha's *Ratnavalli* bear some parallels with Shakespeare's late romance. Kalidasa's *Sakuntala* is much closer than the other Sanskrit plays to the late romances. Kalidasa uses various dramatic devices like the ring episode (as in *The Merchant of Venice*) and Durvasa's curse in order to transform an ordinary tale of love, separation and reunion into a story of sublime love moving from a physical to a spiritual plane. Goethe states that in *Sakuntala* earth and heaven become one.

Examining Shakespeare's plays as religious drama does not necessarily mean that his plays can be understood and appreciated only as theological tracts and religious documents. Such an approach will not do justice to Shakespeare's excellent dramatic art. His plays are mostly enjoyed all over the world for their rich, poetic content and presentation of human nature in its totality. All the same, the profound thought content of the plays with its deeper understanding of the Elizabethan religious background is equally significant and relevant to a study of Shakespeare.

Shakespeare's tragedies merely present the religious and theological background of the age, while the late romances reveal Shakespeare's own religious experience and spiritual enlightenment, transmuted and transformed into something universal. Shakespeare's last plays bring about a sea change in dramatic art and insist on man's right relationship with God. They emphasize the need for man to understand God's ways and the justice involved in them.

NOTES

1. Una Elllis-Fermor, *The Frontiers of Drama*, p. 18.
2. E.M.W. Tillyard, *The Elizabethan World Picture*, p. 1.
3. G. Santayana, 'The Absence of Religion in Shakespeare,' *Inter pretations of Poetry and Religion*, p. 149.
4. H.S. Charlton, *Shakespeare Tragedy*, pp. 231-32.
5. R.M. Frye, *Shakespeare and Christian Doctrine*, p. 90.
6. S. Elias, 'The idea of person and Shakespearean tragedy,' *S.Q.*, Vol. 16, 1995, p. 43.
7. Frye, p. 271.

8. John Gassner and Edward Quinn, ed., *The Reader's Encyclopedia of World Drama*, p. 857.
9. Wilson Knight, *Shakespeare and Religion*, pp. 66-67.
10. *Ibid.*, p. 9.
11. E.K. Chambers, *Shakespeare, A Survey*, p. 223.
12. Wilson Knight, p. 70.
13. Wilson Knight, *The Crown of Life*, p. 39.
14. Kenneth Muir, *Pericles, Shakespeare Criticism, 1935- 65*, p. 313.
15. T.S. Eliot, *Murder in the Cathedral* (London: Faber and Faber, 1958), p. 45.
16. Wilson Knight, *The Crown of Life*, p. 27.

Rama Sarma and the Second International Milton Symposium, Christ's College, Cambridge, 1983 August

RONALD G. SHAFER

The occasion represented my first meeting with Professor Rama Sarma, a pleasant meeting indeed. How fitting that the sacred grounds where John Milton spent his academic career should be the setting. From lectures in the great hall, to receptions on the lawn, to a concert in Emmanuel's Old Hall, to a production of *Comus* in the New Theatre—at all times and in all places we could sense the stirring spirit of the early Milton.

That was exceptional, and it was exceptional as well that, in the judgment of many, this hitherto unprecedented international investigation into Milton's life and poetry should take place in such hallowed environs. The level of scholarship was astounding as the great minds grappled with the great one.

A very real component of that was provided by Professor Rama Sarma who chaired one of the most important of the symposium sessions, "Milton's Christ College Poetry: General Topics." I recall that this session, held in the New Theatre, was one of the most lively and enjoyable of all. Papers read by Professors Coburn Freer, Robert T. Fallon, Ruth Kivette, and Lady Mary Ann Radzinowicz were among the finest at the symposium. Critical responses by Professor Marshall Grossman, Andrew Harnack, and Archie Burnett were excellent as well.

But in my opinion it was the august presence of Professor Rama Sarma that made for the animated interchange and that created such a high intellectual tone for this session. He had been made chair of this particular session by the members of the planning committee because it was such a significant symposium session and because it featured some of the superluminaries of Milton criticism and scholarship today. His handling of the entire proceeding was gracious, poised, and most appreciated.

So now after many years of seasoned reflection upon that international meeting, I think anew of those happy days and Professor Rama Sarma's important role in them. In my mind's eye, I see him strolling beside Milton's

Cottage in Chalfont St. Giles, walking the streets of Cambridge, listening attentively to Professor Robert Ellrodt's keynote address, emoting in the rapturous strains of Poppy Holden singing Purcell. At all times, he was emotionally, intellectually, and spiritually engaged in the varied symposium events. Perhaps that is why he wrote of this international meeting, it was "an intellectual feast" (see *Milton Quarterly*, vol. 17, December 1983). This was high praise from the man who garnered respect from every single delegate from around the world.

As Roy Flannagan wrote in his account of the symposium, "We were a big event, in Cambridge as well as Chalfont St. Giles"; and Professor Rama Sarma contributed much to that induplicable ambience. There were many of who rightly felt that it was the presence of eminent scholars like himself who were the truly big event.

The Stream: The Myth of Ideal Love

DAISY GUNASEELI

Rama Sarma occupies a unique place as a 'myth maker' among Indian novelists in English. The myth underlying *The Stream* is the external myth or the pursuit of the ideal love of man. The *Sillapathikaram*, the story of Kovalan's passion, belongs to this love. The central theme is a troublesome and much-discussed problem—the eternal triangle. The love of Kovalan for Kannaki and Mathavi, the betrayal of the one for the other and finally the convergence of the triangle to this static point is what constitutes the story of *The Stream* too.

Gopalam, his wife Suguna, and Swarna represent the love triangle. Rama Sarma presents the problem in an altogether novel way, tackling it from a purely different point of view, where neither love nor beauty predominates. The situation is solved most effectively by the triumph of justice. The purity, simplicity, contentment and the meditative peace of Suguna is the hero's answer, as well as the gift to his unsympathetic and non-understanding world.

Marriage incites man to be a capricious autocrat. Gopalam, the principal character of the *The Stream*, is one such person. In his romantic idealism he saw himself as Antony, and found that his wife Suguna did not possess the majesty of Cleopatra, nor her infinite variety. He was madly in love with poets like Keats, Shelley and Wordsworth. So he was known among his friends "The Shelley of India." His was an utopian world where love of the purest type was his goal. "Platonic love with all the dream-like unreality appealed to him." His aesthetic tastes and appreciation of poetry made him detest ugliness in the world. With great expectations he married Suguna. For him the moonlit nights were grand and he said: "why don't you feel thrilled by such wonderful sights?" But Suguna's reply shattered his idealistic vision to pieces. "One must be a poet or should atleast have poetic imagination to admire such lovely sights. I am afraid I have none of these qualities."

Gopalam's grand theory was that the moment Suguna was married to him she should think of him and no one else in the world. He little realized that her father did have a prior claim over her affections. He could take liberties with his wife and even insult her, but could not tolerate an affront from her. When he found that Suguna did not have all these desired qualities, he cut himself off from her, talked less and almost observed a 'golden silence.'

> The physical aspect of life was never a strong attraction to Gopalam. Not that he shunned it, but somehow he felt that life was complete and full only when the partners had common aspirations and ideals. (15)

Marriage became a struggle for dominance for Suguna. But she had to follow the destiny of her husband faithfully with love and reverence. She could not step out of the social system having neither the liking nor the will to do so, and so endured the humiliation like Sakuntala of the *Mahabharata.* Like the myths of the past, human relationship and partnership depended on the basis of endurance.

With the greater gulf he had created for himself and Suguna, he thought of the girls in the college where he was working. He no longer felt that they were artificial. Rather they seemed to be a jolly lot. He wanted women in earthly mode with freedom of spirit. He had no taste for the obedient wife in ethereal robes. A woman who had more of the human element, that was what he wanted. And Swarna was able to provide him with all those qualities.

With Swarna, the world was no longer a dreary place for Gopalam. It was on the other hand a thrilling and exciting spot where women like Swarna lived and loved. She satisfied him from every angle. He lent her his plays and poems and she found them 'interesting, intoxicating and enlivening.' "When the world had such dynamic women for him why should be run away from it and renounce its riches?" He took to life again with zest.

Meeting Swarna was an unusual experience for Gopalam. She seemed to be his dream heroine. Swarna came as an inspiration to induce new hopes in him when he had lost all hopes of leading an ideal life. She was intelligent and so could read his frustrated mind like a book. She was quite sympathetic and understood the reason for his unhappy domestic life. She seemed to be a modern woman trying to be rid of the shackles of society and that was the woman Gopalam wanted.

The tragedy of Gopalam was his inability to distinguish his acquired personality from his own inherited personality. He believed in the apparent externals, that too with the help of his wrong awareness of his association with the Romantic poets.

Gopalam valued the concreteness of objects without giving any credence to its metaphysics.

> If men failed to distinguish between their inherited and acquired personalities, it was their own fault. He was thoroughly convinced of

> the prevalence of reason over bestiality, of judgement over ignorance in man. (170)

In the beginning Swarna found her love for Gopalam inseparable. She was optimistic and was hopeful of a bright future with Gopalam. She justified her love for him,

> Society might call her love unconventional but to her it was perfectly natural. She loved Gopalam and he responded. Their hearts beat in unison. What more was necessary? In how many married lives was there such an amount of harmony, contentment and understanding, she asked herself. (45)

The same Swarna who was loyal to him could not stand the test of time when separation came. Gopalam went abroad for higher studies, and on the day of his departure her feminine instinct raised the natural fear: "You may forget me for the beautiful women there. After all I am nothing when compared with those foreign beauties. You may feel attracted towards them and then what will happen to me?" (45) These words got imprinted in his heart as if they were verses from the Holy books:

> Swarna's words were gospel to him. He knew for certain that he could never displease Swarna. She might be far away from him, but her spirit would be watching him, guiding him and saving him from pitfalls. She was his guardian angel and day in and day out her words would brace him against all possible temptations. (47)

While Gopalam maintained his identity throughout his stay in London, Swarna in India started becoming unreliable, and by the time he returned home, their solemn pledge had lost its significance.

Gopalam's mind had misconceived Swarna's love as a substitute for romantic idealism. He had looked into her heart but had failed to see deep into the mind. For Swarna's mind was a weak and diffident one, and she bore no fighting spirit. Nor had she any faith in herself. She doubted her own strength and feared her own shadow. And then there were the conscientious scruples that she had ruined the happiness of a good natured and innocent woman like Suguna.

Above all, Murthy was threatening her. Swarna did not have the courage to defy him because his word carried weight with the members of the rich family that supported her. She became a fatalist believing that all the changes that came over her were only thrust on her through fate. Like a pessimist she looked forward to a bleak future and this policy of passive suffering, proved to be ruinous to her as well as Gopalam.

Her letters to Gopalam became few as she was closely watched by Murthy. Gopalam was baffled by this silence. His predicament became similar to the bewilderment of Hamlet.

Hamlet says,

> I have of late—but wherefore I know not—lost all my mirth, forgone all custom of exercises, and it goes so heavily with my disposition that this goodly frame, the earth, seems to me a sterile promontory; this most excellent canopy, the air, look you, this brave o'erhanging firmament, this majestical roof fretted with golden fire, why it appears no other thing to me than a foul and pestilent congregation of vapours. What a piece of work is man! How noble in reason! how infinite in faculty! in form and moving how express and admirable! in action how like an angel! in apprehension how like a God! The beauty of the world! the paragon of animals! and yet, to me, what is this quintessence of dust? (*Hamlet*, II, ii)

Similarly Gopalan lost interest in life. A darkness had entered his soul and he wallowed in distress and self-pity.

It was at this juncture that he met Joan in London. Joan's acquaintance with him was a turning point in his life. Her pleasing manners and love for Indianism had a spell on him. He said, "Physical attraction is not the only link between men and women. There can be good companionship or sometimes the friendship may be based on mutual admiration." (67)

It was Joan who revived Gopalam back to his normal self. Her words were encouraging and his lethargy started vanishing and he gained a new energy and vigour to write plays. Her magical words were: "Better use all your intellect for a good cause and not allow yourself to drift away into lethargy and frustration." (73) The intellectual companionship with Joan was not changed to physical desires because of the simple adoration of the fervent love for Swarna in Gopalam's heart.

Meanwhile Swarna communicates about her marriage with Rao to Gopalam. Gopalam had never so far thought that Swarna was capable of doing him any harm. He was unnerved. For a moment his faith in himself, in the Triple force, in the ultimate sense of justice was uprooted. Yet he did not go down to the depths of despondency. He developed for himself a certain unruffled mental state. It was one of detachment to the worldly entanglements. He accepted his defeat with no regrets.

> He took to life with greater vigour and he argued to himself that he was not born merely for the sake of falling in or falling out of love. There were mighty projects before him. Love was only a subsidiary object. He might do something constructive to himself or to the country in general. (169)

He was determined to rule out passion for women from his pageant of life. Life had taught him a lesson not to bother about women. He strove for the substitution of all desires for the achievements of one single goal. In his college days he had dabbled in writing verses and plays. He took to it now wholeheartedly.

Incidentally Suguna too suffered violently, caught in the midst of tempestuous relationship between Swarna and Gopalam. She felt she was abandoned, but she had a firm faith in herself and believed that God would be kind to her and all would be well. She hoped that one day justice would be done to her. Her deep faith in the sanctity of marriage gave her strength to endure patiently her misery of separation without complaining.

The fundamental goodness of Suguna's character and conduct was the secret of her strength. It was a strength that her good conscience offered. She stood for all that was good in tradition. Suguna believed in the worship of her lord and master and wanted to conquer him ultimately with her devotion.

Previously when Gopalam told her of his affair with Swarna, she did not abuse him. But her words left him cold and shivering: "So this is what you have done. I suspected as much. But I don't stand in the way of your love. I want you to be happy. I am glad you have found a woman who satisfies you." (34) This silent acquiescence on her part was too much for him. She had shown absolute serenity and even nobility. It was natural on her part to fight for her possession. But she showed no anger and exhibited no signs of jealousy. This was a lesson to Gopalam. It taught him about a woman's capacity for self-sacrifice. Coming as it did from the woman whom he considered to be not upto his expectations, he was baffled and amazed. Suguna scored a point over him. At least in one respect she was superior to him. He was selfish, whereas she was unselfish. He admitted to himself that he was unfair to Suguna in his madness for Swarna. By making Gopalam himself adore Suguna for her patient suffering, Rama Sarma shows that Suguna would win her husband back not only in terms of physical proximity, but also in emotional and mental harmony in life. The dream did come true. Suguna's love was repaid.

Gopalam asked her to join him. She patiently waited for the word and she came and joined him the moment she was asked to do so. His life with Suguna was no longer unbearable and she could enjoy his 'pompous oratory' without getting bored. He tells her, "Man may correct himself or be corrected by others. But one thing is certain. We are not governed by blind chance. We often talk of fate only to excuse ourselves. In fact, we create and destroy, we love and hate, we sin and repent, we are responsible for all our actions." (172)

Adam violated the hierarchy of virtue through his excessive fondness for Eve. Gopalam found the comparison right with his own life. He had sinned. Now was the proper time for him to throw away lust. The right destination to reach was the 'love of Suguna.'

The very concept of love in Gopalam's heart had undergone a drastic change. The physical love he had for Suguna in the beginning faded away to take up the emotional love for Swarna. But the intellectual love for Joan paved way for his better understanding, and the fidelity of Suguna and the circumstances that led to his awakening from the maddening passion, educated him into a better understanding of life. He now learns that life is a paradox, where you cannot expect every ideal to exist in just one person alone. He realizes that he must let the stream of life flow on. Life with all its limitations has to be accepted.

The eternal triangle in Gopalam was brought through his own individual efforts. Peace was attained through his own enlightenment. He grew serene and austere and was always poised. Mentally he was far advanced of his age and he was keen on exploring to himself the riddle of life,

> I now live for nobler ends; not for me the maddening days of love, I want to be a man, a complete man, a perfect one. Passionate longings no longer move me. The nobler element in me moves me to the more balanced and intellectual understanding of life. I have come out of the storm and stress of the stream. Now I look back and heave a sigh of relief. I am not sorry for my experience, for they have chastened and sublimated me. The stream of life now goes on calmly towards the annihilation of animal instincts. (173)

NOTE

1. Rama Sarma, *The Stream* (New Delhi: S. Chand, 1983).

From M.Phil. dissertation, "M.V. Rama Sarma's Novels: A Study in the Light of Myths," Bharatidasan University, Tiruchi, 1987.

'Just are the ways of God' . . . : A Study of *The Farewell Party*

T. ASOKA RANI

A dedicated academic, a distinguished scholar and an astute administrator, which is what M.V. Rama Sarma is, has made a modest but worthy contribution towards enriching the Indian English literature. As a critic, a novelist and a playwright his achievement is such that he can legitimately lay claim to a pride of place among the contemporary Indian English writers. *The Farewell Party* is chronologically the second in the series of his works on fiction, the others being *The Stream, Look Homeward, The Bliss of Life, Pastures New* and *Height of Noon*; all of which reflect Rama Sarma's empirical perceptions on the various emerging situations in life. Couched in terse but lucid style, with simple sentences and aptness of diction. *The Farewell Party* provides right answers, as conceived by the author, for a wide range of subtle and sensitive problems a university teacher is likely to be confronted with. The novel is also innovatively structured by the author in the form of a stream-of-consciousness narration of the musings of Prof. Prakasam, the main character, on the various episodes in his life as a teacher for over thirty years, during the ninety minutes of time before leaving for the farewell party, on the eve of his retirement.

Prakasam is least perturbed at the imminence of the end of his long but chequered career as a university teacher, for over three decades. On the contrary, he muses over the various incidents, in his life, good and not so good, in his long career and exudes a sense of fulfilment and satisfaction.

The novel deals with the vicissitudes of life of a university teacher—his trials and tribulations, hopes and despairs, successes and failures. But the protagonist Prakasam meets them stoically thus vindicating his affirmative vision of life. His unflinching faith in the Hindu tenet 'Karma Yoga'—do your duty and leave the result to God—enables him to nurture a positive and optimistic view of life and an abiding faith that man, who has strayed from the right path, is bound ultimately to return to his innate good nature.

The Farewell Party opens with Prof. Prakasam, reclining on a sofa in his house one afternoon, with the farewell party arranged for him on the eve of his retirement just ninety minutes away, and reminiscing over the series of events his eventful career, spanning over three decades. In the stream of thoughts that cross his mind, he conjures up situations and happenings which enable the reader to evaluate the characters accurately. By this unique method of narration smacking of a semi-biographical rendering, the reader gets the feeling that Prakasam is none other than the author's surrogate to reveal the latter's views and predilection for the life of a dedicated teacher.

Prakasam is a picture of supreme satisfaction as he nostalgically thinks of his self-satisfying career. His students have abundance of love and respect for him. Being a votary of ethical values, he believes that the education imparted to the students in the rural university inculcates in them a sense of true culture and human dignity besides preparing them for a vocation. Thus a positive attitude towards life manifests itself even at this stage in the novel.

Commenting on Prakasam's nature, the author writes: "Prakasam was a great optimist and by nature he was cheerful. So his summer clouds never stayed for a longer time than they should." (55) If and when Prakasam seems to be unhappy with anything, it is only a passing phase.

Prakasam in general worries over the presence of ugliness, hatred and injustice in this world. He cannot understand why man, an image of God, should be bestial. Man has the free will to choose the nobler path or the ignominious one. But Prakasam, the optimist, fervently hopes that the nobler instincts in man would ultimately triumph over the baser elements in him. It is only a question of time and "Man would ultimately go back to his innate good nature after having experienced several pitfalls and failures in life." (3) Prakasam pities the narrow-minded people for whom a change of heart at that age is not possible. But being a confirmed optimist, he sincerely hopes that at least "in their next life, they would be born better." (3)

For Prakasam, the last five years at Hyderabad, before he moved over to the rural university, were marked by turbulence. All the hostile forces conspired against him and under the pressure of such antagonism, he used to be gloomy and dejected. But he would soon get over it and, try to be happy and contented through his total dedication to teaching.

Prakasam loves his student, Sarala, who belongs to a different caste. Thereby they become victims of social opprobrium. Prakasam pays a heavy price by losing his job. For two months, they find themselves in wilderness. Despite all this suffering, Prakasam faces the situation with a rare courage and unflinching faith in God. "His simple faith almost naive faith in himself, that he was destined for an eventful life . . . stood him in good stead. He waited patiently for something to happen." (17) And it did happen; he got a job in Hyderabad.

Prakasam receives three letters, on the day of his retirement, one from his son in London, and other from his daughter, the third from Principal Gupta. Prakasam is visibly annoyed when he sees the third letter from

Principal Gupta of the Hyderabad college, his one-time rival. It is only because of Gupta that he had to come away from Hyderabad after living there for nearly thirty years.

This letter from Gupta makes Prakasam think of his life in Hyderabad. He who believes in the innate goodness of human nature, fails to understand man's degeneracy to the level of bestiality. Commenting on Prakasam's positive attitude to life, the author writes: "There was degeneracy but Prakasam felt that man could be revitalized." (23)

Gupta does not feel secure as long as Prakasam is there. So he slights him and makes his life miserable. Though losing Principalship to an undeserving person affects his sense of justice his genial disposition makes it possible for him to be reconciled with that position. Gupta symbolizes the intriguer. He makes it impossible for Prakasam to stay in Hyderabad. But Prakasam's faith in God saves him. Prakasam "always believed in God's grace and man's innate good nature. The next year brought him an escape from the impasse." (82) Admiring the innate simplicity and unpretentious nature of the people at the rural university, in the last phase of his career, Prakasam tells his wife: "Losing Principalship in Hyderabad has been a blessing in disguise for us." (83) He never finds fault with anything in life. This serves as a striking example of his affirmative approach to life.

This type of outlook on life is exquisitely manifested in yet another instance. His aspiration for professorship, which he richly deserves, is thwarted by the malicious Suri, the Principal's right-hand man at the New College. Prakasam champions the cause of Sundaram, another teacher of the college, who is harassed and given a raw deal by the Principal. As a fitting punishment for Prakasam's independent spirit, Professorship is not created that year. The Principal treats Prakasam's independent spirit as insubordination. Prakasam does not feel sorry at losing the Professorship. He thinks "he could wait for sometime more." (44) Five years later, he does become a Professor, and he serves in that capacity with distinction for fifteen years.

Prakasam loved humanity and "did not condemn vice outright, for he realized that it was a part of man. It was the negative force in him—it was upto him to become divine or beastly. He pitied the unthinking man going down the path from one passionate desire to another." (23) Prakasam has tolerance for others and he accepts life as it is.

Elsewhere, the author writes how Prakasam practises tolerance in his relations with fellow human beings: "To a lover of human nature like Prakasam these little angularities meant nothing. . . . He sincerely believed that it was too much to expect men and women to be faultlessly pure and divinely good. It would be preposterous to do so. One had to live in an imperfect world, with human beings not in any way perfect. It would be sheer folly, if not hypocrisy, if one were to assume for oneself the godhead and condemn others as being beastly and inhuman. Tolerance was needed;

Prakasam realized that." (30) This is a comprehensive view of life that Prakasam develops.

Summing up his own life, Prakasam also emphasizes the virtue of tolerance which he possesses in abundance. "If some were unkind or hostile to him, he always tried to be friendly with them. In fact he did not have any serious quarrel with anyone. Some felt jealous of him, but he tolerated them." (53)

Prakasam stresses, again and again, the goodness of life and its values. Life at Oxford was pleasant though he was a staunch nationalist. Prakasam, who is a humanist, strongly believes that human relationships are more vital than political ties. He echoes E.M. Forster when he says that a Britisher, back home, is a different person—helpful, kind and polite. Prakasam has several British friends and he does not want to tear himself away from them on political grounds.

Prakasam's habit of seeking some good even in evil reflects his humanism. He joins others in condemning war, is concerned about the ghastliness, the horror and the savagery of the war. However, his disposition is such that he finds a core of goodness in the ruinous war itself. He finds that war creates job opportunities for the unemployed and the low paid employees get better jobs, at least till the war lasts. It is, indeed, a blessing in disguise for all those who have been rotting for years.

Prakasam is such a humanist that he sincerely believes in serving humanity and thereby fulfilling his mission in life. Now that he is retiring, he decides to devote his life to the service of others. He says: "Human beings are essentially good. I can never imagine anything exclusively negative. I don't think I have understood life in its totality. But I shall try to get at the truth of it. That will be my major work for the rest of my life." (85)

If Prakasam is undeterred by hurdles, it is because of his unflinching faith in the theory of 'Karma.' It offers him solace and comfort. He believes that a person's past plays a vital role in shaping his present life. That is how he tries to explain to himself the bitterness and unhappiness he has to face in this life for no fault of his. He desires to practise 'Nishkama karma,' to devote himself to the service of others.

Prakasam uses the magic word 'karma' to relieve the agony of Seshu's father. Seshu, a student of Prakasam, commits suicide along with his fiancé, in order to escape the domestic pressure to marry his niece. Seshu's father is broken hearted as he holds himself responsible for this ghastly tragedy. Consoling the old man, Prakasam says: "There is a higher force governing our actions. We are not completely responsible for our actions. And when Fate wills it, human effort is futile. It is destined that Seshu should meet his death that way. You are only an instrument. If he were destined to die, even if you had not done anything to him, he would have died. So don't blame yourself too much. . . . You ought to realize that you are in no way responsible for your son's karma." (64)

Prakasam's unswerving loyalty to God is manifested throughout the novel. He, at the outset, is grateful to God for making him choose teaching as a career where he can serve humanity faithfully and fearlessly. Even Sarala, his wife, often says: "We are indeed grateful to God for this peace and contentment" (83) in the teaching profession.

Prakasam's concept of God is based on the three qualities of Beauty, Love and Justice. He believes in God, but religion with all its ceremonial and ritual has no meaning for him. He is "more inclined to believe in an impersonal godhead and in the existence of an all-pervading Spirit in the Universe." (83)

He has abundant faith in God's grace. Sarala, his wife, has the same faith for she says, "by God's grace we have passed through the storm and stress of life creditably." (67)

Prakasam's affirmation of life is based on his 'rich and varied life.' He says: "I have that feeling of pride and satisfaction, that comes to every successful teacher at the time of his retirement. . . . I can happily look back and feel satisfied." (85) This is the contented life of Prakasam.

Prakasam often refers to divine dispensation. Still he thinks that one should not resign oneself to inactivity. One need not get dejected if one's efforts go waste and plans do not materialize. It means something else is in store for him. He affirms "God's ways are just, though peculiar." (83) Sarala too expresses the same sentiments and together they experience the justness in God's ways.

The Farewell Party presents an ideal teacher who accepts life as a service to mankind.

Look Homeward: Service to Country

N. GANESH

The novel *Look Homeward*, makes one realize the value of detachment and broadmindedness. If man adheres to the ethics of life naturally, the love for his country will get deep rooted.

Attachment and insularity are the root cause for the death of innate good nature. The freedom fighters were detached and broadminded. So, they could sacrifice everything, even their life. But now the young scholars prefer to stay in a foreign country simply because the motherland does not offer all the amenities and affluence they want to enjoy. They are in the mad pursuit of these trifles. Service to humanity and dedication to the country are things of the past. In the midst of this murky atmosphere, Rama Sarma's *Look Homeward* serves as a lodestar to guide the misconceived Indian scholars. It also emphasizes the need of a mighty zest from young scholars to reform the country.

> The title *Look Homeward*, a Miltonic expression from *Lycidas*, 'Look Homeward, Angel, now and melt with ruth' suggests the acceptance of the reality of the situation . . . in the context of the novel it is indicative of the noble ideal that after one's sojourn in foreign lands one has to think of developing one's country with the rich knowledge and experience acquired during the stay abroad. The ultimate fulfilment of all knowledge is to make humanity share the benefits of developments.[1]

Rama Sarma portrays Ravi as a young scholar of India who goes abroad for higher studies and who looks homeward to serve his motherland however discouraging the circumstances may be. He is a rationalist and puts more emphasis on human effort. Ravi being the son of Ramesam, the staunch Gandhian and philanthropist, has an inherent desire to serve his country. On a Fulbright fellowship Ravi goes to the USA to study Mechanical Engineering. There he falls in love with Prem who is studying in Denver to specialize in Drama. One night Ravi and Prem are invited to dinner by the local Drama Society. When the talk is about India, he eloquently champions his motherland and supports everything that is Indian. He is not blind to the limitations of his country, yet he feels that he should not expose his country to the taunting remarks of others. When he returns to India he can be very critical but while he is abroad he is an unofficial ambassador for his country. The members put him searching questions about Gandhi's policy of non-violence and Nehru's political philosophy of neutrality. He argues:

> Gandhiji's creed of non-violence is positive. It does not mean that one should run away from fighting. But one should abhor violence. Applying that ethical idealism to practical politics Nehru propounded the idea of dynamic neutrality. It is non-violence only so far as we are not interested in joining power blocs. But our freedom is a great responsibility and in its defence we do not hesitate to fight.[2]

Ravi wants us to 'maintain our individuality' and he thinks that 'Nehru gives a great image of our country in that way.' (16-17)

After the holiday trip, Ravi is received by his friends Gupta, Sundaram and Ramesh Babu. Gupta is all admiration for the American life. He identifies himself with the customs and manners of the Americans. There is Ham who shortened his name to sound like an American. They all like Ravi even though they cannot very much appreciate his Indianism. Sometimes they pity him for he cannot enjoy life as they can.

Gupta decides to settle down in the USA, and he gets married to Rosie a foreigner. His other friends also desire to settle down in the USA. They wish to convert Ravi to their way of thinking but in vain. "Unfortunately India does not offer the facilities for advanced research work. The Universities have yet to develop" (22) points out Sundaram. He is genuinely interested in research work and is a dedicated worker in Space Research. He is afraid that if he were to come to India all that work will come to a close. "Everywhere in India there is corruption. It is sickening. The government offices, the business concerns, the educational institutions, all seem to be seething in the pool of corruption. There is a lot of nepotism." (22-23) Ramesh Babu vehemently pleads and justifies his plan for not returning to India.

> In India very often there is no right place of opening for the type of research work we wish to do. For instance, the training we receive here in Food Technology, Aeronautical Engineering or other branches of advanced knowledge has no relevance to the employment opportunities in India. We have to depend mostly on the government. We are kept as pool officers or pensioners, or sometimes if we have a good pull we become administrators and all this research work will be a waste, a colossal waste. (23)

Ham argues that even though he loves to be in his own country, it is mean to stay in India. Only Gupta insists on money and the material comforts wealth gives. All others have different views on the matter. Their motivation is mostly based on research and the opportunities that are denied in India. Ravi listens to them with patience and sympathy. He starts slowly but deliberately. He pleads that we are all responsible for all this and have to blame ourselves. He hails the young intellectuals to launch a war against these foes:

> We have to fight it out. What is the use of running away from reality? We become escapists. Scientific research should be useful to society. It should have an applied bias. A developing country cannot afford to spend much on pure research. (24)

Ravi emphasizes a change in the educational system. He points out that everyone has an obligation to his country, to his community. The work and service of an individual will stimulate others and open new horizons and new vistas of knowledge. At least it will shake people out of their complacency. Ravi agrees with his friends that there are several difficulties and one may not get what one deserves. But he points out that an Indian is an outsider and alien in the USA he has a right place only in his country.

All of them want to return to India but they are not sure of their future and often they are doubtful of the opportunities that India may offer to them. But Ravi alone has a greater sense of commitment to his country. "We should work for our country however discouraging the circumstances may be. One day through our efforts a greater India will be created." (25) Ravi unfolds his quest for service to the country and he seems to echo Swami Vivekananda's views: "Let us perfect the means; the end will take care of itself."[3]

A great sense of responsibility to one's motherland has been created in this novel very effectively by Rama Sarma through the protagonist Ravi. He longs to be back in India as soon as he finishes his academic work in the USA. He is every inch an Indian. Apart from his love and affection for his parents, he has a commitment to the country. He feels that every Indian who goes abroad for higher studies should come back and serve his country. His national sentiments as well as personal interest and anxiety to return to India are made clear throughout the novel.

Ravi and Prem go to Berkeley to meet Suguna who is doing her Ph.D. and they are received warmly and affectionately. Suguna is nostalgic and she wants to go back to India. There is Raghu studying in Berkeley and is bent upon settling down in the USA. He has no intention of returning to India. He has already developed a curious attitude towards India. Suguna is in love with him. She cannot wriggle herself out of the complicated situation. Ravi does not like Raghu repeatedly referring to the poverty in India. Raghu is thoroughly disgusted with the Indian conditions. Ravi can understand that deep in his heart Raghu too has tender feelings for his country but only out of sheer desperation he is talking like that. But Ravi also cannot understand why these persons, who are at heart willing to go back to India, pretend to be settling down in the States. Ravi thinks that a certain type of bravado, a recklessness and an abandon, all mixed together perhaps worked on them.

In the evening, Ravi and Prem go out shopping and they have a ride in the cable car. They go towards the bay area. They observe the heavy traffic on the bridges. They think that the Golden Gate Bridge is a marvellous engineering feat. Especially to Ravi all these are of great interest. As an engineer he feels he should build mighty bridges and dams, tame the Indian rivers, control the floods and bring prosperity to the teeming millions of the country. Such noble thoughts fill his mind.

Gupta marries Rosie, breaking the Indian social tradition. He advises Ravi and other friends to get married to foreigners, so that international relationships and world citizenship may be established. Gupta's life with Rosie is all right for a few months. Being an Indian, Gupta naturally longs for a few peaceful moments in life with Rosie. She never allows him that moment of peace. She hurries him all the time through the vast panorama of life as though she has lost something and is trying to find it. It soon occurs to him that she is not happy with him. Gradually Gupta realizes the mistake of getting married to a foreigner. Rosie is disloyal to him. She sues him in the court for divorce for ill-treating her. Gupta has to spend all the money he has saved so far. Everything between him and Rosie is over. He comes back to India penniless and broken-hearted. He sets up practice in Delhi and wishes to recreate himself and live afresh. Gupta takes his marriage with Rosie as a lesson for him: "We have to accept life in its totality, come what may. We cannot shun the tide. We are on it or we are drowned. It does not matter whether we go up or come down. But we have to get experiences in life." (80)

The novel obviously shows how youngmen like Gupta are fascinated by the west and its ways of life. Eventually the motherland alone gives 'the elixir of life' (80) to those who are betrayed in a foreign country. The stream of life can ever be smooth and sweet only in the motherland, this truth is portrayed very effectively:

> The country needed him [Gupta]. He would have been lost to his country if Rosie did not jilt him. It was a blessing in disguise. . . . The commitment and involvement he had for his country was clear to him. Nothing could shake him in his determination to serve the country. (87)

Ramesh Babu has nearly finished his work. He is working for a Ph.D. in Food Technology. He has his own serious doubts about a job opportunity for a subject of that type in India. However, he is prepared to return to India and try his luck. Ravi feels sure that persons like Ramesh Babu would be of great help to the mother country.

Sundaram's return to India is uncertain. He is a dedicated scientist and he wants to win international renown. That will not be possible if he comes back to India. So he decides to stay on. Sundaram is committed to scientific research and it is not like the emotional entanglement of Gupta with Rosie that binds him to America. He is an Indian in all respects. He is neither crazy about western life nor is he too much sophisticated. Ye his love of research and his aspiration to win fame leaves him with no alternative. He has to stay on. He will be a loss to India. Ravi hopes that one day Sundaram will come back because he is not a slave to western life. So there is hope. Ravi presumes that Ham will return to India as he has no definite commitment to stay on. Sundaram confides in Ravi and expresses his nostalgic reminiscences of India on the eve of Ravi's departure to India. Sundaram longs for the warm climate, the sunshine, the moonlit nights which have their own sweetness.

Ravi reaches his village which is situated on the banks of the river Krishna. Rama Sarma vividly shows the contrast between 'the calm, placid life as tranquil as the waters of the river' and 'the busy, sophisticated life in the USA.' (72) The portrayal of Ravi's 'innate simplicity, his essential good nature and his typical Indianism despite his stay in a foreign country for three years,' is very illuminating. Rama Sarma hints that all young men who go abroad should cultivate such innate simplicity, essential good nature and Indianism to build a prosperous and wholesome India.

Ravi leaves for Hyderabad and meets Ramesh Babu who is already there. Ravi admires Ramesh's pluck and courage in sticking to his motherland in spite of unemployment.

Ravi goes to Delhi for an interview and stays in a hotel. He does not like to go and see Prem. He luckily meets Gupta. Gupta having failed in his attempt at establishing peace for himself, wants others to be happy in marital life. Hence Gupta brings Ravi and Prem together. His mind is given to such noble thoughts of doing good for others.

In a developing country like India there is plenty of opportunity for people like Gupta to settle down as a practising doctor and serve the people. The country needs generous, humane, tender and charitable persons. Gupta is a changed man and begins a new chapter in his life.

Ham and Sundaram still remain in the USA Ravi and his friends understand that 'there is nothing so wonderful as the service one renders to one's country.'

Rama Sarma points out that it is not enough if Indians are politically independent. He emphasizes that Indians must cultivate love for their country and develop national spirit: "The day we all feel that in our humble manner we serve the country to the best of our abilities we march towards prosperity." (92) Everyone has to put in the best effort for the good of the nation. The government must develop the will and capacity to serve the nation. "Only a Hercules can cleanse the Aegean Stables." (93) The novelist feels that a superman's effort on the part of young intellectuals alone can set up a healthy and prosperous nation. Every Indian must cultivate a sense of involvement in nation building, dedication to work and uprightness in dealing with others.

Rama Sarma diagnoses the malady that ails India:

> We have private morality but lack public morality. We are puritans at home, God fearing and religious minded. But the moment we come out into the public sector activities we have no scruples. We shirk work. We have a general grouse against humanity. We don't mind subverting public good and negating to fellow men what should belong to them. (94)

The novelist insists that everyone should put in maximum effort in the developmental programmes. Young men who receive education and training in foreign countries should come back to India. Belief in creating a greater India, optimism, faith and love for the nation should be deeply rooted.

Rama Sarma optimistically observes: "If young men and women took it on themselves, they could metamorphose the sick social order into something dynamic. They had the energy and the will power." (100) He desires mighty zest from young men and women for the reformation of the motherland. The novelist also views the young intellectuals as "the knights of a new order believing in service and in love of the country." (100)

No doubt our country has all the natural resources. It needs proper utilization of human energy and natural resources. The politicians who merely garland the statues of the great patriots will never do this noble service. The young scholars alone could do this noble, mighty service to develop the motherland. They could bring real glory to their nation. The novelist exhorts them to make our nation self-reliant, advanced in science and technology, free of poverty and clean in administration. He makes it obvious that this sublime service of building a prosperous and wholesome nation could be achieved only by the younger generation. *Look Homeward* is a novel with 'a message' and it aims to create and cultivate love for the nation and devotion to serve it.

NOTES

1. G. Nageswara Rao, "M.V.Rama Sarma," *Indian English Novelists: An Anthology of Critical Essays*, ed. Madhusudan Prasad (New Delhi: Sterling, 1982), p. 110.
2. Rama Sarma, *Look Homeward* (Madras: Blackie), p. 16.
3. Swami Vivekananda, "Work and Its Secret," *Indian Writing Prose Selections*, Comp. A. Uthandaraman (Madras: Emerald, 1983), p. 9.

From M.Phil. dissertation, "The Quest for Service in M.V. Rama Sarma's Novels," Madras University, 1991.

The Bliss of Life: Temptation Ordeals

SYED MUKHARAM

Although Rama Sarma's earlier novels, *The Stream, The Farewell Party* and *Look Homeward* present a comprehensive picture of life on the physical, social and emotional planes, *The Bliss of Life*, presents life in its totality and complexity. All these planes of life are ultimately made to blossom into a divine love. The entire process is artistically depicted in terms of the life of the poet-musician, Kshetrayya who passes through all these stages and struggles of mundane life, finally attaining god realization. The life of Kshetrayya reveals a clear and convincingly gradual progression of an individual from a physical to a spiritual plane ultimately surrendering to the will of God.

Varadaiah who never loses his original self but realizes his mission, evolves gradually and finally attains the 'bliss of life'. The novel is, as the writer points out, 'an imaginative reconstruction of Kshetrayya's life', a famous poet-musician of Andhra region who wrote *padams*, devotional love-songs. The theme of the novel, thus, is the legendary—historical life of Kshetrayya the celebrated artist of the seventeenth century and his quest. As Nageswara Rao explains, 'This is a tradition beginning with the rishis of the Vedas. . . . The same tradition has been continued by the medieval mystics, the song composers like Chaitanya and a number of others.[1] Kshetrayya belongs to the tradition of music composers.

Kshetrayya was earlier called Varadaiah, and he was a young devotee of Muvva Gopala. The first section of the novel very aptly opens with Varadaiah singing a song and Mohanangi dancing to that tune in ecstasy. To use the words of the novelist,

> He [Varadaiah] enjoyed her company immensely. They had similar tastes, they both belonged to the world of music and dance. But gradually as they grew to be man and woman thoughts of love occupied their minds. Their study of Bharata's *Natya Sastra* and Bhanudatta's *Rasa Manjari*, gave them an intellectual refinement and affinity.

Their passionate association, emotional identification and artistic tastes naturally lead to a deeper union. The novelist's imaginative reconstruction of the scene is idyllic and impressive. Varada tells Mohana, "I am fond of you, desperately in need of you and your company. Without you there is no world for me. I cannot sing unless you dance. I cannot compose songs unless I look at you and feel inspired." Mohana responds warmly,

> Varada, I know your affection for me. I have also noticed the change in you recently. It is no longer that innocent look you have. Your looks communicate to me your desire to be with me, your passionate longing to take me into your hands. Take me, take all I am.

Nageswara Rao rightly gives the social and sociological reasons, particularly 'the social disapproval of the love of Kshetrayya and Mohanangi which actually intensifies their love on the one hand and the love of the couple to the Lord, Gopal on the other. They feel isolated and therefore driven more to the side of God and become more devoted. The effect of this social segregation is more pronounced on Kshetrayya than on Mohanangi.[2]

Varadaiah enters a new phase of experience in life when he has a revelation on a Krishnashtami day. He is blessed by Muvva Gopala to be the great Padam composer and to spread the message of love and devotion for god. After the revelation, mundane life appears dull and drab to him. He surrenders himself completely to Gopala and starts composing Padams in praise of him. During this phase we witness Kshetrayya's transformation from a state of sensuous attachment to life to a state of spiritual realization.

Kshetrayya realizes his mission and gets a clear idea of his goal. At this stage he transcends his physical longings and reaches an emotional perception where he communes with the Lord and becomes a perfect instrument of divine will by attaining total identification with the Lord, Muvva Gopala. He does with joy whatever the Lord prompts him to do. His compositions acquire a new melody, depth of meaning, passion and metaphysical suggestiveness. He becomes fully conscious of the mission of his life, like any other devotee, and dedicates himself totally to the task of fulfilling that mission. He feels a kind of mystic elation in his communion with the divine, not without any aversion to Mohanangi. He tells her, in the typical tradition of 'Madhura Bhakti':

> From now on I am the consecrated bride of Muvva Gopala and He is my lover. I have to woo him, please him, praise him and worship him through devotional songs. I have to celebrate His glory through Padams noted for their literary excellence, musical quality and dance potential. This is my cherished goal.

All the passionate protestations of Mohanangi, that she is his beloved in all planes of her existence, physical, mental and spiritual do not move Kshetrayya. He is so devoted to his task and absorbed in his mission that he feels a mystic elation and spiritual growth. His individual will is fully absorbed in the divine will. He has surrendered himself to God:

> I have no will of my own. I surrender myself to the will of God. . . . I have a noble and purposive life with a mission. I have to fulfil that. I also feel that sublimation of desires comes only through participation in pleasures. I do not believe in renunciation. Through a gradational process of willing and subordinating our physical pleasures to a higher pursuit we achieve the bliss of life, the communion with God and identification with the Lord.

The novelist makes a very creative use of Kshetrayya's pilgrimages and visits to the centres of learning. The novel makes it a mode of expressing not only the evolution of the character of Kshetrayya but also the progression of his spiritual quest. Kshetrayya is exposed to a number of temptations, of wealth, the luxury of court life and all its joys. Presumably Rama Sarma being a Milton scholar feels that his hero should be tempted and tested. He says, "In *The Bliss of Life* Kshetrayya is tempted and tested before he is accepted by God. This is typically Miltonic. Much of the Miltonic thought content permeates my novels."[3] Kshetrayya is unmoved and he takes all these temptations as fleeting incidents, irrelevant to his central quest, the spreading of the message of love, the 'Madhura Bhakti.'

Here, the individual who is blessed through a revelation, is presented in the process of becoming a greater being through a series of temptations. According to *Narada Sutra* (Sutras 46, 47), 'A true devotee crosses Maya, the bondage to matter through sense attractions and selfishness. He should be freed from the *Opposites.*' [4] Rama Sarma maintains in his *Heroic Argument,* in a different context, "Blessed is the man who endures temptations, for when he is tried he receives the crown of life."[5] Varada in his conversation with the King Vijayaraghava says, "God may choose to expose His devotee to a fiery test before He accepts him. The path of celestial glory is a difficult one. So God purposely puts man in the midst of temptations so that he may be tempted and tested and those who go through this process successfully become identified with God."

The first temptation comes from Kamala, a dancer in the court of Golconda. She casts amourous glances at Varadaiah. But Varadaiah's mind, ever since he has the revelation, is given to a nobler path and an ennobling desire to glorify Muvva Gopala through his Padams. This is his inner urge and the driving force in him. So when she proposes that he should stay with her in the court, he expresses his inability and explains to her about his ambition of spreading the message of Gopala. But still she argues,

> But you can do that better by belonging to a court especially to a flourishing court. And this is the right place for you. I shall dance and

> I shall express the emotional content of your songs through dancing. We will make a good team and we will get name and fame.

She tempts him not only with alluring promises of physical pleasures but also with the glory of fame, the natural weakness in great men. But Kshetrayya successfully overcomes this tempting offer by saying, "I am not anxious for name and fame for myself. It is for Muvva Gopala that I want all that glory, not for myself. I am his devotee and I am dedicated to His service." The words demonstrate his conviction and assert his faith in the life-divine and all its bliss.

Kshetrayya becomes a 'Jivanmukta' whose sense of 'mine' has vanished, who is unmoved at 'the sight of fair damsels. . . . He feels no dislike for the world. He is free from joy and sorrow.'[6] *The Kathopanisad* expounds the same truth, that the senses are to be controlled and if one is always of unrestrained mind and devoid of right understanding, his senses become uncontrollable and one who has a controlled mind reaches the goal. Kshetrayya's goal is to sublimate his desires. He has to attain wisdom and establish his right relationship with God and become identified with Muvva Gopala.

After visiting Tirumala Nayak's court in Madurai he proceeds to Kanchi where he has a mystic experience which confirms his belief that he is the blessed one. One night Varada is left in the temple of Kanchi Varadaraja unnoticed. The next morning when he wakes up from his meditation he sees the goddess leaving the Lord's temple and he composes a Padam being thrilled by that vision of the goddess. The priests admire his devotion and adore him as a saint.

He stays at Kanchi for a month and later leaves for Tanjavur where he happens to face another temptation, this time from Kalyani, a dancer in the court of Vijayaraghava. She expresses her great infatuation for him by offering his self to him. But he says, "I am wedded to Muvva Gopala. All my feelings and emotions, all my perceptions and capabilities are given to him," and then gently touches her head as though he is blessing her and goes away.

Thus he successfully steers himself clear of this temptation. Like the sublime individual, he transcends the limitations of the self, of passion and of sublunary desires. He understands the hollowness of the worldly glory which is an insubstantial, airy nothing. He acquires a sort of detachment from honours and rewards and all other material gains. In upanishadic terms he is a 'Jnani' who 'gets anything he likes through the power of his 'Sat-Sankalpa' (perfect will). A Jnani wills and everything comes into being.[8] Kshetrayya reaches a stage where he says that all the glory that comes to him belongs to Muvva Gopala. And at this juncture the king, Vijayaraghava declares:

> You are a Kshetragna. You have attained the sum total of wisdom. You have established the right relationship with God. You are one of the blessed few, knowing everything, seeing everything perfectly. You have the bliss of life, the heavenly joy, the spiritual enlightenment whereby you have annihilated the lower self in you. You have attained divinity.

Kshetrayya's mission of glorifying Muvva Gopala through his Padams has been achieved. He wins the literary contest and thus is established and accepted as a great composer of Padams. His literary fame is established. But then, on his return to Kanchi, he explains to the priest of the temple that he is waiting for the infinite moment to be one with God. In his own words,

> Only I wait for the God-given moment when I surrender my mortal coil and become one with Muvva Gopala. In all our lives there is a sacred moment when the decision is made for us by the great God above. That determines our fate. We have to submit ourselves to the will of God.

Kshetrayya has attained great glory as a composer of Padams and a spiritually enlightened poet. He faces the final and crucial test in the court of the Nawab of Golconda. Kshetrayya is asked to write fifteen hundred Padams in forty days. This serves as a challenge to test his superhuman poetic powers. Kshetrayya accepts it as a means to glorify Muvva Gopala. Kamala, who was once rejected by Kshetrayya, conspires against him by joining hands with Tulasi Murthy, the court poet of the Nawab. She invites Kshetrayya to her house and he accepts the invitation because he has attained a stage of spiritual evolution where he is disposed to regard all with equal love. He accepts the hospitality of Kamala and she gives him a love potion, a practice which was common in medieval India, to make the unyielding yield to love. Mohana devoted to Kshetrayya as deeply as Kshetrayya is devoted to Gopala, suspects some foul play against Kshetrayya's life. She approaches Siddhendra Yogi who happens to be at Golconda and with his help Kshetrayya comes out of the evil effect of the potion just a day before the stipulated time by Kutub Shah. He enters a deep trance of absolute communion with the Divine and all the fifteen hundred Padams are composed on time. The test demonstrates that Kshetrayya has divine grace and he is blessed by the Lord. The intrigues of Kamala and Tulasi Murthy prove ineffective and Kshetrayya ultimately triumphs and his poetic genius is established beyond dispute. During this time of trial, Kshetrayya hears a divine voice, "Varada, very soon you will be with me. Visit the other holy places and come back to Muvva to be identified with me." Blessed by Gopala he visits other holy places like Bhadrachalam, Srisailam and Tirumala. After completing his pilgrimage he intuitively feels as though Muvva Gopala is calling him back. He decides to return to Muvva.

Though Mohanangi fails in her quest to meet Kshetrayya at Kanchi finally she meets him at the court of Vijayaraghava in Thanjavur. She stays with him. But now, her former lover, Varadaiah is totally a transformed man. No doubt, he still retains love for her, but it is of a different kind, it is part of his love and devotion to Lord Gopala. When Mohana reminds him of their youthful life in Muvva, he tells her, "Mohana, we may again sit by the side of the tank, but our minds will be given only to an appreciation of God's ways and to an awareness of objects we see as manifestation of divine beauty and grace."

Finally Kshetrayya returns to Muvva with Mohanangi. He waits for the sacred moment to become one with Gopala. He is acclaimed by everyone as the chosen and blessed one. There is the final consummation when the illustrious Padam-writer starts singing his Padams with divine rapture in Muvva Gopala's temple accompanied by the spirited dance of Mohanangi on the Krishnashtami day. It is a fitting finis. He has that deep experience of being one with the divine. The individual life of Kshetrayya merges with the divine, symbolically, as a small flame merges with the luminous glow of the divine. As the novelist says in the questionnaire, "Mohana sees God in Varada as Varada sees God in Gopala. He for God only, she for God in him."[9]

In the novel, *The Bliss of Life*, Rama Sarma has successfully reconstructed this progression and liberation of the life of Kshetrayya from an earthly to a spiritual plane. As Rama Sarma explains, "the bliss for Mohanangi is romantic life with Varada. It is romantic idealization of love. The bliss that Kalyani and Kamala visualize simply refers to physical pleasures. To Kshetrayya the bliss would mean identification with the Lord, Muvva Gopala."[10] In the portrayal of the evolution of Kshetrayya, the author has rightly laid more emphasis on the depiction of the theme of divine love by showing the hero in the actual process of composing the Padams. The author provides a convincing locale and topography for Kshetrayya's journey through the various stages of his career as a devotional composer and the progress of his character from a stage of passionate love to that of devotional love, ultimately leading to the divine love, the bliss of life.

Rama Sarma employs myth in everyone of his novels, "A myth necessarily deals with an idealized man or a man larger than life and Professor Rama Sarma employs the device of mythicizing facts in order to give his hero an exalted status and the story a universal significance."[11] Varadaiah is given this exalted position in the novel and his "quest gains an extension into infinity by being absorbed into infinity, the bliss of life."[12]

The Bliss of Life with its insistence on *Madhura Bhakti* and willing submission to God's will gives to the reader the concept of a life divine, full of ethical idealism and spiritual illumination.

NOTES

1. G. Nageswara Rao, "M.V.Rama Sarma," Indian English Novelists, ed. Madhusudan Prasad, p.111.
2. G. Nageswara Rao, "The Bliss of Life: A Study," *Journal of English Studies*, Vol. 10, No. 2 (April 1978), pp. 677-82.
3. H.G.S. Arulandrum, "Meeting of Minds: The Creator and the Critic" (Questionnaire), *Journal of Literature and Aesthetics*, Vol. II, 1982, p. 23.
4. E.T. Sturdy, trans., *Narada Sutra: An Enquiry into Love* (London: Longmans, Green, 1896), p. 33.
5. M.V. Rama Sarma, *Heroic Argument* (Madras: Macmillan, 1971), p. 134.
6. Swami Sivananda, trans., *Ten Upanishads* (Garhwal, The Divine Love Society, 1973), p. 61.
7. See Swami Gambirananda, trans., *Eight Upanishads* (Calcutta: Advaita Ashrama, 1957), pp. 95-228.
8. Swami Sivananda, p. 85.
9. Arulandrum, p. 23.
10. Loc. cit.
11. G. Daisy, "M.V. Rama Sarma's Novels: A Study in the Light of Myths" (M. Phil diss., Bharathidasan University, 1987), p. 71.
12. Ibid., p. 72.

Kshetrayya: A Picaresque Saint

V.V.N. RAJENDRA PRASAD

In his introduction to *The Bliss of Life,*[1] "The Visit to Movva," Rama Sarma says that the novel is "an imaginative reconstruction of Kshetrayya's life" (xii). *The Bliss of Life* is different from Rama Sarma's other novels in that here we have a treatment of history and myth. Although the narrative scaffolding is largely historical, the theme is a displacement of the myth or rapturous union with the Divine of the celebrated Vaishnavite tradition. But, then, why did he choose the history of an individual to write a novel? That "fiction seeks a broader and more enduring truth than history"[2] has been the opinion of critics at least since Aristotle. Discussing the difference between historical truth and poetic truth, Aristotle observes, "The difference is that the one tells of what has happened, the other of the kinds of things that might happen. For this reason poetry is considered more philosophical . . . than history; for while poetry is concerned with universal truths, history treats of particular facts."[3] Aristotle also considers works based on history in creative writing, since "even if he [the poet] writes about things that have actually happened, that does not make him any the less a poet, for there is nothing to prevent some of the things that have happened from being in accordance with the laws of possibility and probability, and he will be a poet in writing about them."[4] It follows that "fiction allows the writer greater freedom to draw a moral, to make judgments."[5]

Even a casual reading of the novel seems to prove the assertion that "Novelists seeking 'truth,' even though they define it differently, often make special investigations into social conditions or individual lives that border on scholarly research."[6] Rama Sarma has structured his imaginative insight in such a way that it serves both as a mirror and as a lamp. The novel succeeds not only in presenting complex and, at the same time, unified images of society, but also in throwing light on the Indian socio-cultural problematic. Moreover, as Joan Rockwell has noted,

> fiction is not only a representation of social reality, but also a necessary functional part of social control, and also paradoxically an important element in social change. It plays a large part in the

> socialisation of infants, in the expression of official norms such as law and religion, in the conduct of politics, and in general gives symbols and modes of life to the population, particularly in those less easily defined but basic areas such as norms, values, and personal and interpersonal behaviour.[7]

The Bliss of Life presents the journey—physical and symbolic—of Varadaiah from Movva, his native village to different places and back to Movva; from the state of an innocent village lad to that of *Kshetrajna*. Both secular institutions—represented by the King's court—and religious institutions—represented by the temple—form the various milestones in Varadaiah's journey to the state of rapture divine.

When the novel begins, we find Varadaiah and Mohanangi deeply in love with each other. But marriage is something they cannot even dream of, caste being the insurmountable barrier. Hindu society is not meaningful in terms of Marxian ideology. Both in the city and in the country the significant division of the population is not on the basis of class but on the basis of caste and community. But in spite of the general dislike of the villagers, including their parents, Varada and Mohana become more and more attached to each other and indispensable to each other's happiness. Their love, of course, is not based on physical attraction. They are like the twin wicks of the lamp in the temple of Muvva Gopala. Further, we can say that Varada needs Mohana as much as she needs him; he needs her not only as his companion but also to dance his *padams*, since his *padams* become more effective when accompanied by music and dance; and she needs him as her friend, guide and philosopher. When Varada requests her to be with him in all his life as his friend, Mohana says,

> Of course, I will promise all that. But let me tell you that I have myself come seeking you. . . . I want you, I need you. I shall be faithful to you. I shall always dance merrily only when you are by me, and by the sustenance of your looks I shall dare to overcome everything in the world. And we both belong to Gopala. In our adoration of Gopala we become united as one stream. We are one, inseparable whole. We sing and dance and leave the world to its flat and weary life. (6)

Varada's symbolic journey starts earlier than his physical journey. When Mohana asks him, "why don't you take me in your arms and give me the bliss of life," (11) Varada says,

> Mohana. . . . You amuse me, your looks thrill me, but whether I am physically drawn towards you I cannot say. Perhaps the physical aspect of life does not mean much for me. I look at you as my companion, as an indispensable guide for my literary compositions. I see in you the fulfilment of a dream, of my love for Gopala. I adore

> you. To love you is to love Gopala, for to me everything seems to be His image. My devotional love for Gopala is something real and substantial. It overpowers my physical love for you. (11-12)

In the preceding passage two statements attract our attention: 1) whether he is physically drawn to Mohana, Varada cannot say, and 2) his devotional love for Gopala overpowers his physical love for Mohana. The novelist seems to suggest that Varada's is not yet a completely evolved self. It is sandwiched between the physical and the spiritual worlds. He is not yet free from bodily desires; he cannot resist the temptation to possess her physically. The novelist seems to have a double purpose in presenting the physical aspect of the relationship: it hastens Varada's departure from Movva, to be away from Mohana for at least a few months so that he can conquer his bodily desires; and it also helps Varada in composing *padams* expressing his *madhura bhakti*, the love of a girl for her lord.

Varada finds it very difficult to go away from Mohana. Conflicting thoughts oppress him. Only divine intervention can release him from the shackles of physical desires. Varada sees Muvva Gopala in a vision blessing him and asking him to compose *padams*, visit several places, and spread the Lord's message all over the country. Under the influence of the vision, Varada's passion for Mohana transforms itself into passion for Muvva Gopala:

> He [Varada] pleases Him as a Nayika, and in several ways through Sringara Rasa he would dedicate himself to the worship of the Lord. . . . Nothing else mattered to him, not even Mohana, except his devotion to the Lord. Like a Nayika patiently waiting for her lover he too would wait for his Lord. All his songs would be a dedication to, and glorification of, Gopala. (27)

In many devotional works, the devotee always considers God the protagonist, the hero he loves. For example, Donne, in one of his Holy Sonnets, wants God to "ravish"[8] him; and Crashaw begins his "Hymn to Sainte Teresa." as follows: "Love thou art absolute sole Lord/Of Life and death."[9] This does not mean that Rama Sarma is a metaphysical poet; he is undoubtedly a realistic novelist.

Thus there is a change of roles, Varada becomes Mohana who will offer herself to her Varada, Muvva Gopala: "From now on I am the consecrated bride of Muvva Gopala and He is my lover." (29) An interesting point to be noted here is that though Varada says, "I surrender myself to the will of God," (30-31) he never wants to run away from life. Promising to be faithful to Mohana, he says "I . . . feel that sublimation of desires comes only through participation in pleasures. I do not believe in renunciation. Through a gradual process of willing and subordinating our physical pleasures to a higher pursuit we achieve the bliss of life, the communion with God and identification with the Lord." (31) Thus we have an image of the temple he wants to build in himself, in which his Lord could be consecrated. The sanctum sanctorum that Varada has within himself, perhaps unknowingly, assumes control of his entire physical frame as he evolves and matures in consciousness.

Varada's journey begins with a visit to the Nawab's court at Golconda. Varada is received well by the Nawab. As he watches Kamala, the court dancer, dancing, his thoughts go back to Mohana: "He wondered why on earth he left Mohana instead of enjoying her sweet company. To be with her was bliss. Separation from her was unbearable." (35-36) This clearly shows that Varada is not yet liberated from physical desires. We also notice that this sorrow caused by unbearable separation and the satisfaction of having enjoyed company of the beloved at least once forms one of the themes of Varada's *padams*. He gives an incomplete *padam* to the poets at the Tanjore court and asks them to fill up the last line: "My maids, expecting Muvva Gopala, I have asked for good omens, but seeing many other women enjoying themselves with their lovers I have been sad." (76) When the court poets fail to complete the *padam*, Varada completes it thus: "The woman after having longed for Muvva Gopala finally gets reconciled to her state. She feels that her first contact with Muvva Gopala is itself enough." (98)

But Varada is as loyal to Mohana in his love for her as he is to Gopala in his devotion for Him. He tells Kamala, who expresses her view that even a devoted servant of God need not renounce all pleasures:

> I quite agree with you that from physical pleasures we attain ennoblement. But this happens only if we try and make an attempt to rid ourselves of these physical pleasures gradually. Or else we remain where we are, all the time enmeshed in this corporeal existence. We cannot ascend, nor can we transcend the earthly longings unless we make a desperate bid to control our libidinous inclinations. (37)

He believes that "If at all he wanted physical life, no one could be a better partner for him than Mohana." (38) But he does not like "to surrender himself to physical pleasures" since his goal is "to sublimate his desires and become identified with Muvva Gopala." (38) So, in order to save himself from falling a prey to Kamala's advances, he leaves Golconda for Madurai, where he composes a few *padams,* which "gave mystic elation to the learned and the devout, and the pure and simple physical love appealed to the common man." (41)

Varada next visits Kanchi and from there goes to Tanjore. His stay at Tanjore is important in that here we find him evolved and mature in consciousness. When Kalyani a famous dancer, offers herself to Varada, he does not run away from her, as he did when Kamala made advances to him, but tells her firmly, "I am in love with Muvva Gopala. I cannot love anyone else." (64) He further says that "I am wedded to Muvva Gopala. All my feelings and emotions, all my perceptions and capabilities are given to him." (65) But, as already mentioned, Varada does not believe in renunciation; a true devotee, he believes, must learn to "accept pain and pleasure with detachment." (69-70) Professing *Karma Yoga,* he says to the king, "we have to do our duty, but we need not be unduly excited about the results. We may leave it to God for He knows better when to give the reward for the work done by us." (69) This is in accordance with what Lord Krishna says to Arjuna in the *Bhagvad Gita*: "Your duty lies in doing Karma; never a right to the fruits [thereof]. Let not the fruit of action be the motive nor there be any attachment to non-action."[10]

Rama Sarma introduces two characters, a sanyasi and a priest, who exemplify "attachment to non-action" and interest in the result of the action rather than the action as such respectively. Varada meets the former at Rameswaram and the latter at Kanchi. Varada advises the sanyasi to "Go back to life and accept life with all its limitations. A life lived in a normal way is a fruitful one. By gradational process and by steady detachment you will acquire the nobler self. Serve others and service to mankind is service to God." The priest at the Varadarajaswamy temple at Kanchi thinks that it is difficult to be detached. Varada tries to convince him of the importance of *nishkama karma:* "We have to be Karma Yogis but we cannot stress too much the reward that has to come to us. We must leave it to God." (106) He further says,

> Apparently it looks difficult. Human beings, as we are, we long for fruits. All our deeds are motivated by selfish desires. Even the love we show to others is selfish because we expect something in return. That is the worldly way. But man has to come out of that self-centredness. He has to develop interests that keep him busy in the service of others, or in the devotion to God. (106)

And when the priest feels that God has not been kind to him, Varada says, "Perhaps He is testing you. You have to accept life with all its joys and sorrows, with faith in God." (109) Thus Varada exemplifies *nishkama karma,* and reminds us of what Lord Krishna says in the *Gita*: "he excels . . . who, restraining the senses by the mind, unattached, directs his organs of action to the path of work."[11] Varada is, therefore, not just Kshetrayya but a Kshetrajna.

On his way back to Movva, along with Mohana who joined him at Tanjore, Varada spends a few days in Golconda, where he successfully crosses the last barrier to achieving oneness with God. He comes out of the trap laid by Kamala. In fact it is Mohana who rescues him with the help of Siddhendra Yogi. Maybe he was destined to be in a trance for some time. As he himself says, "we have to accept the fact that in some form Karma also rules our life. While Karma may not be completely binding on us, we cannot altogether dismiss it as non-existent. We have to give some consideration for things predestined for us." (122)

The cycle is complete when Varada returns to Movva after successfully coming out of the labyrinth of the lures of the world and the flesh. No woman could ensnare him and no king could persuade him to lead the luxurious life of a court poet. On Krishnashtami day, Varada sings (his famous *padams*) and Mohana dances to their hearts' content in the temple of Muvva Gopala. Varada experiences rapture divine and becomes identified with Gopala. Mohana gently leans on Varada and looks inseparable from him.

Thus Varada attains the blessed state of union with God through the path of supreme devotion which transports the devotee beyond human, earthly love. What Varada strives after with Mohana as a twin partner, in the spiritual quest is renunciation of material aspiration and recognition of God not as the sole refuge but man as a twin with God in a supreme state of bliss where love not merely ennobles and enthrals the human being but transports him into the world of the Divine.

Varada speaks about the divine mission thus: "from time to time God sends His saints and sages into this world so that they may remind human beings of the ultimate reality and of the futility of earthly longings." (106) These words reveal Varada's conviction about the subtle points of intersection between time and eternity which lead to an ennobling of human endeavour, and man's renunciation of the physical and acceptance of spiritual intimations for a holistic order to prevail in the universe. This esoteric spiritual quest for the integration of man and society passes far beyond the Maslowian version of the ideal social order, Eupsychia.

NOTES

1. M.V. Rama Sarma, *The Bliss of Life* (New Delhi: S. Chand, 1979).
2. Morroe Berger, *Real and Imagined Worlds: The Novel and Social Science* (Harvard: Harvard University Press, 1977) p. 171.
3. Aristotle, *Poetics*, trans. T.S. Dorsch, *Classical Literary Criticism* (Harmondsworth: Penguin, 1965), pp. 43-44.
4. *Ibid.*, p. 44.
5. Morroe Berger, p. 171.
6. *Ibid.*, p. 163.
7. Joan Rockwell, *Fact in Fiction: The Use of Literature in the Systematic Study of Literature* (London: Routledge and Kegan Paul, 1974), p. 7.
8. John Donne, "Batter my heart, three person's God; for you," p. 14.
9. Richard Crashaw, "Hymn to Sainte Teresa," pp. 1-2.
10. *The Bhagavad Gita*, trans. K.V. Iyer (Madras: B.G. Paul, 1966), p. 14.
11. *The Bhagavad Gita*, trans. Swami Chidbhavananda (Tirupparatitturai: Tapovanam, 1967), p. 218.

Towards Eternal Harmony: A Study of *Pastures New*

SYED MUKHARAM

Pastures New[1] is the fifth novel of Rama Sarma. The very title is from the famous line of Milton's *Lycidas,* 'Tomorrow to fresh woods and pastures new.' The narrative appears to be a travelogue centered round the holy places like Kanyakumari, Rameswaram, Varanasi, and Tirupati. The note on the back cover of the edition clearly states that the description of the places creates an authentic background for the socio-religious life in India. Indian tradition feeds, nourishes and shapes the Indian outlook. It holds the communities and races, the rich and the poor together, more strongly than language and region. The individual has to experience life at all levels for he has to sustain himself through the perennial supply of his life-blood from outside. As in the picaresque novel, Rama Sarma chooses to make his chief characters move from place to place, that too the holy ones, so that they experience the thrill of life and fellowship with others. The visits to the holy places constitute a fairly detailed Indian experience out of which Rama Sarma has created his *Pastures New*. Each holy place has an abiding influence on the socio-religious life of the Indian irrespective of the caste, creed or religion to which he belongs. The novel draws its strength from the ingredients that transcend the domestic and social limits of the people.

The novel appears to be a presentation of the life of the individuals who belong to the privileged middle class—the contented domestic life of the pairs, Dr. Madhu and Sarala, Ramu and Suguna, Dr. Raja Rao and Vimala, Mohan and Prem, Kumar and Kamala. Rama Sarma does not like to present in this novel the temperamental incompatibility, the frustration, the despair of the young, the social problems as he does in his earlier plays and novels. In his earlier writings he seems to be keen on presenting problems and problems alone. 'When the problem is presented in its totality,' Rama Sarma says, 'his business is over.' But what strikes one as significant in *Pastures New* is the approach of the novelist towards life and spiritual awareness. In this novel he presents only the harmonious side of life. Not even a single character is disturbed, not a single mind suffers from any complex or conflict. Even in the case of Lalita, who has not been fortunate in her domestic life, she shows an equanimity of mind and is prepared to accept life with understanding. The happy pair Dr. Madhu and Sarala have their fruitful pride. They are happy at the individual level and establish good relations with Rama and Suguna, another good pair with domestic bliss. The ideal pairs lead a contented life.

Thus for the curious reader there is a simple and interesting story which runs smooth mostly concentrating on the little, little joys of domestic life. It looks as though the writer does not like to create any disruption or discordant note in any situation or relationship. Kumar, a dejected son of an ill-tempered mother, is introduced to the reader in Varanasi as a guide. He meets his wife Kamala quite unexpectedly and the situation ends in a happy reunion.

For a serious reader the story is not so simple as it appears to be. The novelist as a visionary dreams of a new world order. For this he centres the narrative round 'a few holy places like Kanyakumari, Rameshwaram, Varanasi and Tirupati, mostly to create an authenticity for the socio-religious life in India and to show the abiding influence of these places of worship on the rich and the poor alike.'[2] So the novel opens with the holy place, Kanyakumari, the confluence of the three seas, the Bay of Bengal, the Indian Ocean and the Arabian Sea, which is believed 'to cleanse a person of all his sins, inherited, acquired or committed in this life itself.' (1) This belief is in conformity with the old established doctrine that ablution in sacred waters will purify the body and soul. The old doctrine is that 'the only real defilement of the soul proceeds from sin which is caused by the perversity of the will.'[3] It is the pious hope of the novelist that men and women absolved of their sins will await a new world order where equity and justice will prevail. So the omniscient narrator Dr. Madhu rightly speaks out that he is there in Kanyakumari to see for himself 'The Land's End with all its glory.' (1)

It is this sublime sentiment of seeing the land in glory and harmony that pervades the entire novel. The novel may appear to be a search for the self or a spiritual quest. But, the novelist with a social consciousness and vision, aspires for a new society, a new social order as a way out for all the ills of life and society. Every event and every visit contributes to the richness of the main theme—to move towards establishing eternal harmony, a better world order in future.

To articulate this vision, an attempt is made at different levels in the form of experience. In the first phase, the experience is a purely human experience at the individual, personal and social levels. Dr. Madhu and Sarala on one hand, Ramu and Suguna on the other contribute to this experience. The husbands draw sustenance from their life-partners. In the life of Dr. Madhu, his wife is a planner in all his affairs. She is his guide. Madhu says that in his family the central figure is his wife. He says,

> the central figure was my wife, the silent witness of our prosperity. With her rich commonsense and unquestioned faith in God she had a way of doing things, of cautioning us about things to come. She had a mysterious way of looking into the future and I relied on her many a time for her guidance and unfailing support. (44)

The second phase of experience is partly human and partly divine—Man sitting at the holy feet of a very great sage, a Guru who shows the *Truth* and gives out a message. It is drawing sustenance from a 'man-divine.' The experience at Prasantinilayam illustrates this fact. The man-divine Bhagwan says, "I have come to bring the light of love to the world. That love will reach the hearts of the devotees and they in turn will let its glow surround them and reach outwards to all they meet. That love is God, it can drive away the darkness."[4] The spread of godly love can move us farther than the physical lures because Love is the ultimate goal. "God is the very embodiment of Love. God who is love can be realized only through love. Live in love."[5] With the second phase of experience the human mind is properly set with the indelible impressions to think of love. Love becomes universal transcending the narrow limits of physical love.

The third phase of experience begins only at the end of attaining a mind that loves. It is purely a spiritual experience which has its basis in religious beliefs and convictions. The holy places are conducive to spiritual experience. This is the strangest and strongest experience where man draws sustenance from the unseen God. Gopal's words echo this sentiment. He says, "I am now on a pilgrimage to all the sacred spots. These religious centres may give me some solace. In moments of depression and desperation we can visit these holy places and get sustenance." (38) In Kanyakumari and Rameshwaram after the holy dips Dr. Madhu sees a radiant glow on their faces. He says,

> We were baffled by the scene and silently went through the ordeal hoping to be purified and cleansed of our sins. . . . The temple fulfilled the spiritual quest of man for he felt that he was one with Lord Rama, Lord Krishna and a host of other saints from time immemorial. He sought refuge in the temple and bathed in its 'Teerthas' for purification. We came out of the temple with a radiant glow on our faces. (27)

The visit to Varanasi "the holy city ever resplendent with divine light" and a dip in the Ganges, the bulky bell in the Kashi Vishwanath Temple "give a sacred sound instilling new faith and new courage in the pilgrims." (83) In this place Kumar, an unemployed dejected young man draws sustenance from the Lord Vishwanatha. He gets a job there. Soon he meets his separated wife and settles well in life. Outwardly it may appear to be man's simple settlement in life, but Kumar who undergoes the ordeal firmly believes that everything has come from the Lord Vishwanatha. So he has made it a point to visit the temple everyday as a sign of his sense of gratitude towards the Lord.

The visit to Tirumala and the mystic experience Dr. Madhu has, is at once revealing. When he sees the idol he feels elated. He says,

> That was a mystic experience. Just for one moment I was one with the Lord in supreme bliss and some inner prompting told me that I had come to the journey's end. Even now, as I think of it after so many years I still feel the divine presence and the message given to me. It was a revelation. (12)

This is the experience of many who visit the temple for the beatific vision of the Lord. William B. Hunter after reading *Pastures New* writes to Rama Sarma about the supreme joy he felt on seeing the Lord in the temple in Tirupati, during his stay as Visiting Professor in Sri Venkateswara University in 1983. He says, "Another part that meant a great deal to me was the worship of Divya Manohara Murti with the complex and profound meanings involved." He finds it "the most moving religious experience of my life—a peace, as our Bible says, that passes all understanding."[6] As the upanishadic words say, God loves the world. If he withdraws his protective hand for one moment, the whole universe will collapse. It is God's love and his benediction that ultimately give solace and sustenance to human existence. It is this inarticulate and inexplicable individual experience which is purely divine that the men at large feel in these holy places outgrowing the narrow prejudices of caste, colour, creed, race or religion. Dr. Madhu very aptly says,

> Fundamentally human nature is the same, east or west. In our ignorance or out of our ego we build a wall around us and create tensions for ourselves and others. Love begets love and in the world of love narrow prejudices and caste feelings do not exist at all. (144)

When one seeks refuge in love that sustains and promotes progress, the individual, the society and finally the world will become a sublime trinity. Thus the three levels of experience echo the ideal sentiment—an all-transcending feeling for a new world order. The novel owes its relevance to these deeply felt convictions that transcend the personal, the domestic and social limits of the people. It is a search of the human mind for a lasting order in the individual and the society which has its base in the sheet anchor of the tradition that leads to eternal harmony in the world.

This sheet anchor holds the novel together providing insights into the mysteries and puzzles of life. The individual has to experience at all the levels to realize the wholeness of his existence. Rama Sarma makes such a lofty attempt in this novel *Pastures New*. K.R. Srinivasa Iyengar rightly comments that "the pastures 'new' are really the age long sacred spots that, as Gandhiji said in his *Hind Swaraj* 80 years ago, hold India together and preserve its inner purity."[8] The novelist aptly concludes the novel on a note of exaltation. "If the poets dream of a millennium, a golden age, we dream of a world order and world citizenship where love of fellow human beings and establishment of peace become universally accepted." (164)

The writer amply illustrates in the novel his firm faith in exploring fresh woods and pastures new that may ultimately lead human beings to a new world order transcending the limitations of caste, creed, race and religion. The motto of the novel, is 'Sarve Janah Sukhino Bhavantu' (Let all people live in happiness').

In fact this novel looks forward to a day when India will lead the other nations of the world in its quest for spiritual enlightenment. The narrator Dr. Madhu feels that when the west is satiated with its pursuit of material gains it will look to the east, especially to India, for a better way of life and for God realization.

NOTES

1. M.V. Rama Sarma, *Pastures New* (Madras: Emerald, 1985).
2. Back cover, *Pastures New*.
3. A.J.A. Dubois, *Hindu Manners, Customs and Ceremonies* (New Delhi: Asian Educational Services, 1985).
4. Charles Penn, *My Beloved* (Prasantinilayam: Sri Satya Sai Central Trust, 1981), p. 44.
5. N. Kasturi, *Satya Sai Speaks* (Prasantinilayam: Satya Sai Publications, 1981), p. 69.
6. Letter October 6, 1985, Huston, Texas.
7. Letter to Rama Sarma, Feb. 3, 1986, Waco, Texas.
8. Letter to Rama Sarma, Aug. 24, 1985, Madras.

From Ph.D. thesis, "The Symphony of Life: A Study of Professor Rama Sarma's Plays and Novels," S.V. University, Tirupati, 1990.

The Karma Yogi in *Height of Noon*

H.G.S. ARULANDRAM

Besides being an outstanding scholar and a critic of English literature and an authority on Milton, M.V. Rama Sarma is one of the leading and prolific Indian creative writers in English who has, through his writings, successfully projected the best social and cultural legacies of our country to Indian as well as foreign readership. He is a delightful creative artist and in all his writings, one can see man's relentless quest for something higher and nobler in life and the synthesis of the best in Indian life, tradition and culture.

With the publication of his recent novel *Height of Noon* (1994), M V Rama Sarma is again in the news. His first novel *The Stream* deals with the need for acceptance of life in all its totality, as our life is very often governed by the triple concept—Beauty, Love and Justice. *The Farewell Party* depicts the life of a distinguished Professor, Dr. Prakasam, who looks back at his long years of service as on efficient and a successful teacher—with a sense of satisfaction that he has been of some use and service to the society all these years. His third novel, *Look Homeward* is an appeal to the Indian scholars and students who have gone abroad either for study or on some assignment to look homeward and come back to their mother country with their rich experience and expertise to contribute their mite to the welfare of their country. In his fourth novel, *The Bliss of Life*, through an imaginative reconstruction of Kshetrayya's life—the famous poet—musician of Andhra Pradesh Rama Sarma demonstrates that the final stage in man's life is surrender to the will of God and it is this absolute surrender to the will of God that ultimately leads him to the bliss of life. The next novel *Pastures New* is a plea for exploration into new pastures—new paths and fresh woods that may ultimately lead human beings into a brave new world order transcending all the limitations of caste, creed, race and religion.

Rama Sarma's latest novel *Height of Noon*, at the surface level, may look a naive life-tale of a teacher—who started his career as a Lecturer in a newly formed University but was finally elevated to the post of the Vice-Chancellor of the same university. But a careful reading and an in depth study of the novel will reveal that it is a serious novel in the sense that many themes have been carefully and dexterously woven together, making it a complex one. It could be examined or interpreted as a campus novel depicting the academic life of universities in India today; as a comprehensive study of interpersonal relationship; as a pointer to the cultural assimilation of the East and the West; as an autobiographical narration of the author's academic life; as an analysis of husband-wife relationship and not the least, as a restatement of *Bhagavad Gita*'s philosophy. The purpose of this paper is to view the protagonist, Dr. Anand, from a comprehensive angle—as a *Karma Yogi* since the main thread in the novel is devotion to work.

Dr. Anand is a *Karma Yogi* in the truest sense of the term. The novelist confirms this thus: "In fact he [Dr. Anand] was a *Karma Yogi* who believed in doing everything with detachment and as a service to God." (134) On another occasion, the novelist says: "Anand learnt the lesson of doing things irrespective of the reward. He became a *Karma Yogi.* " (74) To Dr. Anand, work was his religion and he was committed to his work. He was always aiming at perfection. The novelist records thus: "He [Dr. Anand] was committed to his work and he was thoroughgoing in everything he did. He aimed at perfection and never did anything half-heartedly. Work was his religion, and service to mankind, he thought, was service to God." (35-36)

Anand's life as a *Karma Yogi* could be better studied and discussed in three phases, in respect of the various posts he was holding. The first phase of his life and career is as a young teacher who joined as a lecturer in a college, then migrating to a university as a lecturer and finally, rising to the status of Professor and Head in the same university department. The second phase is the period of his involvement in the administration as the Principal of the University College for a period of six long years. The third phase is his tenure of office as the Vice-Chancellor in the same university—the academic and administrative head—for a fruitful and successful period of three and half years. It is interesting to note that whatever position Anand was holding, be it Lecturership or Readership or Professorship or Principalship or Vice-Chancellorship, his interest was in teaching and in research. The novelist endorses thus: "His [Dr. Anand's] primary obligation, he thought, was teaching, doing research and conducting research. He was consistently true to his objectives." (90)

Dr. Anand, after completing his Ph.D. in the United Kingdom, started his career as a young lecturer in a college in Delhi. He was sincere in his work and very soon he earned the love and respect of all his students. The students loved him as a man and respected him for his scholarship and commitment to his work and above all revered him for his interest in the welfare of the students. Fortunately, an opportunity came to Dr. Anand in the form of Lecturership in a newly formed university. As a young lecturer in the university department, Dr. Anand was very successful and became the centre of attraction. The students found him respectable and scholarly and he was liked by the entire student community. It is no wonder that his student Latha fell in secret love with him even though he was married to Lakshmi at that time. Latha's confused confessionary words go thus: "Because you are so good . . . you are an excellent teacher . . . your teaching thrills me . . . not just the teacher in you, the man in you is of great appeal to me." (32-33) Such was Dr. Anand's magic spell over his students. He was soon promoted Reader in the same department and Anand continued his teaching and research. He was instrumental in upgrading the department into a post-graduate one to felicitate and augment research in the department.

When a vacancy for Professorship in the department arose, the Vice-Chancellor, very much impressed with Anand's work, saw to it that Anand was promoted to the post, brushing aside cleverly all political and other obstacles that stood in the way of Anand's promotion. Anand was a lovable and respectable Professor and whatever he touched he turned into gold or something far richer.

When the Principalship of the University College was offered to Anand, he accepted it even though he liked teaching and research. He was mentally prepared that if any administrative responsibility was placed on him, he would not shirk or shun, for in a developing country like India, the educated had a greater obligation to work for the well being of the country. But at the same time he was determined that he would accept his new assignment with a sense of detachment. The novelist records thus: "Whatever he did, it was wholehearted service to the University and it was considered to be good. That way he was quite involved also in his work." (92) As a Principal, he was very successful. He avoided groupism in the college and he was always fair and just to everyone. He had the knack of solving all the local problems posed and created by the staff members or by the students and he always chose the middle path—the path of mutual adjustment and reconciliation. He was so successful as the Principal that he became the central figure on the university campus. The novelists says: "For six years Professor Anand was the central figure on the campus. He was on every commission and the Vice-Chancellor had full faith in him. He left him free and never questioned any of the decisions. All academic matters and all college affairs were completely left to Anand. He was the deciding factor. Even in important administrative decisions he had a major role to play." (92) It is interesting to note that even during his tight schedule as the Principal, Dr. Anand did not forget his primary vocation—teaching and research. He could be seen taking classes and conducting research in the forenoon session in his parent department and attending to his duties of the Principal in the college premises in the afternoon.

Anand's commitment to work was recognised and rewarded at the right moment. Just five days before his retirement from the university service, he was appointed the Vice-Chancellor of the same university. It was an irony that the farewell parties were turned into welcome parties and it was the first time that an internal Professor was elevated to the highest post in the same university. Anand accepted Vice-Chancellorship as a God-given post and he thought that it was a covenant between him and God and he had to fulfil his duty in the name of God. He took it as a Holy Mission. He thought that God had chosen him for doing some good to the university and therefore he should perform his duty with sanctity as if he was God's agent to do justice to all. During his tenure of office as the Vice-Chancellor, Anand was very fair, impartial and sincere in performing his duties: he was also true to his primary obligation—teaching and research. He was still teaching post-graduate students and conducting research in the department. The students liked him: the teachers respected him and the Government backed him and acknowledged his good leadership in the university. The Government selected him for "Meritorious Teachers Award" twice and that too in consecutive years. In fact, Anand was at his height of noon when he was the Vice-Chancellor of the university. He spent three and half years as the Vice-Chancellor, doing yeoman's service to the university and introducing new programmes in collaboration with foreign universities. At last he was relieved of the Vice-Chancellorship when he was earnestly, praying and yearning for relief when the domestic calamity—the death of his beloved wife Lakshmi—took place. Even at the time of affliction, he accepted life in its totality with a sense of stoic resignation—let his will be done. Even after retirement his thirst for work had not yet quenched and he was waiting patiently like the scholar gipsy for the God-given moment of surrendering himself completely to the will of God.

To conclude, while discussing Dr. Anand as a *Karma Yogi*, one cannot escape noticing the philosophical overtones in the *Height of Noon*. It is through Dr. Anand, the *Karma Yogi*, that Rama Sarma explicates and advocates the *Gita's* philosophy of detached attachment to work. The ultimate message, in the words of the author, seems to be this: "He [Dr. Anand] knew that God would give him what he deserved at the right time and his duty was to do his work patiently, sincerely and faithfully. His work had to be judged by God and not by human beings. So he had to do it flawlessly and to the best of his abilities. This patient waiting for God's grace and not getting unduly excited if things did not happen as he planned was developed by him through some experience he had in life. He realised that if he did not get what he asked for, it only meant that God had other plans for him and he had to wait. He submitted himself to God's will and he found to his surprise that what God gave him was much better than what he had asked for or planned for." (36) It is precisely for this reason that the novel acquires universal significance, global appeal and epic grandeur.

Height of Noon: A Critical Study

DEVA RAJENDRA

The protagonist of the novel, *Height of Noon*, Dr. Anand, seems to be a thinly-veiled portrayal of the author himself. Anand is an ideal teacher and administrator in the ancient Hindu tradition of 'Guru.' His birth and early life in a Gandhian family, his British education and above all an innate catholicity of outlook contribute to his liberal attitude towards fellow human beings. Anand's conversation with Mary amply brings it out. His comment on Indian caste system is realistic and it serves as a good repartee to the prejudiced thinking of the westerners. Mary asks Anand, "How about your caste system?" Anand readily replies:

> "As bad or as good as your class system. The same barriers hold good in both cases. Ours is based on social customs and yours is based on economic conditions."

Anand is a multi-faceted personality. Principal Gupta pays a great tribute to him when he says, "You are a good teacher, a good researcher and above all a good man. You love to be useful to others. It is difficult to get a person like you."

Dr. Anand is a great humanist who believes in the essential goodness of every man. Anand has cultivated quite early in his life a certain poise. Reacting to Mr Singh's criticism of one of their colleagues, Anand says in an Upanishadic vein: "Mr Singh, when you see a good man thank God that He has created a good person. When you see someone wicked, feel sorry for him for after all he is also a part of God's creation."

Anand is generous by nature and he never harbours any grouse against anyone. He loves humanity with all its good, bad and indifferent people. His reaction to the supposed lack of gratitude among some people reveals his generous temperament. While talking to Ravinder, Anand expresses his view on gratitude: "So my thinking has been that when I do a good turn, I need not expect anything in return. I have the satisfaction that I have made someone happy." (104)

As an administrator, Anand has earned the love and respect of everybody with his fair-mindedness and open nature. His concern for his students is such that he is always willing to be of some help to them. True, he has to face some tricky situations as the Principal of the University College and later as the Vice-Chancellor. Keeping his conscience and common sense as a guide, he is able to solve all those problems to the best satisfaction of the students, teachers and various other authorities. Anand is quite independent and is not in the habit of collecting a group of teachers for advice or for carrying news to him. He never believes in a coterie.

Though the character of Anand is idealised to some extent, the novelist has not ignored the objectivity needed for an artistic creation. Certain drawbacks of Anand are also touched upon. The chief among them is egotism. In the raw years of his life Anand has presumed too much on his intellect. His thinking in those days was that every man's character was his destiny. He gave little allowance to the divine dispensation. Overpowered by intellectual snobbery he had looked down upon his wife Lakshmi and began to feel that he had done a great favour in marrying her. These views of Anand however, change drastically in the course of his life. He realises soon than man's efforts alone can never give him success in life; he needs God's grace too. Further, Anand finally comes to understand the value of Lakshmi's companionship for him. He recognises, in due course, the role of Lakshmi in shaping his life and career.

Justification of the ways of God to men, is one of the striking aspects of the novel *Height of Noon.* Anand has a firm belief that his life is in the hands of God. When he was working as a lecturer in Delhi, he was tempted to enter the Civil Services. He did apply for one or two placements, but failed to secure any despite his exceptional educational qualifications due to the machinations of the powers that be. But soon he realises that he has to submit himself to God's will. This belief is again confirmed when he is appointed Vice-Chancellor of the University just five days prior to his retirement as Professor: "Anand somehow developed a new faith that the Vice-Chancellorship was God-given and no one could check him out for three years. He said repeatedly that it was a covenant between him and God and he had to fulfil his duty in the name of God. He took it as a holy mission."

Height of Noon is a highly realistic novel which graphically sketches the academic scene in independent India. The aspirations of the students for campus leadership, the professional jealousies among the teachers, favouritism and nepotism in the appointment of teachers in the universities, the fall of standards in research in India, all these are discussed at length in the novel. No other Indian novel has so deeply analysed these academic issues as *Height of Noon* does. Dr. Anand's talk with his former students Vijaya Kumar and Prathap brings out the role of an ideal teacher. His dialogue with Dr. Ravinder of North-Eastern Hill University provides an opportunity to discuss threadbare the problems plaguing research in Indian universities at present. His comments on the state of research in Indian universities have a ring of authenticity about them and they seem to have arisen from the rich experience of Rama Sarma as the Research Supervisor. "And very often the topics chosen for research tend to be survey types and do not yield genuine original work. In our anxiety to produce more and more Ph.Ds, we are sacrificing quality for quantity." The views Dr. Anand expresses in his press conferences held on the occasion of D.Litt., being conferred on him by a neighbouring university hit the nail on the maladies of the educational scenario in modern India.

Parallel to the academic world, Rama Sarma also presents in *Height of Noon* the domestic world with a lot of warmth and understanding. The reader is transported to an ideal world of marital felicity in which wife and husband play complementary and not contradictory roles. It is a world where the Hindu Dharma is implicitly followed. Anand is blessed in having an understanding wife who has stood by him through all their trials and tribulations in life. Lakshmi provides Anand a sweet home where peace and harmony prevail. "In those days of trial, he realised that Lakshmi was his true partner. He was touched by her loyalty. He also felt that she had no illusions, and delusions like him. She was steady and balanced with a pragmatic approach to life." Most of Anand's success in life is largely due to the happy homely atmosphere in the house. In the evening of his life when Lakshmi is taken away from him by a deadly disease, Anand loses much of the meaning in life. "A spiritual vacuum overpowered him." The relationship between Anand and Lakshmi is analogous to that of Rama and Sita in the *Ramayana.*

In the *Height of Noon* Rama Sarma's fictional art has attained new heights of maturity and complexity. In it there is a judicious admixture of narrative and dramatic techniques. Though for the most part of the novel the third person omniscient narration is adopted, the dramatic devices are also liberally used. The author has put the traditional story-telling method to good use when he makes Lakshmi narrate to the grand-children in a relishing manner Anand's early life as well as his father's Gandhian life. This flashback adds to the realism of the novel apart from providing the historical touch. The conversation Dr. Anand has with his students Vijaya Kumar and Prathap as well as his dialogue with Dr. Ravinder give the dramatic touch to the novel. In *Height of Noon* language attains a remarkable depth and lucidity. One can safely conclude that Rama Sarma has undoubtedly enriched the Indian English fiction by adding to its stock 'a wellmade novel' on the theme of Indian academic life and the search for identity of a highly conscientious intellectual.

Height of Noon: A Study

K. SANTHANAM

M.V. Rama Sarma is one of the foremost creative writers in English in India today. He is a renowned Milton scholar with quite a good number of critical studies on Milton's works. Besides being a critic, he is also a creative artist who has written novels and plays which have become quite popular with the reading public in India. *Height of Noon* is Rama Sarma's latest novel published in 1994. It is a 'campus novel' for it depicts the academic life of universities in India today. At the same time, the novel deals with the life of the protagonist Anand the ideal teacher and administrator, his hopes, disappointments and struggles and finally his belief in the willing submission to God's will.

The novel begins with Anand taking charge as Vice-Chancellor just five days before his retirement as Professor. In fact, Anand was looking forward to a peaceful retirement from the university which he had served in various capacities for more than two decades. The news of his appointment as Vice-Chancellor was a bit of a surprise to everyone including himself. He says very humorously that "the farewell parties organised earlier now became welcome parties." (4)

Anand came from a prosperous middle-class family with landed property. He had no idea of going to school, for he always used to spend his time on the fields having got attracted by the rustic language used by the villagers. One day Anand happened to listen to a young man reading a book on Swami Vivekananda and was fascinated by it. This inspired him to read and write and so Anand was sent to the local school. His father was surprised to see his son reading everything very fast and retaining everything in his memory so much so he created a sensation in his village for the excellent grasp of the subject and good memory power which stood him in good stead in his later years. After finishing high school, he pursued his higher studies in a local college much against the wishes of his father. But Anand convinced his father that his fate would be different from that of the other unemployed graduates. Anand proved himself perfectly correct in acquiring educational qualification which brought him many honours, titles and awards in the course of his life. After finishing post-graduate studies, he became a lecturer in a college near his village and became a popular teacher. There were a few Boswells for him even among girls and they considered him as their hero and ideal teacher. This was the time when Anand got married to Lakshmi. Being proud and egoistic, he thought he had done a favour in marrying a girl without taking dowry. He had a feeling that she was not his equal in intellectual attainments. Still, Lakshmi remained a devoted wife to him and she began to tolerate the angularities in his behaviour. Anand's love and affection for Lakshmi grew with the passage of time.

On his return to India after getting his Ph.D. from a British university, Anand first got a job as a lecturer in a Delhi college. Lakshmi and children liked the cosmopolitan atmosphere of Delhi. Anand felt completely at home in Delhi surroundings. The students in the college loved him and respected him for his scholarship. Later after five years Anand joined the new university in the South. Anand wanted to establish his reputation as a good teacher and began to work hard towards reaching his goal. He felt a bit disappointed when the university did not make any efforts to start a postgraduate programme. At this time, Anand was lucky to be selected to visit a few universities in America and study their general educational programme. He found from his own experience that lecturing in American universities was quite informal unlike the British. The seminars in the USA and the tutorials in British universities prepared the students for originality and creativity.

Anand could not very much like the Principal for he used to indulge in unfair methods like encouraging Anand's colleagues to flout his authority as the Head of the Department so that he would fall in line with the Principal. But Anand was always upright and independent and never wanted to compromise with his principles. This conflict came to a head when the Professorship was advertised. Anand could not be promoted as Professor for he was considered to be too young for that post. Anand remained a devoted teacher. He was always decisive in his views. His colleagues had a fear that Anand would become a virtual dictator if he were made Professor. Some even wrote anonymous letters to the Vice-Chancellor to spoil his chance for Professorship. But the Vice-Chancellor knew Anand's good work, and when the next opportunity came, he was appointed Professor. Anand's colleagues felt jittery and even thought that Anand would take vengeance on them. But Anand by nature was never petty-minded and vindictive. He requested his colleagues to forget all about the past and work as a united team.

Anand always maintained a dignified aloofness as a Professor and never involved himself in the university politics. His main interest was teaching and all the students adored him as an ideal teacher. Anand also served as Principal of University College for two terms and that provided him with an opportunity to move with the students and observe their behaviour. He was sympathetically disposed towards them and he wanted them to be the good citizens of the country. Anand in his own classic style used to solve the student problems much to their satisfaction. Very often students could appreciate and understand Anand's impartial attitude towards them.

Anand always had the students' welfare in his mind and strived hard to bring about harmony and understanding among the students. As Principal, he was very fair in his admission policy, and merit alone was the criterion in the matter of admission. Throughout his career, he always helped people unmindful of the ungrateful attitude of some, for, according to him, "gratitude is so burdensome" (104) and it is difficult to be grateful all the time.

When Anand was made the Vice-Chancellor, everybody thought that he fully deserved the post. Anand accepted his new responsibility as something God-given and worked hard in maintaining the high dignity of the office. As the Vice-Chancellor, he was accessible to one and all. Anand also received many honours and awards. He was selected for the Meritorious Teacher Award that year, and D.Litt. was conferred on him by a neighbouring university. He was made Fellow of the University College, Cardiff for the distinguished work done by him. There was domestic harmony and contentment at the home front. Just as Anand's fortune touched the peak, it came full circle in the declining fashion in the next few months. He was worried about his wife's health. Life was good for him so far. And now suddenly he was confronted with the cussedness of life. He thought that God, after placing him at the height of his glory, suddenly dropped him down, rather unceremoniously. After his wife's death, Anand did not want to continue as Vice-Chancellor since life had lost all its attraction for him. Still he had to continue for some more months much to his disgust. He was frequently praying to God for some relief. Finally the relief came to him when he was informed that his extended period of six months was over even though a few more days were left. Anand felt happy that God had finally answered his prayers. But he still wanted to serve the society, "but he had to wait like the scholar gipsy for the God-given moment."(136)

Thus the novel deals with the life of the protagonist Anand, who is an ideal teacher, a good scholar, an able administrator and finally a humanist who always believed in the essential goodness of man. Anand was the 'karma yogi' who believed in doing everything with a sense of detachment, and to him, service to mankind was the service to God. He had an absolute faith in God and believed that God's ways were mysterious and He helped man in an unexpected way—a fact proved by his own experience. Anand learnt the efficacy of willing submission to God's will by undergoing a process of trials and tribulations in life. He always remained an optimist throughout, which was further enlivened by his wife's feminine grace and charm sustaining him to bear the burden of life.

The title of the novel proves the strange irony of life. As the author himself says, man is often taken to the heights of noon by divine grace only to be dropped suddenly to a shadowy afternoon. Anand reached the zenith of his life and in the same way, there was a declining phase in his life which started with his wife's death. Anand comes to the hard realization that man should always try for spiritual illumination.

Height of Noon is a campus novel that portrays the academic life of the universities in India with all its attendant problems like teachers' rivalry and their petty politics. Further, the novelist presents many details of Anand's life by resorting to flashback techniques. A careful reading of the novel reveals its semi-biographical nature in that the novelist seems to narrate his own life experience at various stages. The reader comes to know certain important facts about the life of the protagonist through the form of dialogue which lends objectivity to the narration. The novel ends on a note of calm acceptance of life with all its joys and sorrows.

Gradational Process of Understanding God's Ways: *Height of Noon*

P. SOMNATH

M.V. Rama Sarma's sixth and latest novel, *Height of Noon* (1994), chiefly presents the unfolding of awareness of the meaning of life and the subtleties of divine dispensation in the mind of the sensitive, learned protagonist, Dr. Anand. Being intensely autobiographical in content, the novel also turns out to be an objective examination of the author's own life and career.

The story is woven round the central character, Dr. Anand. He comes from a prosperous middle-class family in a village in Andhra Pradesh. As a boy, initially, he is reluctant to go to school but soon he develops interest in studies. Even as a student of Intermediate, he is married to Lakshmi. As a lecturer in a college, he is liked by his students. As a young man he believes that every man's character in his destiny. He applies for admission to Ph.D. in a British university. After an initial failure, he is offered a seat by a Professor in Cardiff.

On his return to India with a Ph.D., he joins Delhi university as a lecturer. Meanwhile, the Vice-Chancellor of a new university in Andhra Pradesh named after the Lord of the Seven Hills offers him a teaching post. Dr. Anand joins it as a lecturer after his selection in an interview. Fortunately for him, this turns out to be beginning of a glorious academic and administrative career. Soon he gets U.G.C. selection for an assignment to go to the USA to visit various universities for hundred days. At the end of this period, he is invited to visit the UK by the British Council. Back at home, his elevation to professorship is stalled by the jealous principal. Only after the exit of the principal from the university, Dr. Anand is selected for professorship giving him a sense of achievement and fulfilment.

This leads to a series of laurels. He becomes the principal and continues in that position for six years. On the verge of his retirement, he is made the Vice-Chancellor of the university. His trips to the US and the UK help him establish contacts with some departments in his university. He is elected twice for the Meritorious Teachers Award by the government and he is also conferred D.Litt. by a neighbouring university. Towards the close of his career, dark clouds hover over his personal life. His wife Lakshmi dies of cancer. It makes him lose interest in life and he prays for retirement. And when it comes, he accepts it with a sigh of relief.

The novel has a single theme, namely, the 'gradational process of understanding God's ways' woven round the growth and development of Dr. Anand's personality. It has a two-pronged structure with the juxtaposition of the present and the past. Chapters 1 to 3 deal with Anand's career as Vice-Chancellor. Chapters 4 and 5 are recapitulative dealing with events after his return from England with Ph.D. till his appointment as a professor. Chapter 6 deals with his boyhood days and ends with his trip to the UK for Ph.D. Chapter 7 deals with his career as a principal of the university. Chapter 8 is a continuation of chapter 3 showing him as Vice-chancellor. The last chapter deals with Lakshmi's death and with the end of Anand's term as Vice-Chancellor.

Besides the major theme, the novel contains the episodes of Mary and Latha in chapters 2 and 3 respectively. Mary's episode shows her disappointment in a love-affair and her reconciliation with life by taking up creative writing as 'a way out of this impasse' on the suggestion of Dr. Anand. It drives home the point that 'we get what is destined for us.' The episode of Latha is another instance of "patient acceptance of life as it came to her despite her inward craving for a different life." Even as a student of Anand, she was fond of him. Yet she concealed her love in her 'unfathomable mind.' She gradually endeared herself to Lakshmi and it is only through Lakshmi that Anand comes to know of Latha's love for him after many years. Thus, the episodes of Mary and Latha are aimed at their coming to terms with life in spite of their disappointment. The two episodes are woven into the main plot by way of showing how the protagonist exercises his benign influence on the two characters.

The fictional focus throughout the novel is on Anand and the gradual ripening of his personality and thinking forms the thesis of the novel. A distinct feature of his personality is 'a stubborn faith in himself.' When his father was discouraged by his relatives not to send Anand for higher studies, "Anand's own argument was that his fate would be different from that of the others" and that "he was born for better things in life." (85) Even as a boy, he displayed a thirst for knowledge. "He seemed to be a prodigy" and "created a sensation in that little village for his excellent memory power and quick grasp of the subjects taught to him." (77)

Anand's supreme faith in himself is strengthened by his success as a lecturer. He indulges in 'self-glorification' and assumes 'intellectual snobbery.' He claims credit for his 'indomitable self-effort' for his success. Anand's supreme faith in himself is rudely shaken when he fails to get admission for Ph.D. in some universities in Britain: "Anand's pride was hurt, but there was no alternative. . . . He never thought that he would receive negation and rejection in life. This was a new experience for him, a bitter experience. He was terribly upset." (25)

When Anand is steeped in bottomless despondency, a professor whom Anand meets by chance in Cardiff offers him admission to Ph.D. course. It is a 'miracle' for Anand for he realizes that man's effort can be crowned with success only with God's grace.

> For the first time in his life Anand realized that God's grace was needed before anything could be achieved. . . . This was a new awareness that came to Anand. He accepted his defeat. He no longer over-emphasized man's almightiness. He was humbled and this was the first stage in the gradational process of his understanding God's ways. (26)

After coming back to India with Ph.D. degree, Anand is selected by the Delhi university. His trial for a job in Hyderabad fails and he leaves for Delhi. With this "it occurred to Anand a second time in his life that he had to submit himself to divine direction." (38) Even during his stay in Delhi, Anand "still struggled to assert himself as an independent intellectual not to be deterred by the inhospitable happenings in life." (44) He does not realize that God's intervention has caused his obsession to join the new university at Tirupati in Andhra Pradesh. "Even though divine dispensation repeatedly showed itself to be stronger than human effort, he did not as yet surrender himself to the will of God." (44)

Anand's appointment as Professor, after his failure in his first attempt, gives him not only a deep sense of fulfilment but also brings about a subtle transformation in his attitude towards God: "He realized that all his merited work was nothing as compared with divine disposal. Anand was slowly getting reconciled to the worship of the Lord." (71) Further, Anand identifies himself with the university with a sense of devotion. The dedicated teacher in him now reigns his consciousness. Now, "it became his faith, solemn faith to be useful to other fellow human beings" (74) and he becomes a 'karmayogi.' This is distinctly yet another elevated, ripened aspect of his personality:

> He understood that his destiny was with that university and he surrendered himself to the will of God. He never asked for anything, but from that time onwards everything was made ready for him by the protective hand of God. Anand learnt the lesson of doing things irrespective of the reward. He became a karmayogi. His contention was that when God was kind to him, in return he should be helpful to others. (74)

Anand's conviction in divine dispensation is further strengthened when he reaches the pinnacle of his glory with the assumption of the office of Vice-Chancellor of the university. He takes it as God's will: "He knew it was providential. God's blessing had come to him. He realized once again that divine Providence had always played a greater role than his individual effort in life." (2) Anand accepts his new responsibilities as 'a holy mission' and feels himself as a chosen one:

> He was like Thomas Becket 'wishing subjection to God alone.' . . . Anand and Lakshmi firmly believed that God's grace was extended to them. This belief gave him supreme moral strength to uphold and maintain a sense of justice in administration. He affirmed and asserted that God chose him for doing some good to the university. (108-9)

When Anand's wife dies of cancer, his faith in God is shaken. He is seen 'wrestling with God's justice': "Like Adam he questioned why God had given him all those good things of life almost unasked for, and then had abandoned him to a life of suffering. For one moment he could not reconcile himself with God's ways." (128) In a dejected mood he says to himself: 'no more Gods for me.' He is overpowered by 'a spiritual vacuum.' Now he turns to God once more to come out of the impasse knowing full well that God's ways are 'mysterious and inscrutable.' He prays to God for relief 'persistently and almost doggedly.' When ultimately he is relieved of his duties as Vice-Chancellor a few days before his term ends, Anand is surprised that his prayer is answered rather swiftly and abruptly:

> That sudden and unexpected manner in which he was sent out could be God's way of dealing with unruly children like him, Anand felt. . . . Anand did not know whether the relief given to him was God's blessing or ire. (135)

Thus, Anand attains the wisdom that there is no other way except accepting God's will in pleasure and pain and that one should consider oneself an instrument of God with equanimity of mind. Besides developing this major theme, the author seeks to show how Anand is essentially a self-made man. Equipped with knowledge by sheer effort and dedicated to teaching, Anand is helped by fortune to come up in life and in his profession. Inspired by his uncle and father in his boyhood, Anand develops a thirst for knowledge and a sense of nationalism and patriotism. During his stay in England "he was so full of national spirit that he often felt annoyed if anyone spoke slightingly of his country." He is pained to hear Indians telling him that they would like to settle in England.

In spite of his high education and refinement, 'the rustic in him never left him' in the sense that "he could never talk with a twisted tongue and flatter anyone. He was invariably courteous with everyone but he was frank and open in his talk with others. It was indeed difficult to see when his rustic truthfulness overpowered his acquired sophistication." (45) Another important feature of Anand's character is 'his deep involvement in his professional work' shunning publicity. Hence he is adored by students. He loves teaching and is a good researcher. Even as a principal and as a Vice-Chancellor, he continues to take classes. The goodwill he has achieved helps him as an administrator too. He is generous to those who have tried to stall his promotion as a professor. He is never petty-minded or vindictive.

As the chief focus in the novel is on the character of Anand, other characters do not gain much importance. However, the character of Lakshmi, Anand's wife, emerges quite distinctly. Mostly, she is sketched out from Anand's recapitulations. She was only thirteen when she was married to Anand. But emotionally she was more matured than Anand who was seventeen. She bore Anand's egotism patiently 'like patient Griselda.' She has unshaken faith in Anand. So she encourages him to go abroad for Ph.D. without any wavering.

> He was amazed to see the simple woman show such firm faith in him. He was touched by her loyalty. He also felt that she had no illusions and delusions like him. She was steady and balanced with a pragmatic approach to life. Lakshmi became his source of strength ever since he planned to go abroad. Anand's love and affection for Lakshmi grew with the tide of time, and they looked inseparable for the rest of their lives. (89-90)

It is again due to her total faith in Anand that Lakshmi never feels jealous of Latha even after knowing that the latter has been nursing a secret love for Anand.

At times, she acts as a guide to Anand. While he is not particular about building a house, Lakshmi takes the initiative in the construction work with the help of her son. Once a beautiful building has come up, Anand begins to like it immensely. "Then he realised that he was foolish in denying the gift of God." (73) The peaceful atmosphere created by Lakshmi at home contributes to Anand's success in his office. "Lakshmi looked like the presiding diety in the house. Anand never did anything that might displease her. Harmony prevailed. There was domestic peace. Anand could devote himself to the service of the university wholeheartedly." (74) Anand's assumption of office as Vice-Chancellor is a great moment for Lakshmi. Anand acknowledges her role for the last twenty-five years leading to the eventful day: "All these years she was with him as a partner sharing with him his experiences, pleasant and unpleasant, with an unswerving loyalty to God." (3-4) Hence, naturally, when Lakshmi dies of cancer, Anand feels inseparable loss: "Lakshmi was no more, the light was gone, and Anand's life was given to darkness. . . . Life had lost its glamour and dreariness overpowered Anand." (131) Thus, Lakshmi emerges as the quintessence of Indian womanhood. In her strength of character and clear vision of things, she is as fascinating as her husband.

Rama Sarma chiefly uses the telling method rather than the showing method in his narrative technique. The third-person point of view is employed uninterruptedly except where Anand's boyhood is narrated through Lakshmi. Very often the author sums up some of the traits of Anand's personality. For instance, he says:

> Anand was a dedicated teacher and a conscientious administrator. (136)
>
> Anand on the whole was warm hearted, friendly with others. Only occasionally the pride in him made him too critical of others. (88)
>
> Anand was not orthodox, nor did he believe in any ritual. (4)

Occasionally, the author intersperses the 'telling' method with the 'showing' method by probing Anand's thoughts, feelings and motives and comments on them. For instance, while tracing Anand's reaction to his appointment as Vice-Chancellor, the author says:

> He talked as though it was God's will. He knew it was providential. . . . He *realized* once again that divine providence had always played a greater role than his individual effort in life. He *felt* that things were made ready for him by the benevolent hand of God. (2, emphasis added)

Similarly, Anand's feelings are traced when he is honoured on the assumption of office as Vice-Chancellor:

> Anand realized that his task was a stupendous one as so many wished for his success. He should live up to their expectations and not falsify their hopes about the development of the university in his term of office. (5)

Dissecting Anand's bent of mind when he was fresh as a lecturer, the author writes: "He was very young, imaginative and very intelligent. He was an intellectual not to be classified with the generality of mankind, he thought. One might call it intellectual snobbery." (87) After Lakshmi's death, Anand's gloomy thoughts are traced: "his life was so far sheltered under the benevolent hand of God. Anand felt that God for one moment withdrew His protective hand and he fell." (129) He is found 'wrestling with God's justice' in his stupefied mind:

> his mind was racing fast with all those interrogations of God's ways. Hitherto he talked of God's essential justice all the time with gusto, but what had happened to him, he mused. For all his faith in God he was left with a tragic fate. (130)

Though it helps project the character's state of mind and renders his mental process, Rama Sarma's method is undramatic method, "since we are conscious of the author standing beside his characters on the stage, and our attention is divided between them and him."[2]

Height of Noon is realistic in more than one sense. First, there is autobiographical realism since Rama Sarma maintains a very thin veil between Dr. Anand and himself. For instance, Sri Venkateswara University at Tirupati in Andhra Pradesh in which he worked is referred to as the 'university named after the Lord of Seven Hills.' It is also true that Rama Sarma had worked in Delhi University before he came to serve S.V. University, Tirupati. His Vice-Chancellorship is also corroborated by the description given on the title page of the novel.

Apart from the realism at the personal level, there is historical realism too. The amount of Anand's boyhood is narrated by Lakshmi against the background of Freedom Movement during 1920s and 1930s. Gandhi's visit to Anand's village and his magnetic influence on the people are re-lived in the novel. This link with history is again taken up when the death of Gandhi is reported during Anand's student days in Cardiff.

Further, the novel amply brings in 'academic realism' relating to the conditions in Indian university. Certain important problems of the university are highlighted as Dr. Anand grapples with them and finds solutions to them setting certain standards. For instance, the jealousy and animosity of the Principal towards Dr. Anand come in the way of his elevation as professor in his first attempt. He succeeds only in his second attempt in due recognition of his merit. As a principal, he does not involve himself in the group politics of the university and plays fair and impartial in tackling problems. As such, he gets ample co-operation from the students and the teachers. In solving the disputes of students, Dr. Anand is convinced of the essential goodness of students. He says:

> My own feeling is that basically students have no deep- rooted hatred for one another, and their abnormal behaviour is only the creation of their teacher leaders who use them for their ends. . . . And students do it partly because of caste affiliations and partly because of a fond hope that they may get a class in their examinations. (95)

The author also throws light on the sorry state of research in the universities. Research work is done hastily sacrificing quality. Foreign examiners are done away with to help the candidates. In some cases, candidates expect their guides to write theses for them. Further, in the case of giving promotion to university teachers, he decides "that an overall picture of teaching, research and publications would be demanded of every teacher." (114) Another important issue is limiting the stay of university teachers to their States. As such "the best in them is not properly exposed and utilised." (113)

Coming as it does from a former professor of English, the language of the novel is free from unnecessary embellishment and ornamentation. A distinguishing mark of the language of the novel is the apt use of a host of literary references bearing the scholarship of the novelist. For instance, Anand is reminded of Becket's martyrdom on his visit to the Cathedral at Canterbury in England. Similarly, his visit to Dover reminds Anand "of *King Lear* and the scene where Gloucester imagined himself to have fallen from the cliffs." (27) It is also interesting to note that "Anand often likened his daughter to Perdita of Shakespeare's *The Winter's Tale*. Perdita brought prosperity to a barren land, and his own daughter Padma, he felt, had given him peace and prosperity to the family." (71) That is why, after Padma's marriage, "her parting reminded him of Sakuntala's separation from Kanwa, her foster father." (122) Similarly, whenever Anand saw two groups of students fighting, he "was always reminded of *Romeo and Juliet* where the Capulets and the Montagues were all the time fighting." (95) Sometimes, they fought "like the Big Endians and the Little Endians in Swift's *Gulliver's Travels*." (99) After Lakshmi's death, Dr. Anand strives to overcome his personal grief and wishes to dedicate himself "to serve mankind, but in what manner, he himself did not know. He had to wait, like the scholar gipsy, for the godgiven moment, whenever that might be." (136)

The title of the novel, *Height of Noon*, is symbolic of the pinnacle of Dr. Anand's glory in his personal life as well as in his academic and administrative career like the sun at noon. On the one hand, the pinnacle overlooks the steps he has climbed to reach his present state with God's benevolence. The title seems to suggest that one should learn to accept God's will and to accept life as it is and that wisdom lies in such affirmation of life.

NOTES

1. M.V. Rama Sarma, *Height of Noon* (Guntur: Maruthi, 1994), p. 35.
2. J.W. Beach, *The Twentieth Century Novel* (Ludhiana: Lyall, 1969), p. 180.

Themes in the Novels of Rama Sarma

S. HARI BABU

Rama Sarma's novels exhibit his social awareness. The pattern of life presented in his novels revolves round primarily on issues concerned with social realities. These realities and themes may be broadly categorised as the exploration of the inevitable interaction between man's attitude of his own self and his attitude towards life.

Georg Lukacs[1] has pointed out in "Art and Society" that it is as a social being that man can become a human individual and not a mere natural entity, a view that Rama Sarma seems to endorse. Man, in his relationship with society may create in himself an attitude which may prove to be wrong both to him and to the society on account of his too much stress on the concreteness of his existence on the physical plane. Therefore, he with the help of his mental attitude, should strive to establish an equilibrium between his subjective mind and the objective world of things and then try to fight tooth and nail the imperfections of the society by finding ways and means for the evolution of a new social order. In the next stage he must create within himself an attitude on the spiritual plane to work for humanity without aspiring for any reward. These ideas occupy centrality of position in the novels of Rama Sarma drawing attention to allied themes like exploitation, caste system, corrupt practices in the academic life and the pathetic plight of intellectuals in search of their livelihood in a foreign land.

Thus in all his novels what is manifest at the surface level is nothing but the theme of awareness of the being in relation with his subjective mind and the objective world or society. The theme of self perfection or upward progress then has its growth not only in one novel but in a series of novels from the physical stage to the most advanced spiritual stage, with the intermediary mental and intellectual stages. The growth of the individual as a being of self perfection is possible only in a society and not in isolation. That is why Rama Sarma's protagonists seek their identities in relation to their attitudes stemming either from physical or mental or intellectual or spiritual levels and in their relationship with the society.

Rama Sarma is of the view that man shall acquire sanity only on learning the bitter lessons. There are so many layers of sanity ranging from the physical, concrete object to that which embraces a world wide view. This belief of sanity has its genesis in man's intellectual power of discrimination.

This essential factor in him will definitely help him in his quest for better alternatives in this material world. To Rama Sarma this is to be found inherent in the human being as an inherited personality highlighting the hallmarks of cultural heritage and values. Man to him is not an ordinary being but a being 'noble in reason and infinite in faculty.' Therefore we find his protagonists have in them such an inherited personality with its roots in their deep contemplation on the theme of detachment which is not withdrawal from worldly partakings but involvement and right action. Thus Rama Sarma's concept of faith in man lies not in his renouncing action but in renouncing the result of action, a philosophy and practical wisdom which constitutes the Indian culture. Thus his men contemplate on the value of detachment in human terms.

In his first novel *The Stream* the theme of detachment has taken a wrong direction on account of the protagonist Gopalam's wrong mental attitude and lack of reason. His concept of love and beauty are illusory in nature. His understanding of the Romantic poets too will claim him to be a man of passion without any iota of reason.

The tragedy of Gopalam is his inability to distinguish his acquired personality from his inherited personality. He believes in the apparent externals, that too with the help of his wrong awareness of his association with the Romantic poets. He values the concreteness of objects giving any credence to its metaphysics. This is all due to his lack of reason. "If men failed to distinguish between their inherited and acquired personalities, it was their own fault. He [Gopalam] was thoroughly convinced of the prevalence of reason over bestiality, of judgement over ignorance in man."[2]

Gopalam's marriage with Suguna is also born out of the misconception of taking her external beauty as the fitting expression of 'Romantic Idealism.' In fact his love for her is not born out of pragmatic reason but out of romantic passion. Similarly he has misconceived Swarna's love as a substitute for romantic idealism. Here too he fails to look deep into her mind rather than her heart. Finally it is through Joan, he comes to understand the real value of life with its stress on justice and reason.

So far as he is caught up under the influence of his acquired personality with its roots deeply laid in passion, he is made to suffer in the stream of life. Finally when he is made to interact with the metaphysical and platonic concept of love of Joan, he acquires an intellectual awareness which is reflected in his concept of triple force. Similarly it is through Joan's friendship that he realises true love. Though love is a dominating force in life, it is only a part of life. Only towards the close he understands that there are many other useful things to be done for the society than 'falling in love or falling out of love.'

> He took to life with greater vigour and he argued to himself that he was not born merely for the sake of falling in or falling out of love. There were mighty projects before him. Love was only a subsidiary object. He might do something constructive to himself, to society or to the country in general. Social service, creative writing, political work—any of these, he could take up and anyone of them should surely absorb him completely. He was determined to rule out passion for women from his pageant of life.
>
> His love for Swarna became an obsession with him and in those hectic days it was impossible for him to think of any other object except Swarna. His nature was such that he would go the whole hog and never do things by halves. He even thought he might die if Swarna failed him in her promises. Now life taught him a lesson not to bother about women. (169-70)

Rama Sarma gives a clue in this novel that if an individual can by some method, adjust his awareness, he can gain a certain victory over the external world, which is the first stepping stone in the direction of meaningful detachment. Gopalam observes,

> Passionate longings no longer move me. The nobler element in me moves me to the more balanced and intellectual understanding of life. I have come out of the storm and stress of the stream. Now I look back and heave a sigh of relief. I am not sorry for my experiences for they have chastened and sublimated me. The stream of life now goes on calmly towards the annihilation of animal instincts. (173)

The theme of self perfection is balanced with the optimistic view of life and this is realised through the theme of mental awareness. In fact this theme forges a broader bond of unity between the individual and the society. Rama Sarma's noble creed takes the dimension of individual's annihilation of animal instincts through his awareness of sanity or the preponderance of justice. Rama Sarma feels that man with his power of thinking and mental attitude can grow as an individual of perfect being thereby in a way influencing the community to which he belongs. Therefore the theme of self perfection or upward progress is complete when the individual strives hard to establish some perfection in the society.

The Farewell Party depicts how the individual's self-perfection gets shifted from the physical plane to the intellectual plane with the tools of tolerance and detachment and how it establishes a healthy relationship with the society. The theme of tolerance as we find in Prakasam in *The Farewell Party* is another dimension of awareness to establish harmony and peace among the disjointed groups. Prakasam's tolerance and detachment serve as the life boat for him to reach his destination of self-perfection. When these two aspects of tolerance and detachment are properly blended, it will earn the individual a permanent and lasting victory in the realm of marriage: "Professor Prakasam was a dreamer, his wife Sarala a realist. He was an utopian, she was practical minded. The difference in nature did not produce any conflicting results, on the other hand the one supplemented the other."[3]

The entire portrayal of the novel about the corrupt contemporary academic atmosphere is realistic in a sense that the writer focuses his attention not only on the sick academic order like the "divide and rule oriented administrator, a faculty divided by notions of first class, second class and third class, besides the divisions of Ph.Ds and non Ph.Ds and the student body eager to learn and willing to co-operate on the slightest show of warmth, but left hungry and unfed and hence indulging in mischief" but also suggests its remedy in the human form, that is Prakasam, "a rare and dedicated teacher"[4] thereby introducing the theme of the co-existence of good and evil.

The tolerance of Prakasam has taken its fuller dimension only when it is made to interact with social beings, and in a sense this tolerance is one of the phases of the social consciousness to maintain a balanced relationship with the society to which he belongs. Even though the theme of tolerance has its seeds of growth in the individual consciousness its resultant success is not the individual's practice of it in personal life but in the practice of the same in the social plane.

In practising this as a correct mental attitude Prakasam does not rise in revolt to root out evil from the phase of his campus community nor accept the same in total silence. This is because of Prakasam's humanism at the pragmatic level. He sees Sundaram, his colleague, a being deliberately treated as a kind of underdog on account of Suri's evil influence on the Machiavellian Principal Gupta. It is Prakasam who has found out in Sundaram certain brighter patches which are enough for a teacher to handle undergraduate classes. He takes up the task of getting some fair deal for Sundaram all in human terms.

The theme of detachment is reflected through Professor Prakasam who is not expecting any material gain but at the same time wants to be useful to the society.

The theme of detachment that consists of right action is limited in scope in this novel whereas the same theme is further expounded in the next novel *Look Homeward.* As a social being Prakasam has achieved his self-perfection through his attitude of tolerance, faith, love and fellow-feeling. As a man given to thinking he has already killed his animal instincts through his mental awareness that is rooted in tolerance and detachment and has emerged out as the supreme intelligent being in the evolution of man. His love and concern for fellow beings are directly linked with his quest for an ideal way of life in human terms. His tolerance is exhibited not only in his association with his colleagues but also with a foreigner like Margaret. Maintaining that human friendship is essential rather than throwing brick bats on each other out of envy, hatred and injustice. Thus his tolerance, when it is to find its expression through friendship with Margaret, emerges out as human love. From his relationship with Margaret we learn the value of human love. But what is much more essential is patriotism—love of one's country.

> "Prakasam, I wonder why there should be bitterness between our two countries. Don't you think it is silly to go about like this hating each other?"
>
> "Yes, there is no point is spreading ill-will, but yet, we want to be independent. That's our legitimate right."
>
> "Of course, you ought to be independent. But do you really think you can manage it by yourself now? Don't you think that your country will have to wait for sometime more before it can be independent?"
>
> "That is what your politicians tell us. But some beginning has to be made, the sooner the better."
>
> "I think so."

The love for his country is reflected through his attitudes of tolerance and detachment. It is a spectacle through which he looks at men's good qualities on the social plane. This awareness of Prakasam has elevated him from his sensuous existence to intellectual existence and thereby he, as a being has attained his self-perfection due to the fact that all his individual attitudes become his conversion of social attitudes.

In this novel the theme of exploitation is found in the social behaviour of academicians like Shastry, Sekhar and Ramesam. Shastry knows the weakness of his wards. Sekhar knows the weakness of the educational system. Ramesam knows the weakness of his colleagues. But none comes forward to rectify the sick and corrupt academic order. They never realise the importance of their holding such a responsible position that offers them ample scope to show the future generation the right path. Instead they all make the best out of the existing order by means of remaining themselves 'blind mouths' showing special care and attention for their personal gains and comforts at the cost of moral and social responsibility.

The same awareness of tolerance and detachment in *Look Homeward* is allowed to emerge as a unifying force to root out all the evils of the nation. It takes the dimension of not only love for fellow beings but also the theme of nationalism firmly grounded on the commitment for the country's progress.

Ravi, besides being a lover of mankind, is a true patriot who approaches the problem of brain-drain and reveals to his friends their lack of social awareness. When all of them find fault with India's lack of scope for advanced scientific research. Ravi tries to instil the spirit of patriotism in them: "But we cannot run away from the country. With all its shortcomings, the country is lovable. If people, who have gone abroad, come back and serve the country, a new outlook may prevail."[5]

Ravi explains to them that any protest against the nation's shortcomings without trying to bring about a change through their acquired knowledge in the foreign land is nothing short of shirking their social responsibilities. Ravi patiently listens to the caustic comments of his friends against India.

> "Unfortunately India does not offer the facilities for advanced research work. The universities have yet to develop" put in Sundaram.
>
> "Everywhere in India there is corruption. It is sickening. The Government offices, the business concerns, the educational institutions all seem to be seething in the pool of corruption. There is a lot of nepotism. You can't expect any fair deal from anyone. I would never go back to India" vehemently pleaded Ramesh Babu.
>
> "In India very often there is no right place or opening for the type of research work we wish to do. We have to depend mostly on the Government. We are kept as pool officers or pensioners, or sometimes if we have a good pull we become administrators and this research work will be a waste, a colossal waste. So we mean staying here even though we too, love to be in our country," Ham argued.
>
> Only Gupta insisted on money and the material comforts wealth would give. All others had different views on the matter. Their motivation was mostly based on research and the opportunities that were denied to them in India. Ravi listened to them with patience and sympathy. He started slowly but deliberately: "What you say is true. Those who go out, in any country, are the adventurous ones. They are more than average. Their intellectual equipment is greater than that of the others. So they seek new paths, new pastures to graze. But after having fed themselves they should go back." (23)

The above conversation reveals how the awareness of Ravi's friends is at variance with that of Ravi, all because of their lack of meaningful action. Further, they are not ready even in a humble manner to serve the country to the best of their abilities so as to make the nation march towards prosperity. Ravi's social awakening with its stress on patriotism seems to be like the view of Kennedy that one should not ask what the country has done for him but one should ask what he or she has done for the country.

The problem of brain-drain can be solved provided the intellectuals develop love for their country. Ravi's social consciousness stems from the love for his country. For the betterment of the society he has cultivated the spirit of oneness. Man as an individual should love to work for the sake of the country, so as to rebuild not only the objective world but also to rediscover the truth of self-perfection which is nothing but rendering service to mankind. Service to mankind is service to God. Thus Ravi's intellectual existence in this novel is shown to make an honest attempt to reach the cherished goal of man's ultimate 'upward progress' or inner revolution of attaining non-involvement through involvement. This absolute blissful stage of spiritualism is nothing but the attainment of inaction through action itself which is superior to asceticism. This has taken the form of *Bhakti* or absolute surrender to God in spiritual terms in the next novel *The Bliss of Life*.

Bhakti is intense love of God. It is a powerful emotion arising in man from a vivid sense of the greatness of God, and his goodness and love for all. It is an attachment to the perfect God who is responsive to the needs, and sensitive to the wishes of man. By His saving grace He liberates man from his bondage—*Samsara*. *Bhakti* presupposes faith in the existence and majesty and acceptability of the Lord. . . . It is popular because it is basically a human emotion. To love and be loved is the human effort to fly from loneliness. . . . Under normal circumstances, men in general are prepared to make all kinds of sacrifices for their love. Love is an emotion, and it is all-consuming and universal. It is total and is at times self-effacing and self-emptying. Its divine analogue is *Bhakti*. Human love is directed to other fellow beings, who are imperfect and are all of the one type. our loves are based on infatuation [Moha], a projected picture of us about others. . . . *Bhakti* is the love of the perfect lord based on the clear knowledge and deep conviction of his majesty and love. . . . It is the replacing of self-love by God love."[6]

The principal aspirant of *Bhakti* in this novel is a symbol of the above definition of *Bhakti* that Kshetrayya shows to his Lord Muvva Gopala. The path that he has chosen is self-surrender. His surrendering soul sees no other than his Lord Muvva Gopala. Right from the beginning of this novel Kshetrayya who is otherwise called Varada in his early days sees only his Lord Gopala in animate and inanimate things. He lifts the burden of his spiritual welfare from his helpless self and places it into the hands of the Lord. He feels that he is a *Nayaki*, a property of his Lord, suffering greatly in the consuming fire of love. For this act of replacement, he needs displacement. Displacement means self-emptying and this is done in his case through music. It is only in music the divine rapture can be experienced in the concrete form. His *Padams* are the expressions of this rapture since they please, "all those who look for *Sringara* at the surface level, for others the *Padams* stand for the spiritual experience of the devotee. The devotee's love for the lord and all the varied feelings that come to him in the pursuit of the devotional love, sometimes in hope and sometimes in despair, are like the alterations of bliss and suffering that may be the experiences by a Nayaki waiting for her lover."[7]

His love for Mohanangi is his fulfilment of his dream that is his love for his Lord Muvva Gopala. His Mohanangi is not an ordinary being with imperfections. If Muvva Gopala is Varada's lord, to her Varada is her lord. The theme of self-surrender attains full effulgence in their case. To Lord Muvva Gopala, Varada is his devotee or *Nayaki*. Similarly to Varada,

Mohanangi is his *Nayaki* or devotee. Both of them have attained this mental detachment and the bondage between the two pairs is a sign of ceremonial purity. Both of them have led a God-centered life and practise the living presence of their respective God in their devotional love pronounced through their harmonious blending of music and dance. Both of them lead a total dedication of life to their gods. Varada and Mohana in their own selection of their respective Lords of surrender have attuned their individual wills to the wills of their Lords. The spiritual union is born out of their total identification of their self-surrender to experience the divine essence of love. There is no caste or colour or creed barrier to stop them from their spiritual experience. Their devotion is born not out of physical affinity but out of reason and self-control.

In this context Rama Sarma attacks certain ancient caste beliefs which are not rooted down to reason. "Kshetrayya belongs to the ruling niyogi brahmin caste and Mohanangi to the *devadasi* community professionally dedicated to the worship of God in temples, mostly through dance and song." (112) Rama Sarma's portrayal of Mohanangi in that community is really thought provoking since he shows through her to the world how our glorious culture of Indian womanhood has its firm faith in purity and chastity especially in their worship of their husbands as their gods. Mohanangi tells Varadaiah, "I may be a dancer but I have decided not to lead the life of a dancing woman and surrender myself to the highest bidder. That life is not for me. I know I am for you and you are destined to be my lord."

Thus we find in all his novels a juxtaposition and interaction of man's individual mental make-up and the objective world. If the protagonist acquires proper equilibrium, between these two entities, then he can have a fuller and richer view of life as well as about his own self. Such a juxtaposition strengthens the conviction that man with such mental poise will definitely bring a newer light not in his isolated mental abstractions but in his association with society.

NOTES

1. Qtd. Hirendranath Datta, "Creative Writing and Social Consciousness," *Indian Literature*, Vol. XIX, No. 3 (May-June 1976), p. 74.
2. Rama Sarma, *The Stream* (New Delhi: S. Chand, 1983), p. 80.
3. Rama Sarma, *The Farewell Party* (Hyderabad: Orient Academy, 1971), p. 6.
4. G. Nageswara Rao, "Rama Sarma," *IEN*, p. 105.
5. Rama Sarma, *Look Homeward* (Madras: Blackie, 1976), p. 111.
6. Dr. P. Nagaraja Rao, *The Heritage of Vendata* (Madras: Jyothi Nilayam, 1968), pp. 56-57.
7. Rama Sarma, *The Bliss of Life* (New Delhi: Chand, 1979), p. 136.

From M.Phil. dissertation "Social Consciousness in the Novels of Rama Sarma," Bharatidasan University, Tiruchi, 1985

Rama Sarma's Novels: Novels of Ideas

G. NAGESWARA RAO

Like Shaw's plays of ideas Rama Sarma's six novels, *The Stream, The Farewell Party, Look Homeward, The Bliss of Life, Pastures New* and *Height of Noon* are centred round thought provoking ideas. Apart from the readable story presented in every novel, there is the element of edification generated through a clustering of ideas related to our human values and traditions. The concept of the Triple Force of Beauty, Love and Justice in *The Stream,* the plea for good teaching in *The Farewell Party*, the brain drain and the call for the exhilarating love of the country in *Look Homeward*, 'Madhura bhakti' and man's willing submission to God's will as a desirable goal in *The Bliss of Life*, the glory of India as a leading country in the world in *Pastures New* and finally the imperishable significance of doing one's own duty as an act of faith in God in *Height of Noon*, all these comprise the social, religious, political and educational conditions of the present day. These novels can rightly be called the Novels of Ideas.

According to Rama Sarma life understood in a proper perspective is bound to be glorious. Depending upon man's attitude to life, he can make his life what he wishes it to be or mar it in more ways than one can describe. In a view of life based on this attitude there is little scope to believe that some are lucky and others are unlucky, or that the quality of life depends on money or wealth or power. Every human being has to go through an inescapable process of life before realizing what life really is.

Rama Sarma's first novel *The Stream* depicts the painful quest of Gopalam. Beginning as a boy slow to learn, he grows into a brilliant but somewhat hypersensitive young man and finally after a trip to England for education, he becomes a fully evolved individual. All the rough edges are rounded off and several conflicts are ironed out by his encounter with reality, by the inevitable tempests, cross-currents and whirl-winds in the stream of life. His true being is shaped by three women Suguna, Swarna and Joan with whom he comes into contact.

We find the influence of four British writers on *The Stream*. The retrospective recollection of Wells' Mr. Polly has influenced the opening section of Rama Sarma's novel. The realistic narrative technique and semi-biographical form of the *The Stream* reminds us of the art of Maugham, particularly his *Of Human Bondage*. The concept of the Triple force developed in the novel reminds one of the concept of 'life-force' as presented by Shaw and the way in which Rama Sarma artistically unfolds it in the course of the action of the novel reminds us of the art of Thomas Hardy. Like Sue in *Jude the Obscure* Swarna is always in two minds.

This opening scene in *The Stream* reminds us of the opening of *The History of Mr. Polly*. Polly is disgusted with everything, his wife, and life in general. He retrospectively thinks of his boyhood days. In *The Stream*, Gopalam too wistfully recollects his early life, as an escape from the mood of frustration. Swarna's beauty and full blooded warmth takes Gopalam through the pleasures of passionate love. But it is his platonic love affair with Joan that illuminates Gopalam's intellectual life and his sense of justice is fully realized and fulfilled through his friendship with her. Love, Gopalam realizes, though a dominant force in his life, is only a part of life, whereas it is the whole being for Swarna. If Suguna, Swarna and Joan symbolize Beauty, Love and Justice, Murthy and Rao serve as foils to the central figure of the novel, Gopalam.

The skilful organization of characters around the vital triple concept of Beauty, Love and Justice gives a rounded fullness to the structure of the novel. Otherwise the novel would have become a philosophical treatise. Rama Sarma makes the whole concept a living experience through the conversation of Joan and Gopalam, without himself stepping on the stage, as it were, like Maugham in his *Of Human Bondage*.

The discussion of Joan and Gopalam shows that one achieves the fullness of being liberated from passion not by a theoretical acceptance of the triple principle, but by participating in a life of quest. One acquires realization by living through the strife of life, by the painful voyage of exploration through violent storms and fair weather of the sea of life.

The whole action in the novel *The Farewell Party* is centred round three letters which Professor Prakasam receives that day, one from his son, one from his daughter and the third from his formal rival. The novel presents a three-dimensional picture of several aspects of life in all their complexity and entirety. It gives a true picture of an ideal professor who is shown as 'a man thinking' than as a 'mere thinker,' as a contemplative type of person pondering on the predicament of life.

The Professor's quest is also shown in certain aspects of his domestic life and eventful academic and social life. His quest makes him examine his behaviour, being and bearing in all areas of life. This quest for an ideal way of life, a way of life which liberates from passion and his constant objective self-criticism makes him "an honest soul—a sound scholar, an affectionate father, a loving colleague, a friendly neighbour, and a good husband and a beloved Professor."

Within this framework, the novel also portrays the three-fold aspect of the contemporary academic scene; a rare and dedicated teacher like Prakasam, the spicy campus politician like Suri and a variety of other teachers modest, selfish, mercenary and even comical. The whole picture is so true to day-to-day campus life that one feels that the author has immortalised many mortals whom one meets everyday. Professor Prakasam, among this group of living teachers, may look like "an utopian." But who has achieved anything worthwhile without being an utopian?

The rich panorama of life is presented as the reverie of the Professor between half past three and half past five, just before the farewell party on the day of his retirement. Stream of consciousness technique of narration and the semi-autobiographical mode of projecting experience are admirably suited to the nature of the vision. The novel presents a vital area of Indian life surprisingly left unexplored by Indian English novelists and a form and technique virtually left untouched. In both, the author has achieved a remarkable success and has made a rich contribution.

The Farewell Party presents infinite riches in a little room. The type of experience presented offers immense scope, perhaps an irresistable temptation as well, to indulge in cynicism, satire and even lampoon. Only an artist like Rama Sarma with wide sympathies and tolerance could steer clear of these temptations. After reading the novel one is bound to echo Mrs. Prakasam's words: "Professors are lovable."

Look Homeward, Rama Sarma's third novel, is a remarkable one not only because of its fascinating theme and the vital issue of life and society involved in it, but also for the way in which these aspects are artistically projected in the form of an inner quest and the realisation of the main character and the style in which they are presented. In this novel the author uses the fictional semi-biographical mode of narration—a technique he successfully used in his first novel, *The Stream* and later meaningfully combined it with the stream of consciousness technique in *The Farewell Party*. The semi-biographical form in *Look Homeward* is elegantly spiced with retrospective narration and direct dramatic dialogue wherever they are called for by the exigencies of art. The style which is crisp, direct and forcible, fits the technique and the theme so naturally that the medium becomes the message. So the whole novel as one reads unfolds as naturally as a flower blossoms. Such is the mastery Rama Sarma has acquired over the form and the medium. As K.R. Srinivasa Iyengar perceptively comments, *Look Homeward* "tells a straightforward story with a pointed relevance for India. The characters have been delineated with a few bold strokes, and there is variety in character, scene and incident. The book has a timely message too."

Appropriately set in an intercontinental background of the beautiful American lake city and idyllic Andhra riverside cultured village, with New Delhi as a connecting link of the two cultures, the novel deals with the thoughts, feelings, ideals, dreams, aspirations, love and actions, in a word, the quest of a variety of young Indian intellectuals, Ravi, Ramesh, Babu, Gupta, Sundaram and Ham. The theme acquires a remarkable immediacy and concreteness because the intellectuals are torn between the innate desire to serve the motherland and a helpless acceptance of opportunities for the realisation of their innate potentialities offered by the affluent American society. The quest of these intellectuals is to find a path which gives them job satisfaction, opportunities to actualize their innate potentialities and yet to remain rooted and thus retain cultural identities. The whole quest acquires spiritual and ethical dimensions, almost tragic in its intensity, when the young men realise that it is not enough if one looks homeward, the home must be able to accommodate and accept them: if accepted the conditions must be such that the people who return can accept them.

Look Homeward thus explores in a compelling fashion one of the complex and vexing problems of India: the irreparable brain drain sapping the life blood of a developing nation struggling to recover from centuries of foreign exploitation.

The title *Look Homeward*, a Miltonic expression from *Lycidas*, 'Look Homeward, Angel now and melt with ruth' suggests the acceptance of the reality of the situation. Thus in the context of the novel it is indicative of the noble ideal that after one's sojourn in foreign lands one has to think of developing one's country with the rich knowledge and experience acquired during the stay abroad. The ultimate fulfilment of all knowledge is to make the humanity share the benefits of developments. In the last section of the novel we find the meeting of Ravi, Ramesh and Gupta in Delhi on their return from Manhattan.

The theme of *The Bliss of Life* is the spiritual quest of Kshetrayya, Rama Sarma rightly claims that it is an 'imaginative reconstruction.' The fundamental quest of Indian life, art, literature and music is to attain the joy of spiritual realization, the rapture divine. This is a tradition beginning with the rishis of the Vedas who composed the melodious hymns, the upanishadic sages who composed the deep philosophical and poetic passages of the upanishads. The same tradition has been continued by the medieval mystics, the song composers like Chaitanya and a number of others. The sufi mystics contributed their share to it. None can afford to ignore or be indifferent to such saint composers as Dadu, Ravidas, Rajjab, Meerabai, Kabir, Chaitanya and Thyagaraya. Tagore, who imbibed and rejuvenated this tradition, remarked:

> India has a spirit and tradition of her own, which have survived through all political upheavals. This spirit and this tradition do not obey the mandates of the holy books, and, are little influenced by scholars. In fact, neither has been incorporated in any theological or social code, and their roots are deep in the hearts of the masses themselves against restrictions and dogmas, and their prophets came from the commonest of the common people.

Kshetrayya belongs to the tradition of the composers I have mentioned earlier. But there is one vital difference. He composed *padams*, musical compositions, which have literary as well as musical value. More than this, the *padams* are chiefly intended for dance, dance of the tradition popularly known as Kuchipudi dance. Scholars claim that this is in the direct tradition of Bharata. In fact, the very name Bharata stands for the union of Bhava, Raga and Tala. This is the ideal combination of literature, music and dance. Kshetrayya composed such *padams*.

The novel begins in a very striking way with the singing of Kshetrayya and the dance of Mohanangi at a special function of the village temple of Muvva Gopala. Both are dedicated to this God and in fact each song depicts an aspect of Gopala, each stanza ends with the refrain Muvva Gopala. In a flash-back the blossoming of the love of Varada and Mohanangi along with their training in music, dance and song at Kuchipudi is brought out in a very poetic way. The idyllic rural background of the Krishna valley, its colourful green fields, mango groves, golden paddy fields, innumerable flowering trees, making the breeze fragrant, the brimful tanks covered with lotus flowers and the rural life brightened by Yakshagana performances and musical narratives full of sound movements, colour and melody. This forms the real background for their deep love. Kshetrayya belongs to the ruling niyogi brahmin caste and Mohanangi to the 'devadasi' community, professionally dedicated to the worship of God in temples, mostly through dance and song. The social disapproval intensifies their love for each other on the one hand and together their isolation from the rest strengthens devotion for Gopala on the other.

In this isolation from society because of his love for Mohanangi and their oneness in their devotion to Gopala Kshetrayya's quest for realization begins. His quest is intensified and given a spiritual direction by the revelation he attains in the temple. He gets a vision which a distinct voice tells him that he is born to serve the Lord. The voice says that he should go from place to place spreading the message of 'Madhurabhakti,' the message of the divine love of Gopala. The voice also declares that he will be the most illustrious composer of *padams*. After a painful leave-taking from his parents and Mohanangi, Kshetrayya goes to Golconda to the court of Abdulla Kutub Sha, the great patron of *Kuchipudi* dance and Telugu literature. It is at this court that some of Varada's relatives worked as ministers and it is under these Sultans of Golconda that the great composer Ramadas, also relative of Kshetrayya, perhaps lived, worked and built the famous temple of Rama at Bhadrachalam. Ramadas too composed a number of songs in praise of God. Tactfully avoiding the shares of physical pleasures offered by Kamala, the court dancer, Kshetrayya goes to the court of Tirumalanayak, another patron of art and literature. It is at the court of Tirumalanayak that Kshetrayya develops the deep philosophical outlook and becomes an enlightened soul. Tirumalanayak was very much impressed by Kshetrayya's insight into religious issues and philosophical maturity. Kshetrayya develops an enlightened detachment to all issues of life and becomes equally averse to fame and blame, pleasure and pain.

The next significant event in the quest of Kshetrayya is his visit to Vijayaraghavanayak's court at Thanjavur. It is here Varadaiah attains the status of Kshetragna. Here he comes into a trying encounter with the great Pandits in Natyasastra, Alankarasastra, Rasamanjari and the art of literature. Kshetrayya proves by demonstration that an artist is not bound by the rigid classifications and theories of the Sastras. He silences the court poets by showing their limitations by giving them a problem which they cannot complete and which he completes fulfilling the technical requirements of literary art and music and dance the pandits themselves speak of. Vijayaraghava is shown as a great rasika and *sahrudaya.* He is delighted by the love-devotion *padams* of Kshetrayya and readily accepts his greatness as a composer. Being a Sringarapurusha himself he approves and praises Kshetrayya's presentation of divine love and devotion in terms of physical love through music, dance and songs. The king's admiration for Kshetrayya is so deep that even when the poet describes him as Vitaraya he is not offended. The philosophical discussions on poetry, dance and literature in which Kshetrayya solves a number of difficult issues shows the high level of the court life beside its intrigues and evils. The intrigues of the court, petty jealousies among court poets and officials, narrow-minded rivalries among artists, musicians, and the typical court professionals do not have any effect on him. In all these issues we are made to realise that the creative genius, the artist, is above the rules of grammar or music or any art and his insight into aesthetic and philosophical issues is something that proceeds from his experience and his vision of life, not from dry learning. It is in this court that Kshetrayya is reunited with Mohanangi who comes in search of him enduring many troubles and tensions. He is styled Kshetragna by the king himself.

The most important trial of Kshetrayya's quest for salvation occurs in the court of the Nawab of Golconda. He achieves the incredible feat of composing 1,500 *padams* in 40 days. The limitations of human energy and the impossibility of attaining any success without divine aid is presented in unmistakable terms by the events of life Kshetrayya had gone through in this court. He becomes a victim of sexual jealousy, of love potions, and of black-magic. It is through the blessings of Siddhendra Yogi that Kshetrayya is released from the troubles. Kshetrayya finally gets *mukti*. This is not the salvation as described by the modern Indian philosophers, which is often called *moksha*. *Moksha* is simply salvation. It is not liberation in this life. This liberation is called *mukti* in the Upanishads. The concept of *moksha* and salvation are not there in Indian thought upto the time of Kshetrayya. *Mukti* as shown in *The Bliss of Life*, is the attainment of *ananda* here and now. There can be bliss in this life only.

The trials and troubles—physical, intellectual and spiritual through which Kshetrayya passes, make him a sage. He transcends the limitations of human desires. He acquires a humility which is endless.

Pastures New looks like a prophetic vision that India will soon be the leading country in the world. When the West is satiated with its material gains it looks to the East, especially to India for spiritual illumination. That is the time when India offers sustenance and ennobles mankind. *Pastures New* is an exploration into new paths and fresh woods. It envisages a new world order based on equity and justice. As Dr. Madhu, the narrator concludes, 'If the poets dream of a millennium, a golden age, we dream of a world order and world citizenship where love of fellow human beings and establishment of peace become universally accepted.'

The narrative is centred round a few holy places only to show that the rich and the poor alike, even in the present day, visit the temples partly as an act of purification and also as an indication of their abiding faith in the great traditions of the country. The temples, and all such religious places of worship indeed signify man's quest for something nobler in life.

Pastures New opens with the delightful picture of the Land's end, Kanyakumari, with the three seas meeting together. Picturesquely as the sun rises on the hills in the morning, the waves come and dash against the shore, attesting their joy in the sun rise and sun light driving away darkness.

The first-person narrative gives to the novel a realism and an authenticity as though Dr. Madhu has seen and experienced everything that is recorded in the novel. Lalitha emerges as the most engaging character, full of curiosity and capable of participating in the rich panorama of life, however disappointing her own life may have been. Dr. Madhu and Sarala, Ramu and Suguna, Prem and Mohan, all these represent the typical conventional domestic life with all its little joys. On the whole the novel gives a vast picture of the present-day life in India, its socio-religious life, the political scenes of liberal promises, the deteriorating education system, love-lorn young men and women coming together under the benevolent influence of Viswanath—all these give to the novel epic dimensions. Like Fielding's *Joseph Andrews*, *Pastures New* is in the picaresque tradition and it reads like an epic in prose. With all its kaleidoscopic life, the novel also traces the influence of godmen like Sai Baba of Prasanthinilayam on men in mundane fetters. The novel also shows the east-west cultural assimilation with the wholehearted participation of the Smiths in everything Indian. The novel closes with a wish fulfilment that all human beings should lead a happy life, an optimistic note indeed.

Rama Sarma's sixth novel, *Height of Noon* has a sweetness and light in its portrayal of varied experiences, ripeness in understanding the complex problems of life, and a refreshing mellowness of tone in verbalizing them. Its background is as significant as its central theme of Dr. Anand's life. It presents the protagonist's father who is a Gandhian idealist and his involvement in the freedom movement in rural India. The background very touchingly deals with a mother's concern for the education of her son, the boy's education at different places away from home, early marriage, the painful process of the identity. It is this background, rural, simple and idealistic, that equips Anand to face the problems of life with equanimity and detachment.

With a firm faith in God, so rare in our troubled times, Anand encounters the failures, successes, joys, sufferings, fulfilments, disillusionments, domestic peace, official problems and professional rivalries, unruffled with a philosophical calm. At a point of time when Anand is looking forward to a peaceful retired life, comes the tragic blow of his wife's death that leaves him to a world of retrospective reflections. These imaginative reconstructions form the basis of the novel.

This varied and rich life creates an absorbing interest in the *Height of Noon*. The novelist achieves this by artistically forging the stream of consciousness technique with flashback semi-biographical narration and dramatic projection of crucial incidents in the dialogue form, which often reminds us of his plays.

What imparts artistic unity to this complex and varied thematic material is the enlightened, optimistic outlook of Dr. Anand. *Height of Noon* begins with the delightful news of Anand's appointment as Vice-Chancellor, a day before his retirement as Professor and ends with the relinquishing of the Vice- Chancellorship after the tragic bereavement, the death of his wife Lakshmi, who has been a loyal partner and a sustaining force in his life. Dr. Anand, after his wife's death, ironically enough, furiously prays for relief. The height of noon is over, and he thinks that he has fallen to a shadowy afternoon like the setting sun.

Lakshmi's character is brought out with a subtle all pervading feminine grace as Anand's active but detached life is posited with vigour. *Height of Noon* is a further expansion of the frontiers of a campus novel as it shows the disturbed and disturbing campus life in the Indian universities.

Height of Noon on the whole is a comprehensive study of human relationships with faith in the manifestation of divine providence.

The first three novels of Rama Sarma—*The Stream*, *The Farewell Party* and *Look Homeward*—may be called the novels of situation because each novel begins in a situation which is a vital aspect of the perennial human predicament. The central theme of the novel emanates from the situation and the whole vision of life Rama Sarma projects, unfolds itself through the theme. Everything in the novel, the story, the characters, the incidents proceed from the central situation and powerfully communicate the author's vision of life as well as his view of life. *The Bliss of Life* is unique in the sense that the fundamental quest reflected in the whole fabric of the fable and the incidents is a spiritual quest beginning in a conflict and ending after the trials and tribulations, in total surrender to and acceptance of Muvva Gopala as the supreme Lord.

The two novels—*Pastures New* and *Height of Noon*—are more novels of ideas than of situations. Sarma's creative vision seems to take a mellow fruitfulness after the *Bliss of Life*. As the title indicates *Pastures New* is a further exploration into various spatial perspectives of the spiritual aspects revealed in terms of visiting the holy places. Various streams of thought, like the East and West cultural associations and the three seas meeting at the Land's End, Kanyakumari, harmoniously blend together. *Height of Noon* too moves from the clutches of Egoism to total acceptance of the destiny that shapes human life and endeavour. What begins as a complex quest in *The Stream* entity ends in enlightened acceptance of Divine Grace in *Height of Noon*.

The Theme of Marriage in *Towards Marriage*

A. VIJAYA RANI

Rama Sarma's play *Towards Marriage* depicts various facets of problems in marriage. Even though the child marriages have almost disappeared, arranged marriages are traditionally favoured by the Indians. In this play Rama Sarma deals with the temperamental differences that can be adjusted as well as exaggerated. And also he suggests that marriage has to be accepted with certain limitations which become unavoidable.

Towards Marriage opens with the joy and mirth of the newly wedded couple Prakash and Lalita. It is an arranged marriage. Prakash is a poet and an idealist. He is a man who has a high poetic sensibility. The desire to become a poet is so dominant in him, that every word he utters expresses his love for beauty. For instance he says to his wife on the very first day: "In the evening we will sit in the garden. I will read to you my verses and you will listen to them. The birds will come and join us. Perhaps they may wonder who we are."[1]

His only dream is to become a poet. Like all the poets he always wanders in a different realm. Prakash is always in his height of imagination and he expects warm-hearted response from his wife. On the other hand Lalita is a simple woman without any particular taste for poetry. Like any other normal middle-class housewife she is satisfied with her ability to manage the household duties. She has no appreciation of beauty and poetry. Since she is an unimaginative woman, naturally she is unable to understand her husband's plight to become a great poet. And she does not show even the least interest in her husband becoming a poet, when he expresses his intense desire of becoming a famous poet. Like all other marriages their life also starts in a stupendous manner. They hardly notice any difference at the beginning as they are satisfied with the physical part of life. But as the months pass they become slowly aware of each other's personality. Lalita, seeing her husband always engrossed in his poetic endeavour, gets dissatisfied. She thinks that he is completely neglecting her without giving any importance to her wishes. Lalita, a pretty woman, thinks that nothing can take her husband away from her, especially her beauty will never allow him to drift away. But when she finds that her husband's primary interest is only poetry and not so much her beauty she cannot accept the fact so easily. It is rather foolish on her part to expect her husband to be by her side always and spend all his time with her. She sometimes acts senselessly, argues arrogantly demanding more of her husband's attention. Her persuasive feminine tenderness turns to be arrogance when she loses control over herself because of her disappointment in Prakash's actions. Without making a little effort to understand her husband, she jumps to the conclusion that she no longer can live with him. Being extremely peeved she says: "I am really fed up with you. I want to go back to my parents. There I'll be free and happy, nothing amuses me here, and your cold, austere personality repels me." (135) But if she has understood him, or his deep rooted wish of becoming a reputed poet, she would not have felt that way.

But Prakash thinks from a different angle. He feels disgusted with his life when he finds that Lalita is completely off the track. And he does not even try to convince her in a loving manner, agreeable to her mental calibre. Finally both of them go to the extent of saying that they would not have married if at all they knew each other before. Prakash says in despair: "If I were to marry today, I would never choose a woman of your type." (134) They both accuse each other without trying to understand each other. They could have adjusted if only they had known each other before. Understanding is possible even in arranged marriages, provided, the couple is willing to make an effort to adjust.

Lalita here fails to give any respect for her husband's wish. She is not humble enough to yield to Prakash's taste. And also she fails to realise that it is wrong to expect her husband to be the same as she is. Prakash expects too much from his wife. Even though he is an intellectual he is unable to adjust himself with reality. He expects his wife to fit in every aspect of his imagination. And he wishes his wife to come up to his level in all aspects. But he completely forgets to adopt compatibility. He expects Lalita to shower love and understanding abundantly on him. But he is least bothered to move the ball in his court. So here the personalities do clash. All the pleasant memories about their marriage are gone. Now stand the two completely different personalities in a tie. Without proper understanding their marriage goes to the point of breaking.

Lalita thinks that external beauty alone is enough to lead a happy married life. But happiness depends upon other factors also. The reason for the absence of happiness is the difference in their temperament. The intellectual and emotional gap which exists between them is revealed by Prakash's words: "But there is always a barrier between us. I receive no response from you as far as my emotions and intellectual aspirations are concerned." (136)

Prakash and Lalita are poles apart. Without considering his poetical aspirations she blames him "as an intellectual snob, an egoist" who does not care for her, his better half. When he blames her indifference and misunderstanding she furiously throws a tea-cup at him. This is a parallel to Rupa in Shiv Kumar's *The Last Wedding Anniversary*. When she is at the height of her bickering with her husband, she loses control over herself and smashes the flower-vase. In both the cases this may be taken as a symbol of break up of their happy relationship.[2]

It is at this crucial hour, Prakash goes on to blame the marriage system itself: "I think it is a defect of our marriage system that men and women of totally different tastes and temperaments are joined together in wedlock." (136) Of course no two persons are the same in God's creations. The creator is the originator of the family arrangement. As it is given in Genesis 2:18 of the Bible the first woman was made to be 'a complement of her husband.' God has recognised that the man and woman have a different make-up.

Real love begins where nothing is expected in return. So the difference in their tastes has to be accepted. Relationship built on genuine love will stand the test of time. As it is said in the song of Solomon of the *Bible:*

> Love is as strong as death is. . . . Many waters themselves are not able to extinguish love, nor can rivers themselves wash it away.[3]

Love is not self-centered. Though strong tender feelings are certain to be involved, they are balanced by reason and deep respect for the other person. When one is really in love with the other, then one will definitely care just as much for the other person's welfare and happiness as he cares for his own. More than everything one should view the other realistically seeing his or her faults, yet loving that one anyway.

A key to family success according to the Bible also lies in the way a husband views and treats his wife. A husband should try to love his wife as he loves himself. In Ephesians 5:28, 29 it says:

> Husbands aught to be loving their wives as their own bodies. He who loves his wife loves himself. No man ever hated his own flesh but he feeds and cherishes it.[4]

Yes, husband should love his wife and what is more important is that he must know how to express his love in such a way that his wife accepts it. And wife also has her part to fulfil. Wife should have a deep respect for her husband. Showing love and respect for each other, requires understanding on the part of both. No two human beings can possibly live together in the most intimate emotional relationship known, without sometimes frustrating each other. Understanding is needed because, when love is blocked it turns to anger and hate. If the husband and wife make an effort to understand each other, the marriage will prove to be a successful one. In *Towards Marriage* neither Prakash nor Lalita is willing to take the initiative. Even after a year they never seem to give any room for understanding and love.

Now enters the character Jaya whom Prakash happens to meet in the city club. She has a great admiration for his poetry. The minute he comes to know that she is a devoted lover of his poetry he starts drifting towards her. She is an outspoken, sophisticated girl with much interest in poetry. And Prakash being her favourite poet she develops a sort of liking for him. Prakash also finds her speaking in an appreciative and encouraging manner unlike his wife. He feels that she will be a perfect match to him as he is totally dissatisfied with his wife. When Jaya finds out that his life is a failure, her sympathy towards the poet turns to love. She repeatedly says that she wants to help Prakash out of his problem, but the fact is that she has made his problem a bit worse than before. Instead of making him to understand his wife to establish a good relationship with her she tries to occupy her place. Their love almost comes to the verge of marriage. If she is really an intelligent girl she would not have desired to marry a man who is already married. She does not consider the fact that marriage is a sacred one and marriage bond is an inviolable one. She wants to make hay while the sun shines. She unintentionally makes use of the misunderstanding that prevails between Prakash and Lalita. If she is really interested in the welfare of Prakash she would have advised him not to leave his wife alone whatever the situations may be. But instead, she herself paves the way for the breaking up of the marital relationship by deciding to marry him.

Prakash does not want to hide this love affair from his wife. He tells her that he is going to marry a girl called Jaya, for he cannot continue to live with her, without proper understanding. He says: "Unfortunately there is nothing common between us except the physical aspect of life." (156) So when Lalita comes to know his decision of marrying Jaya, she becomes wild and in utter dismay she leaves the home.

In *Towards Marriage* Lalita has completely failed to co-operate with her husband. Woman's duty in the home is to maintain peace and harmony. This requires a sacrificing tendency on the part of the woman. Lalita totally lacks this tendency. She is not ready to give up anything for the sake of her husband's happiness. But here one cannot say that Prakash is blameless. He also is to be equally blamed. He does not even speak in a kindly, considerate manner to his wife. Moreover, Jaya also insinuates the idea of marriage to him and paves the way for Prakash to get separated from his wife. If she was really an intelligent girl she would have tried her best to mend the relationship of both Lalita and Prakash.

The problem almost reaches its climax in the third act. When Prakash is waiting eagerly for the arrival of Jaya in his home. Lalita enters as a completely different personality altogether. Prakash cannot believe his eyes seeing his wife with total submission and repentance. But even at this moment he is not willing to accept her as he has promised marriage to Jaya. But Lalita says that she is very much determined to live with him. She speaks with a complete realization of her mistake: "I was an ignorant fool, I couldn't understand you. Now I realise that a woman's place is with her husband and not with her parents." (171)

And she goes one step forward by permitting him wholeheartedly to marry Jaya. She too wants to stay with them at least as a servant. When Prakash points out the awkwardness of the situation if the three live together, she says in a total submission: "I too will stay with you, but you need not treat me as your wife. It will be a great satisfaction to me if only I can live under the same roof with you." (172) Wondering at the miraculous transformation of Lalita's character and listening to her kind words, Prakash is really moved and he finds himself in a dilemma whether to marry Jaya or accept Lalita. At this point Jaya enters and she is taken aback on seeing Prakash and Lalita together. Listening to all the facts told by Prakash, and seeing the drastic change in Lalita's character, she feels that she is not justified in ruining her happiness. Now she is ready to sacrifice her love for the welfare of Prakash and Lalita. When Prakash pleads that he needs her so much, Jaya is able to convince him that even if he does not marry her, she will always be the inspiration for his poetry and finally she says: "You can't have everything in life. Love means sacrifice." (175) And with these words she leaves them with satisfaction.

This ending of the play *Towards Marriage* can be compared with what happens in John Osborne's *Look Back in Anger*. Jaya's decision to leave Prakash and thus making way for Lalita is almost like Helena making her exit from Jimmy's house on the arrival of Alison. But the complexities of the situations in Osborne's play are absent in the Jaya-Lalita-Prakash triangle. Here in *Towards Marriage* it is a case of simple rivalry which culminates in a rather unexpected turn whereas in Osborne's play there is no such rivalry between Alison and Helena. "Though the element of surprise is equally dramatic in both and will be equally effective on the stage, the situation in the ending of *Towards Marriage* does not have so much to convey as that of *Look Back in Anger*."[5] But the similarity itself is interesting. Here the motivation for Alison to return is clear enough arising as it does from the psychological emptiness she suffers on account of the loss of the child, but Lalita's return is typical of the woman's lot in Indian society. "Lalita's return has a number of parallels in Indian fiction as for instance Savitri's return in R.K. Narayan's *The Dark Room*." Not all Jayas make room. From this point of view Rama Sarma's play is typically Indian and true to Indian social conditions.[6]

Through this play Rama Sarma intends to bring out the importance of understanding and harmony between the couple in order to have a happy married life. The companion is the one with whom one has to spend his or her life. Without proper understanding of the mate, certainly the marriage will be a failure.

Here it is appropriate to compare Shiv K. Kumar's *Last Wedding Anniversary,* regarding the incompatibility and the domestic discord due to temperamental differences between the husband and wife and also the extramarital relationships of the husbands. The *Last Wedding Anniversary* presents the same story, the incompatibility of the upper middle class couple, Lalit, a suave, sensitive editor of a popular magazine and his wife Rupa, a shrewish ambitious socialite. Their second anniversary becomes the last wedding anniversary due to the strain in their marital relationship. "Though the immediate cause of the problem is the appearance of Lalit's first love Neela, the root cause is a basic clash of wills of personalities which are headstrong to abide together."[7] The placement of the characters in a triangle in *Towards Marriage* is similar to that of Shiv Kumar's play, the treatment and the denounement are different.

In *Towards Marriage* the playwright attempts to convey a message that the solution to the problem of the breakdown in marriage system lies not in dissolving the inviolable bond, but in the husband and wife making an effort to understand each other sympathetically and not critically. He goes on to say that men and women are bound to get on well in their marital relationship as long as they realise that no man or woman can be god or goddess and are intelligent and willing enough to accept marriage with certain limitations.

The characters Lalita and Prakash can be called a replica of the characters Suguna and Gopalam in *The Stream*, the first novel of Rama Sarma. Here Gopalam being captivated by the beauty of Suguna marries her. But within a few months the happiness begins to deteriorate slowly, due to temperamental differences. Like Prakash, Gopalam also always dwells in his world of poetry, always speaking about Keats, Shelley and Wordsworth to his wife. Like Lalita, Suguna never appreciates the poetic aspirations and the intellect of her husband, and Gopalam also fails to come down to her level. And so the result is breakdown in their relationship. At the end of the first chapter the novelist comments, "He [Gopalam] could see that the tastes were different, there was no mutual understanding. She had nothing to offer him spiritually. She did not belong to him. But did he make any effort to come down from his ethereal plane, his utopian world? Was he at any time interested in knowing her mental make- up? Unfortunately not."[8] Here the novel depicts the painful evolution of Gopalam, the hero from the passion of life, into a balanced acceptance of the stream of life which is governed by the triple concept of Beauty, Love and Justice. But in *Towards Marriage* the transformation of the characters Lalita and Prakash from ignorance to self-realization is clearly seen.

Rama Sarma's play successfully conveys the message which the author intends to, namely the temperamental differences between a couple need not ruin their domestic happiness, provided they adopt a give and take attitude.

Rama Sarma's approach is traditional as he says that 'marriage is a sacred and spiritual union.' His approach is purely subjective. Rama Sarma's *Towards Marriage* conveys the message that marriage is a sacred and inviolable bond between man and woman, and peace and harmony depend upon the mutual understanding between the couple.

NOTES

1. M.V. Rama Sarma, *Towards Marriage* (Madras: Pearl, 1982), p. 132.
2. M.N. Sundara Raman, *Indian Drama in English—A Thematic Study* (Autonomous Post-Graduate Centre, University of Madras, Oct., 1983), pp. 204-5.
3. Solomon, *New World Translation of the Holy Scriptures* (New York: Watchtower Bible and Tract Society, 1984), p. 888.
4. St. Paul, "Ephesians," *New Word Translation of the Holy Scriptures* (New York: Watchtower Bible and Tract Society, 1984), p. 1462.
5. M.N. Sundara Raman, "The Plays of Rama Sarma—A Study," *Indian Scholar*, Vol. II, No. 2, July 1979, p. 133.
6. *Ibid.*, p. 134.
7. M.N. Sundara Raman, *Indian Drama in English*, p. 203.
8. M.V. Rama Sarma, *The Stream* (New Delhi: S. Chand, 1983), p. 18.

From M.Phil. dissertation, "The Theme of Life and Marriage in Rama Sarma's Plays," Bharatidasan University, Tiruchi, 1989.

The Carnival: A Plea for Harmony

P. OBULA REDDY

Rama Sarma'a play, *The Carnival* discusses the theme of love and marriage from various aspects. Suresh and Prem meet at a party of the Progressive Youth Association. Prem is an elegant, educated and cultured young woman. She is a teacher and loves teaching. Suresh also likes his job as Secretary to Shiv Lal, the industrialist.

In the very first meeting, Prem understands that Suresh is an idealist. She too is an ardent admirer of beauty. She says:

> Beauty, in fact, stands for ultimate perfection. And that perfection is synonymous with God. By admiring anything beautiful we admire God's workmanship. This workmanship is often reflected in the physical appearance of a woman, in a landscape or sometimes in a man's attitude towards others. But surely we all of us admire harmony in life.[1]

Suresh imagines that the multicoloured roses are a symbol of the essential peace and harmony in the world. Suresh and Prem get nearer to each other in their attitude towards life. They discuss various aspects of life and move about as good companions.

The image of the creeper twining itself around the sturdy tree symbolises for Prem the concept of support and companionship. She insists that Suresh should have some time for the warmth of a woman and understand the language of love for it is essential to remain human. The moment Suresh agrees to marry her, she becomes happy and says: "Sincere love always ennobles its subjects, it makes them develop within them a spirit of sacrifice and nobility. . . . I feel as if I have entered upon a new life, a life in which I always feel the nearness and comradeship of someone else." (194-95) This is the world of ideal love presented through Suresh and Prem. Ramesh and Rekha offer the contract. Ramesh has no faith in the idealism and perfection of life. He has no appreciation of the beauty and harmony of nature. He tells Suresh: "You are a great dreamer. You are an idealist. I am sure you will have many a disillusionment in life." (184)

Ramesh feels that ideals do not feed hungry stomachs. When he understands that Suresh is in love with Prem, he says that the happy days for Suresh are over. He does not want to be a philosopher. He is a realist, he is down to earth. He does not have the idealism of Suresh. So he observes, "That's the whole trouble with you people, who call themselves idealists. You look through coloured glasses, and women appear to be beautiful, charming, wonderful." Suresh asks in an amused manner, "What else?" And Ramesh replies, "You consider women to be roses and jasmines. But of what earthly use are these lilies and roses? After all what is beauty? Lipstick and powder, plus the lover's dream of his lady-love's supernatural beauty!" (187)

Ramesh is a devotee of commerce and industry. He has no belief in the aesthetic aspect of life. He says: "You are all in the land of beauty. I see no such exhilarating picture. To me the busy call of the factory, the bustle and activity of the worker, the thrill of production—these, these alone will be the objects of attraction." (188)

Ramesh is quite the opposite of Suresh. But even Suresh has his problems. True love never runs smooth and his love for Prem gets into difficulties. When he arranges a garden party in connection with the birthday of his employer Shivlal's daughter, Shobha, her attention is drawn to Suresh. She finds Prem with Suresh and Shobha wants to settle things with Suresh. He is called to her room. She feels happy when he says that he likes her. She wants to know about Prem. When she talks about the prospect of riches coming through a woman he reveals his attitude towards life:

> To many, life is a big gamble. To others it is just a matter of 'cursed fate.' And all these persons accept life in a blind unthinking manner. To me it's plain that life is based upon a system—a great plan of Beauty, Love and Justice . . . it is a synthesis of these three dynamic forces that keeps men and women balanced and righteous. (219)

Shobha's admiration for Suresh grows and she proposes to marry him.

Suresh is removed from service when Shivlal comes to know that his daughter is in love with him. He does not want to take his Secretary, Suresh as his son-in-law. Suresh's dismissal puts his marriage with Prem in trouble. But Suresh continues to be optimistic and feels that he would get some other job based on his merit. When Ramesh says that money is the sustaining power of all life, Suresh disagrees:

> Perhaps you are justified in saying that most men marry for the sake of money. But the inevitable urge in man—to love someone, to annihilate selfishness—is bound to come out even after marriage, perhaps in the shape of children! No one is free from that great quality of love. (240)

At this opportune moment Asha brings the news that Shivlal has called back Suresh into his service. This is made possible by Shobha.

The story of Suresh and Prem runs like a fable. They belong to a world of idealism. They do not change even when they face troubles.

Manohar is another interesting character in the play. He has no set ideal. He is prepared to marry Asha though he has not entertained that idea before. This is arranged by Shivlal. He is acceptable to all. He wins the favour of Pratima and Ravinder. Asha is a golddigger. She wants money and the comfort it brings. She has no set views. She is prepared to marry Manohar provided he has a competent wealth. So Shivlal promises to bestow an annuity on him. Ravinder in a weak moment proposes to marry Asha, and he has to get rid of her. So he too is willing to offer a good amount to Manohar. All this frivolity in serious matters like love and marriage reminds us of the Restoration comedy and its world of flippant, non-serious lovers.

If Suresh is a man with a vision, Shivlal is a shrewd worldly type of man. He knows how to manage any situation. He patronises Manohar so that Ravinder is free to marry his daughter Shobha. In the world of Shivlal money alone matters. He is proud of his wealth and he is an industrialist. He is like Sir Andrew Undershaft of Shaw's *Major Barbara* in his analysis of people and situations. He does not approve of the marriage between Asha and Ravinder. He says that the rich should protect their tradition: "It is our duty to uphold our tradition. In almost all the countries we find differences of caste or class. The underlying idea behind these differences is the same. It is to preserve and cherish one's own culture. It is not for nothing that these differences are introduced." (217) He has nothing but contempt for the word 'love.' He tells his daughter Shobha, when she says that she is in love with Suresh,

> There is no such thing as love. It's a mad man's job, an idle man's devilish thought. Nothing more than that. It's a delusion. For goodness sake, please do not allow yourself to be deceived by this fascinating but hypocritical term. (217)

His argument is that men and women get together purely because of a physical urge. He cannot understand the language of love expressed by his daughter. He does not want the unfortunate alliance between his daughter and Suresh. He feels that riches alone offer comfort. His argument about riches is specious and outwardly convincing. He tells Shobha: "It's no use being poor. Everything goes by riches. In this busy modern world who cares for spiritual values or for lofty ideals? As a matter of fact no one likes to be poor. Even the Communists who are supposed to be champions of the poor do not like a life of poverty." (220)

Shobha plays her role as a chastiser. To some extent she makes her father see the truth in her argument. She boldly tells her father that his pairing of men and women solely on the basis of money is repugnant to her. Even Ravinder has to apologize to her for his behaviour at the party. When Ravinder himself promises to wait and get Shobha's love through his sincere adoration, she softens a bit towards Ravinder. She agrees to consider Ravinder's changed attitude towards love. At least for her sake Ravinder will give up his capitalist mentality and learn to love Shobha wholeheartedly as a true lover. She realises that she cannot altogether displease her father to whom she is everything. One is inclined to think that she is like her father shrewd and pragmatic. She may even be angelic like her mother as her own father Shivlal praise her. So the transformation that is seen in Ravinder and Shobha need not be taken as concession to popular taste. Such situations in life are not uncommon.

The title, *The Carnival* is mostly an interrogation. Is life a carnival or a festival? Presumably the answer is that life is for a nobler aspect, not for simple jollity or dalliance. However one cannot ignore the fact that life is for living, and living well. The characters in *The Carnival,* as in Eliot's *The Cocktail Party,* make the best of a bad bargain.

The play has a complex plot involving several types of love and marriage. The ideal love is presented through Suresh and Prem and like Touchstone and Audrey in *As you Like It* Manohar and Asha seem to exist in a world of marriages of convenience. Shobas's acceptance of Ravinder, conditionally, is like an arranged marriage. In a way it is an approximation to the conventional arranged marriages still prevalent in our country. There seems to be a likelihood of Pratima, the rich widow, with an affectionate disposition becoming the partner of Shivlal, the widower. The ending of *The Carnival* reminds us of the happy ending of *As You Like It,* even though melancholic persons like Jaques meant for 'other than dancing measures' may find it disturbing and unpleasant to see so many lovers on the stage making the best of life.

Rama Sarma apparently suggests in all his three major plays, *Towards Marriage, The Carnival* and *Sakuntala* a world where domestic peace prevails and harmony exists. The endings in all these plays show that 'All is well that ends well.'

NOTES

1. M.V. Rama Sarma, "The Carnival," *Collected Plays* (Madras: Pearl, 1982), p. 188.

Thematic Concerns in the One-Act Plays of Rama Sarma

S.A. KHAYYOOM

Indian drama in English, not primarily meant for the stage, is yet to develop and acquire its phenomenal dimension to emerge as a distinct literary form and make a mark in the contemporary literary world despite its native themes and myths and indigenous setting. Still, it deserves to be adjusted and appreciated in the Indian context and within the scope of its linguistic constraints and thematic relevance. Rama Sarma's *Collected Plays*[1] is but an endeavour to popularize Indian drama in English, especially in three-acts and one-act, picturing the on-going living reality to the common native audience. His creativity and conceptual innovations have given us new insights into and better perspectives of art and literature in general. Though not rich enough in variety of content and vitality of characterization, there is in his one-act plays the vigour of the evocation of fundamental human issues making his plays more secular within the limited framework.

Rama Sarma's plays have artistic value as expressions of feelings and ideas about human love, marriage, cultural conflict and value systems. The thematic concerns of Rama Sarma ranging from pre-independent to contemporary situation in India under the impact of the West, spreading over four decades, reflect his own perception of life and living and socio-political crises in the country. Some plays are in the romantic vein with poetic exuberance, while others are less poetic with a tone of protest presenting the conflict between the youth and the aged in Shavian tempo but tinged with optimism. *The Mahatma* (1979) presenting only the last phase of Gandhiji's life in just two scenes, speaks of spiritual values in the final acceptance of martyrdom in the face of struggle and disappointment. Rama Sarma's deep concern for human problems and affairs might have prompted him for viable solutions to social evils and human predicament in symbolic terms through poetic imagination. The playwright, as a believer in the rich Indian cultural heritage, assumes his role though not as an artist, as a serious thinker and a far-sighted counsellor to direct the confused youth in the materialistic world.

Rama Sarma conforming to the thematic design and structural pattern of one-act plays—without variations in scene, action and characters and without complexity in the plot, has skilfully rendered his ideas and thoughts into a single theme to make each of his playlets a sort of 'criticism of life.' The plays are not episodic and the characters do not significantly contribute in the unfolding of the plot. But his characters rise above the plane of mere triviality and are considerably potential signifying much more in the present world. Though his one-act plays do not preach any specific philosophy, they present with clarity and in unambiguous terms his world-view and philosophical assumptions that illumine the human heart and mind. Even if the prime object of his plays is not self-expression, his plays are self-revelatory of his thinking and family.

The one-act plays are concerned about the social man and the moral man, Tradition vs Modernity. Unlike in his plays in three acts—*Towards Marriage, The Carnival* and *Sakuntala* where the theme is marriage, a sacred social institution for domestic felicity and harmony, in some form, the one-act plays deal with the varied aspects of love and relationship with the opposite sex. In *Youth and Crabbed Age* (1942), Ramu is an easy-go-lucky man soaring high above unfettered into the lofty ethereal regions of Keats and Shelley, unmindful of cares of life, poetic in his thoughts and philosophy, nourishing Browning's optimism and anticipating a prosperous future. Indira, his wife, is an ordinary Indian woman representing a different attitude and vision of life, deeply concerned with the factual world. But Gopalam and Lakshmi represent old norms and conservative values of the society, not happy with the shifting values and rampant corruption. Ramu is Shavian in his social protest and defiance of age old customs and traditional norms and in his optimism to overcome the trials and tribulations of life in his onward march into the 'wilderness of Nature.' He symbolises the new spirit of the age craving for liberty, unfettered by tradition. Exploring the theme of Tradition vs Modernity, the author has exposed the two generations and their attitudes toward the other, their misconceptions of values of life leading to misunderstanding and incompatibility.

Like to Like portrays the couple, unhappy alliance with divergent views about love, living and happiness and with disparity in age. Gopalam at the age of forty, after the death of his first wife, remarries Swarna, a twenty year young lady, self-conscious and given to modernity. He proclaims male supremacy and his traditional right to remarry, denied to woman, the authority of which is questioned by Swarna in Shavian tempo. She demands equality with men in every respect including marital status, right to remarry and economic independence. When she champions the cause of woman and her dignity: "To lift the woman's fallen divinity upon an even pedestal with man," (12) Gopalam admits: "Each has what the other has not, each completes the other and is completed by the other." (12) But he is not for equality and freedom for woman. Sukumar is a young man of five and twenty, very optimistic and given to ultramodern views, nourishing socialistic ideology and having his own ideas about the progress and improving economy of the country which are not palatable to Indira his wife, and Gopalam, representing the rich class of society. Indira, a graceful, affable and amicable woman, a widow marrying Sukumar at thirty, acts as a foil to Sukumar and to Swarna who takes pride in her juvenile charms and angelic beauty and who would refuse to be a conventional type of woman. Swarna thinks the marriage of Sukumar and Indira with diverse ideas, tastes and temperament would only mar the bliss of life and make life a woe 'too deep for tears.' Through Gopalam, the playwright seems to uphold the inviolable sacred bond of marriage based on mutual trust, love and equal social status since divorce is not the right solution to any kind of disharmony and defiance in the family. Swarna representing physical life of gratification and external charm tries to justifying her craving for a man like Sukumar whose intelligence and capacities she admires. She says that her liking is not mere obedience and servitude to man but for harmony and true love, and intellectual union which she calls 'platonic love' not physical. The author's reformatory ideas seem to approve widow marriage, conceding also to woman the right to remarry.

The theme of love between the mortals and the immortals in *Marpessa* (1944) is drawn from Greek mythology. Marpessa, daughter of Evanus, incarnating 'grace invincible' and 'charm undefiled,' resists the temptations and lures of Apollo, son of Zeus, and prefers Idas' human love, and also suffering in friendly union on earth to supernatural powers and celestial bliss. She argues that earth-bound life with trials and affliction is enjoyable and worth living since suffering is the noble heritage of mortals. Marpessa has implicit faith in God and His creation and accepts unquestioningly common human life with perils and hardships as she believes that 'All is right with the world.' Marpessa and Idas are transformed into symbols of impeccable human love and virtue, in a sense human life itself by which Rama Sarma appears to suggest that life is but to live and man should aspire not for everlasting, celestial joy, but a life of tribulations and suffering, and make nature his home as Marpessa and Idas, to lead a calm and happy life.

This Busy World uses the Greek myth to explore the intricacies of modernity and of age old conventions as well. The characters symbolizing modernity, as true disciples of Epicurus, concerned with the present and worldly pleasures, find fault with traditional customs and living. Manohar blames men and women for their incapacity to taste the fruits of modern civilization. Rekha is critical about the familial ties between man and woman in an orthodox family. Rup Rani too joins them in advocating individual freedom from dogmatic assertions of society, liberation of woman from the narrow confines of her family and servitude to man and her freedom to think and progress. For Rup Rani and Rekha contentment is the root cause of degeneracy and indolence. Manohar as an Epicurean does not believe in the existence of life hereafter and in the "imagined bliss in ignorance and sweetness in adversity." (35) Prakash does not favour the contention that concentration of wealth would lead to wars and promote social sins and finally ruin art, culture and humanity in general. But he justifies wars between nations if fought to develop and for the balancing of power, which are unlike old wars waged to satisfy the ego or whims of a mighty ruler. Inhuman practices and rituals, superstition and worship of deities only to please them are denounced. The moderns hate even the mystification of the Infinite Being in sublime verse by poets. But the playwright, not approving of Epicurean philosophy, also cautions against those who champion individual freedom, indulge in mere eating, drinking, and merry-making as Bacchanalians and worshippers of Epicurus.

In *Ignorance and Idiocy* (1945) Sundar, Lalita and Swarna represent a divided self accommodating new values but adhering to utopian idealism and also conscious of stark realities of mundane life in the changing society. Sundar contends that since the society is flexible, its customs which are man-made are liable for periodic change and that following tradition for long is but human bondage and hypocrisy. Lalita by being inflexible and unaccommodative faces her tragic end for her sheer ignorance of change. Sundar curses himself for his idiocy in misunderstanding his wife and for not adhering to social norms and morality. Here the playwright merely exposes the attitudes of men and women toward each other, and their misconceptions of ethical values and social morality in the society in transition. The emphasis is on the need for reformation through character building of both individuals and the nation.

Urvasi (1947) like *Marpessa* speaks of the grandeur of human life with toils and affliction. A change in the dramatic style is noticed here as the playwright assumes the role more of a social critic than a dramatist in presenting the human problem. Urvasi, the divine damsel decked with captivating grace and celestial beauty is subject to Arjuna's infatuation. But Arjuna who symbolizes human virtue, like Marpessa conscious of the miseries and limitations of human life successfully resists the temptations of Urvasi and prefers life on earth despite its uncertainty and transiency, to heavenly bliss.

Inspector Raghavan (1959) is a humorous presentation of several aspects of the Indian system of education which includes the condition of the teacher, attitude and behaviour of the teacher and taught at the time of the inspection of the school. Raghavan's final words reveal the significance of the role of the teacher in imparting true education and also by making himself a good model for students to emulate. A teacher should provide adequate training and instil in his students patriotic fervour to make them good citizens of the nation. The author cautions and inspires the teacher to rededicate himself to his noble profession.

Rama Sarma, influenced by G.B. Shaw and T.S. Eliot, chooses martyrdom as the theme of *The Mahatma* (1979). The emphasis is on the total submission of martyrs and mahatmas on sacred mission, and withdrawal from the material world, to the will of God, even if "God's ways are mysterious and inscrutable." (264) The process, in respect of the themes of his playlets from physical existence and human aspirations to martyrdom, the final acceptance of death, spiritually speaking liberation of soul, is complete in *The Mahatma*. Gandhiji's statement, "courage and heroism do not lie in brutally assaulting and murdering people. On the other hand heroism lies in tolerance and magnanimity," (260) echoes Rama Sarma's concept of hero and heroism in *Paradise Lost*. When there was a bomb blast, Gandhiji was serene and unperturbed and was even ready to go to Pakistan and walk across the country on his mission of peace and love to bring unity and harmony between the two countries.

In the second scene, Gandhiji is hailed as the father of the nation, the liberator, the light of India and as the undisputed leader of the three movements—Boycott of British goods, Salt Satyagraha, and Quit India. His philosophy of non-violence or Ahimsa which he himself practised and symbolized, has become his gospel to the strife-ridden world. His humanism with abundant love for the harijans and the oppressed, made him the world's first socialist and Christ like figure of this century. After death, Gandhiji has been canonized as a saint to guide mankind in this era of scepticism and religious disbelief. *The Mahatma* also presents along with human virtues and saintliness of Gandhiji, the views and mixed reactions of people on his socio-political achievements, going even to the extent of eliminating him disgracefully.

The one-act plays of *Collected Plays* reveal that Rama Sarma does not dwell upon abstract speculation about real beauty and felicity, as the focus is on the human condition, Indian cultural tradition and socio-political aspects of national life. Rama Sarma, presenting different views and perceptions of systems of values and cultures but upholding neither, appears to have denounced too much sophistication and also traditionalism and immorality in the two cultures—native and alien, and further, misconceptions of innovative institutions and progressive systems, a legacy of colonialism. But the underlying emphasis in his playlets is on the basic traditional values like truth, beauty, virtue, love, freedom and tranquillity. The one-act plays, though not theatrically entertaining, presenting conflicting ideas of the young and the old, irreconcilable forces in the society, and dealing with the common issues of life of the ordinary man and the woman, have generated interest in the common reader.

Rama Sarma's plays have not been tested in the theatre. Though lacking in intricate plot-structure, the plays are suggestive and contain a deeper meaning relevant to the modern times. These one-act plays have not received adequate recognition, but some of them are refreshingly original with characters symbolizing mythological consciousness.

NOTES

1. M.V. Rama Sarma, *Collected Plays*, ed. G. Nageswara Rao, (Madras: Pearl, 1982), p. 12.

Rama Sarma's Plays: A Study in Social Realism

BASAVARAJ S. NAIKAR

Indian drama in English has not made much progress although regional drama has been thriving in India, though slowly. The Indian English drama has not been growing in the same manner mainly because of the alien medium of English language. Even if there are good plays in English by able dramatists, they fail to have a large audience. Even in universities there is nothing like a drama society as in the west. There are no theatrical troupes in India that are interested in promoting Indian English plays. Most of the Indian theatres are unfortunately controlled by bureaucratic and regional forces. That is the reason why even if there are good Indian English plays they cannot be realised in theatrical terms but remain alive only in class-rooms, seminar halls and scholarly journals. Stage-worthiness being the test of a good play, there is no way of judging the excellence of the plays written in English.

Rama Sarma's plays have the same limitation of not being exposed to an audience. But being a formidable scholar, an ardent admirer of Bernard Shaw and a serious student of Milton he writes because he must. There is the urgency. As a creative writer he feels he has to express himself either through plays or novels. These are the two areas where he has done something substantial. He has eleven plays and six novels published so far and this can rightly be considered a major contribution to Indian writing in English.

A close study of Rama Sarma's plays reveals the emergence of a common pattern. As he himself says in the 'Preface' to the edition of the *Collected Plays* he is influenced by George Bernard Shaw. As Shaw deals with the burning problems of the British society and presents them on the stage through his plays, Rama Sarma is mostly concerned with the problems of the Indian society and gives them a dramatic expression. Since there is a preponderance of ideas in his drama, there is a natural and proportionate reduction of physical action in his plays. Like the Shavian drama Rama Sarma's plays exhibit moral action. It is the thinking man, interested in social criticism that engages our attention in his plays.

Rama Sarma's plays can be classified, according to a broad thematic taxonomy, into two categories: one, social and socio-political and two, mythological. Each one of them is discussed here in some detail.

Youth and Crabbed Age is a socio-philosophical one-act play which depicts the conflict between orthodoxy and modernity represented by crabbed age and youth respectively. Though the setting is not specified by the dramatist, the names of the characters indicate that it is a South Indian town. The abstract title of the play naturally has something in common with the medieval allegories. It also reflects the generation gap and its antipathies. The gap between the old generation and the new is depicted through the intra- domestic dissidence among the members. Ramu and Indira are man and wife belonging to the younger generation. Indira being an ordinary woman cannot understand the poetic fibre of her husband. Ramu's poetic approach to life appears to be impractical in his wife's opinion. Yet her goodness lies in her tolerance of his special trait of personality.

But the matrimonial conflict seems to be nullified by the greater conflict between the younger generation and the older one which is foregrounded in the play. This conflict happens to be between the said couple and their elders. Gopalam and Laxmi who happen to be the parents of Ramu, do not like the modern youth and their society which is vitiated by corruption, licentiousness and a lack of respect for the aged ones. Likewise Ramu also does not like the superstitious beliefs of his parents. Thus the play presents two attitudes or points of view that are at loggerheads with each other. The play is mostly centred round this clash of opposing ideas with not much physical action.

Temperamental incompatibility happens to be the main thematic concern of *Like to Like*, a one-act play, suggesting the gradual change that the Indian society has been undergoing. It delineates the conflict between the practical approach and the Platonic approach to life. Although the main thrust of the play is on the psychological aspect of man-woman relationship, it presupposes the changes in the society allowing a new freedom of choice for the life-partners. Gopal is a widower who has married Swarna after the death of his first wife. But now both of them have realised the inappropriateness of their choice and their unsuitability to each other. They begin to dislike each other on account of ideological differences and temperamental incompatibility. Swarna being a Shavian woman has no sympathy for the view of Gopalam. There is a strong feeling of resentment in Swarna who frequently remarks that "widowers must marry widows" and "To be the wife of an aged man is a perpetual source of torment to a young woman." (12)

This domestic tangle takes a new turn with the introduction of Sukumar and Mrs. Indira on the stage. Sukumar is an admirer of Swarna as there is a perfect agreement between their temperaments. Swarna, who constantly carps her husband Gopalam is finally rejected by him. Consequently Swarna and Sukumar gravitate towards each other. Likewise Mrs. Indira, the widow, feels a great deal of sympathy for the widower Gopalam and goes after him. She says: "Poor man, I am all affection for him. He is bereft of sympathetic company and it is my duty to instil hope, faith and courage in him. His gloomy face has endeared itself to me. I will go, catch him." (19)

Thus, each woman selects her own partner according to her temperament and view of life. Gopalam and Indira come together because of their practical approach to life, whereas Sukumar and Swarna like each other because of their Platonic philosophy. Though the play is quite realistic in the presentation of the problem of clash of temperaments, the solution offered by the dramatist seems to be enigmatic. One wonders whether Rama Sarma is rather sarcastic in bringing birds of the same feather together. The Shavian satirical touch is imbibed by Rama Sarma in producing such situations of social satire.

Another aspect of temperamental incompatibility is treated very elaborately in the three-act play *Towards Marriage*. Rama Sarma deals with this theme more cogently in this play. The life of any poet in the world, especially in India, becomes very problematic when he is burdened with a non-poetic wife, who not only fails to understand or inspire him, but even becomes a stumbling block in the path of his progress and happiness. The problem of adjustment between an imaginative husband and a stark materialistic wife has been so universal that it assumes the significance of an archetypal theme in literature.

The play is set in a South Indian city (which is not specified) and deals with the life of a poet called Prakash. The protagonist being a poet, naturally wishes to lead an ideal and simple life. He has an exquisite taste for beauty of things and beings. But his taste is not unfortunately matched by his wife's as she happens to be a non-poetic, physically beautiful and proud woman. Lalita, like a majority of Indian wives, delights only in material success, glamour and pleasure and cannot, therefore, rise to the level of her husband. Prakash has to suffer like many Indian husbands for being not understood by the woman he has married. He is bound to his wife only physically, and therefore, partially. Total marriage involves not only physical but psychic and even spiritual dimensions. The psychic dimension is obviously missing in their marriage.

When disappointed with his wife, Prakash is naturally in search of a lady who can be his intellectual companion. Jaya who is an intellectual and imaginative young lady happens to meet Prakash in a club and appreciates his poetic talent. Although Jaya is sophisticated and likes social work she is extremely fond of poets and their writings. So she likes Prakash. Their mutual appreciation develops gradually into friendship and finally results in love. By this time, Lalita the egocentric wife of Prakash deserts her husband and goes to her parents' home. The absence of his wife has been quite congenial to Prakash's search for a new partner. He, therefore, decides to marry Jaya and invites the latter to his house. When Jaya goes to his house, she is surprised to see his wife there. She, further, learns that Lalita has returned with a newly acquired meekness and realisation of her folly. Jaya is so sensitive and understanding that she refuses to ruin Lalita's happiness by marrying her husband, but on the contrary promises to inspire him. She equates 'love' with 'sacrifice.' The matrimonial conflict between Prakash and Lalita is resolved by the spirit of sacrifice in Jaya. The writer upholds Jaya as a noble woman even though she appears to be westernised.

The play projects an ideal rather than a reality. The first part of the play presenting the matrimonial discord is very realistic and representative, whereas the latter part showing Jaya's understanding and sacrifice is very idealistic. This situation reminds us of Osborne's *Look Back in Anger* where the woman who comes as a rival withdraws, like Jaya, of her own accord leaving the old pair to adjust to a way of life that may lead to domestic peace.

The play holds a mirror to Rama Sarma's contemporary consciousness of social realism. He shows the contract between Jaya and other snobbish ladies like Suseela who hate even to talk about poverty, let alone sympathise with it. Similarly Prakash is contrasted with other club members who are interested only in the passionate pleasures of drinking, dancing and eating without ever caring for the higher pursuits.

Rama Sarma, thus, introduces certain social types of characters like the intellectual husband, the unimaginative wife, the inspiring beloved, the snobbish gentleman and the society lady who easily bring to our mind the Jonsonian types. The dialogues are simple and straightforward. The situations are clearly conceived and their sequence is logically arranged. The play reads like any modern play dealing with the puzzling problems of life.

Ignorance and Idiocy is a one-act play which dramatises the conflict between materialism and aestheticism/spiritualism or between convention and freedom in the realm of man-woman relationship. There are only three characters in the play. Sundar and Swarna represent the religion of aesthetics and therefore, admire each other. Both of them are lovers of beauty, music and poetry. Sundar describes Swarna as a rare type of woman who combines in herself "Cleopatra's majesty and Helen's matchless beauty." (44) Similarly Swarna admires Sundar's exuberance of thought and richness of expression which "run like the undisputed waves of that mighty ocean." (44) Both of them belong to the higher world of beauty and naturally look down upon the modern world which is overwhelmed with materialistic philosophy. They are contemptuous of modern man's hurry to achieve materialistic greatness and his consequent loss of finer aesthetic powers.

But Lalita, wife of Sundar does not like either her husband or his intellectual companion Swarna, as she lives on a lower plane and therefore is unable to appreciate the truth of the higher plane. She wants to go away from her husband on account of ideological differences. She goes away from him to drown herself in the sea. The ignorance and idiocy of the unthinking wife are pitiable indeed. The play, thus, shows the symbolic victory of aesthetic and idealistic life over the sheer pragmatic, mundane existence.

The Carnival, a play in three acts, deals with the problem of non-alignment between love and money which are two fundamental problems of human life in general. It also depicts the interaction between middle-class people like Suresh and Ramesh and aristocrats like Shivlal and Ravinder.

The play, in the true Shavian fashion, stresses the intellectual aspect of the problem of love and money. The industrialist Mr. Shivlal and the capitalist Mr. Ravinder are naturally embodiments of stark materialism who believe that money is the sole means through which all the happiness and comforts of life can be had. Consequently they believe that love and such other fine emotions are all momentary phases of life and could be bought with the help of money. Being members of the Progressive Youth Association, they believe that human progress is mainly materialistic.

The central conflict in the play is between the monied class for whom money means everything and the world of love that transcends all such material life. Shivlal, the industrialist, has a daughter of 21 whose birthday he celebrates with great pomp. This happy event stirs the tender emotion of love in Shobha's heart for their secretary Mr. Suresh. After a few days when Shobha expresses her love for Suresh before her father, Shivlal is simply horrified and attributes it to her adolescent inexperience. But when Shobha persists in her emotional attraction for Suresh, Shivlal tries to convince her of the extraordinary importance of money and status in life and the relative insignificance of emotional infatuation called love. Shivlal is like the industrialist in *Major Barbara* for whom Mammon worship is the noblest form of human existence.

But Shobha is not influenced by her father's thoughts or arguments. In order to divert her mind, her father decides to offer her in marriage to another rich young man called Ravinder. But Shobha has set her heart on Suresh who is a man with a fine character and sensibility. She considers Ravinder to be a very dull creature. Shivlal grows really anxious when he notices the growing admiration of his daughter for the poor young man. He tries his best to dissuade her, but she boldly argues with him from her own point of view that love should not be tainted by considerations of money or position. Now Shivlal grows desperate and takes a drastic step by dismissing Suresh from service as his secretary.

Suresh is not bothered about his dismissal from service. He believes in the balancing powers of God in the world. Ramesh considers Suresh's philosophy of life as childish and impractical. But paradoxically enough,

Asha comes and breaks the news that Suresh has been reappointed by Shivlal on Shobha's persuasion. Thus the conflict is finally resolved by the triumph of love over money. The solution offered by the dramatist is again idealistic with its inbuilt satire on the modern worship of Mammon. The title of the play *The Carnival* is an interrogation. Is life a Carnival or a fiesta? Apparently the writer suggests that life is no merry-go-round. One has to work hard and cherish human values.

Inspector Raghavan is a one-act play which deals with the theme of corruption even in the educational rung of the Indian society. It dramatises the dichotomy between the expected academic standards and the poor performance by teachers. Raghavan appears to be a very strict and honest Inspector of schools insisting on good teaching. The Headmaster of the High School is worried about the Inspector's strictness and the possibility of his writing a bad report about the school at the time of inspection. He is afraid that incompetent teachers like Ramesam may not do well in the inspection.

But, Sundaram, who is the loyal, trusted follower of the Headmaster, is very practical and knows how to wriggle out of the situation. He suggests that they need not worry about the inspector's strictness, as they can easily bribe him and also please him with flattery. Or they may say that the Inspector has demanded a huge amount and he is prejudiced against them because they have not obliged him. The Headmaster leaves everything to Sundaram to manage. As expected, Ramesam fares very badly in the classroom during Raghavan's inspection and fears that he might be suspended from service. But Sundaram manages everything adroitly and flatters the Inspector in the function. The inspector Raghavan falls an easy prey to the corrupt practices of the school and no action is taken against the erring teacher.

The play is a fine satire on the modern Indian educational system which is vitiated by corrupt practices. It shows how anybody can be bought anytime and how all the ideals of life—in this case educational standards of excellence—are thrown to winds. Though the play is concerned with a South Indian School, what happens in it is applicable to a vast majority of schools all over the country. The play is neatly structured. It is intensely realistic and satirical.

The Mahatma is the only play in Rama Sarma's *Collected Plays* that deals with a political theme. In this one-act play, the playwright intends to depict the martyrdom of Mahatma Gandhi by showing the conflict between Gandhi's ideal of Hindu-Muslim unity and the fundamentalism and fanaticism of the Hindus represented by Nathuram Godse and his followers. One is reminded of K.A. Abbas' play *Barrister at Law* which deals with the early life of Mahatma Gandhi and provides a contrast to Rama Sarma's present play.

The Mahatma seems to be modelled on Shaw's *Saint Joan* and other plays of martyrdom like Eliot's *Murder in the Cathedral.* The conflict is more ideological than physical. There is not much physical action in the play. It is more a conflict between two points of view, the Hindu fundamentalism and liberal humanism, than between two individuals. On account of the preponderance of ideas and ideological conflict, the play assumes the form of heated discussion and consequently becomes Shavian in its texture. For example, Nathuram expresses his frank views which show his Hindu separatism and fundamentalism. He says "Unity! It's impossible. The East and the West may come together one day but not the Hindus and the Muslims." (258) He claims, "We must establish a Hindu Raj." (259) But, Mahatma Gandhi preaches the ideal of the unity of humanity from the platform: "We must live like members of a large family." (259) "We should love our enemies and pray even for those who persecute us." "The Hindus and the Muslims should live together amicably." (261) "India belongs to all, to the Hindus, the Muslims, the Sikhs, the Christians and various other sects who have made India their home. This is greater India." (261) Gandhi thus expresses his concept of India which is governed by the principles of equity and justice.

But Gandhi's views are not accepted by his opponents who have a narrower vision of an exclusively Hindu India. They, therefore, explode a time-bomb near the platform in order to kill him. But luckily Gandhi escapes from danger which his admirers attribute to God's will. Undaunted by any fear, including the fear of death, Gandhi wants to go to Pakistan and try to win their love for Hindus. "Even though I am still not physically fit, I would like to walk across the country and go on a pilgrimage, on a mission of peace and love to bind the two countries India and Pakistan, together." (263)

At the prayer meetings Gandhi's followers admire him for his 'tremendous sacrifice' and call him a 'saint among politicians' and a combination of the Buddha and Christ. They rightly consider him a saviour of the Harijans, a protector of women's rights of equality, besides being a great freedom fighter. But the people of the opposite group like Gopal are not convinced by Gandhian ideals as they believe that "he will be more a hindrance than a help to the country." (270) They, therefore, want to get rid of him so that they can have an India of their own choice. Nathuram Godse, the leader of the opposite group shoots Gandhi to death by pretending to salute him. Mahatma Gandhi dies uttering 'He Ram'.

Thus Gandhi becomes a martyr and a Mahatma by practising great ethical ideals and by dying for them. Although his political rivals led by Nathuram Godse, are successful in putting an end to his life, Gandhi becomes a martyr. Whereas Nathuram triumphs over Gandhi in the physical sense, Gandhi triumphs over Nathuram in the spiritual sense. Gandhi's death, far from becoming a tragic end, becomes a symbol of the affirmation of sublime ethics. Gandhi, thus, emerges as a spiritual hero in spite of his physical death, like Becket in *Murder in the Cathedral*. Rama Sarma is successful in giving expression to his affirmative vision within the limits of a one-act play with all its directness and simplicity of language and the limited number of characters. Because of the Shavian preponderance of ideas in it, the characters remain mouthpieces of the two dominant points of view, without becoming full-blooded characters contributing to the complexity of the theme. It is gratifying to note that Rama Sarma has just written a three act play on Gandhi, entitled *Hail, Deliverer* showing the relevance of Gandhi to the present-day India.

Apart from the social and the political plays, Rama Sarma has written two mythological plays—*Marpessa* and *Urvasi* dealing with Greek and Hindu myths respectively. *Marpessa* is a dramatisation of the Greek mythical theme suggested by a poem of that name by Stephen Philips. In the very selection of a Greek myth, Rama Sarma reminds us of Sri Aurobindo, although he gives it a Shavian treatment peppered with Tagorean lyricism. The central conflict in this one-act play is between mortal love and immortal one. *Marpessa,* daughter of Evanus, is a pretty young girl who is loved by the immortal Sun-god, Apollo, and the mortal Idas. Both of them compete with each other for her love and try to influence her. But Zeus the supreme God arbitrates by asking Apollo not to pressurise her but allow her to choose her lover by her own sweet will. Both the lovers, of course, offer a picture of their own prospective life of hope and joy. After a careful examination of their promises, Marpessa rejects the immortal god and accepts the mortal Idas. Her argument is at once plausible and convincing. She says, "Mortal that I am, with the lapse of years, I shall grow old and lose my beauty. Then I should try to captivate you by little devices and artifices. But if I marry Idas, we will feel delight by looking at our children lisping and prattling." (27) The conflict is finally resolved in favour of a mortal life. Marpessa wants to live happily with the mortal husband, Idas.

The play is poetic infused as it is with lyrical excellence. The lengthy dialogues read like beautiful lyrics, but may not be very handy for actors on the stage. One may, therefore, say that this is a closet play for reading rather than for staging. In fact, it is best suited for the radio.

Urvasi is another mythical play dealing with the love between Arjuna and Urvasi. Urvasi, the celestial damsel, is known for her extraordinary seductive charm. There is, perhaps, no man who does not fall in love with her. Rama Sarma brings an intellectual aura to bear on the mythical story after the Shavian fashion. He highlights the contrast between mortal and immortal life and finally affirms the excellence of the beauty of the earthly life itself. When Urvasi is sent by Lord Indra to entertain Arjuna, the guest, she is overjoyed to do so, as she has fallen in love with him. She promises to give him the heavenly joys and a carefree life by loving him, but Arjuna prefers mortal life. He says: "Still, I prefer a life which is full of uncertainty, a life in which every day brings new pain or pleasures. Human life with all its limitations is lovable." (118-19) Arjuna also tries to disarm Urvasi by expecting only filial affection rather than amorous love from her. His reply, "But I have no other feeling for you except that of a child for its mother. Please don't be angry with me" (121) brings out his nobility of feeling. But Urvasi who is an embodiment of amorous passion curses him: "I curse you! You will have to pass your time among women unregarded as a dancer and as one destitute of manhood." (121) One can easily perceive the similarity between the visions of *Marpessa* and *Urvasi* and their relevance to the human life with all its limitations.

This Busy World is another play presenting the Greek myth of Epicurus. Epicurus boasts that Epicureanism has become universal for it knows "no distinctions of caste, creed, colour or race. Nor does it have any territorial distinctions." (32) Then we see young men and women defying moral norms and indulging in excesses by condemning our traditions as obsolete and irrelevant. Rama Sarma successfully exposes their technique of idealising everything unconventional as liberation from social bondage. The whole play is full of sarcastic humour and all the dialogues have a rich literary flourish.

Rama Sarma's next play, *Sakuntala* is closely modelled on Kalidasa's *Sakuntala.* It is presentable on the stage taking an hour and a half and is easily manageable by the college students or an amateur dramatic group. The play seeks to highlight a clear-cut ideational pattern of contrast between physical love and spiritual love. As Rama Sarma declares, his object "has been to focus the attention of the reader on the sublimity of love, in the juxtaposition of the physical and the spiritual worlds." (57)

The theme of the play is the Gandharva marriage of Sakuntala with King Dushyanta in Sage Kanwa's hermitage. King Dushyanta offers a ring to Sakuntala as a token of his love-marriage and returns to his palace. In course of time, King Dushyanta immersed in the routine life of his kingdom forgets all about Sakuntala. Sakuntala who is expecting a child goes to his palace to join him. But the King fails to remember his marriage with her and, therefore, cold-shoulders her. Sakuntala is really shocked to see herself rejected by her husband. When asked by him to produce a proof about her marriage with him, she fails to do so as she has lost the ring in the river. She, therefore, returns from the palace and seeks shelter in Sage Kashyapa's hermitage where eventually she gives birth to a child called Bharata.

Later a fisherman gets the ring and when Dushyanta sees the ring, he remembers everything that had happened in the past and, therefore, repents for having rejected his legal wife. When he happens to visit Sage Kashyapa's hermitage he is able to see his own child Bharata and identifies his wife. The son Bharata as Marina in Shakespeare's *Pericles* is responsible for bringing together Dushyanta and Sakuntala, parents separated for years.

The dramatist's intention has obviously been to show how the physical love has been transformed into the spiritual one through the patient and uncomplaining suffering undergone by Sakuntala. Rama Sarma has avoided some scenes like Sage Durvasa cursing Sakuntala or Sakuntala losing the ring in the river and a few other incidents in order to achieve a cohesiveness that is needed on the modern stage. Some of the ascetic and the supernatural scenes have been relegated to the background with the main focus on the importance of love, patience, forbearance and sacrifice in life.

The dialogues are short, simple and direct without the stilted wordings of many Sanskrit scholars in India who write about such themes. Rama Sarma has deliberately made the scenes short so that they could be managed easily by the modern actors. Likewise he has removed the lengthy lyrical dialogues of Kalidasa to make the play more intellectual or Shavian. But he has rightly retained the original symbols of Kalidasa's play like the bees, the flowers and the ring for giving the play a ring of authenticity.

A close study of the eleven plays of Rama Sarma reveals to us a profound growth of vision from interrogation to affirmation, protest to acceptance and Dionysian intensity to Apollonian serenity. His plays are concretizations of his contemporary consciousness, keen sense of human nature, wide scholarship and amazing self-control that is evident in his dialogues. He has a clear conception of scenes and an ability to arrange their sequence. Because of the preponderance of intellectual element and the underlying moral tone, his plays tend to look like the Moralities. Like Ben Jonson, he has created certain memorable types of characters—the imaginative or intellectual husband, the unimaginative or non-poetic wife, the inspiring beloved, the heartless capitalist, the snobbish industrialist, the society lady and the blind fanatic, thereby enriching the Indian English drama.

Although Rama Sarma is not obsessed with dramatic technique, he experiments with it where necessary. The use of a philosopher, Epicurus, to bracket off the hedonistic philosophy of the modern man, or of a Voice bemoaning the loss of Gandhi are some instances of experimentation with technique. As far as the use of language is concerned, one may notice a significant change from the early plays to the later ones. Whereas the early plays are written in very lengthy dialogues studded with several scholarly quotations from diverse authors, the later plays are written in relatively shorter dialogues which are free from quotational interferences. The earlier plays written before going abroad have a literary flourish, an exotic imagination. The later plays tend to use a language nearer to the spoken one. Both the categories of plays can be enjoyed by making the right use of them. For example, the early plays with lengthy or lyrical dialogues could be adopted to the radio, and the later plays can be enacted on the stage or used as teleplays. One hopes that they will capture the attention of a director who can transform them into spectacular visions for edification and enlightenment.

Rama Sarma the playwright can justifiably be compared with many other Indian English playwrights in different aspects. As far as lyricism is concerned, he is comparable to Rabindranath Tagore. In the selection and treatment of classical themes, he is comparable to Sri Aurobindo. As far as the treatment of burning issues of the contemporary society are concerned, he is comparable to Harindranath Chattopadhyaya and Asif Currimbhoy. But in the intellectualisation of the dramatic themes, he is definitely Shavian. Rama Sarma's plays like those of several other Indian playwrights, are still confined to the page. It will be fine if they are revived on the stage. Until then "these can be read and enjoyed for their thought content and for the relevance they have to perennial problems of life, East of West" as Rama Sarma himself states in the 'Preface' to his *Collected Plays*.

The Distinguished Miltonist

M.S. NAGARAJAN

In India, Milton scholarship is what most aim at but few manage to achieve. More than any other writer it is Milton who refines our sensibilities and helps us in our inner growth. In the western world, Milton has always been the major source of attraction for the best minds. Right from Samuel Johnson, almost every critic has felt impelled to offer thought provoking comments on Milton's subject or poetic style. Eminent critics like Hanford, Douglas Bush, Tillyard, Herbert Grierson and Basil Wiley have been quite conventional in their views and estimates regarding Milton's poetry. With Eliot's twin essays, our century witnessed, as never before in the past, a literary controversy of awesome magnitude with Miltonoclasts and Miltonators accusing one another, along with their followers, over the long drawn battle on Milton's books.

In India, however, two names stand paramount as regards lasting contribution to human knowledge on Milton studies—B. Rajan and Rama Sarma. They are decidedly the two most acclaimed scholars on Milton. Rama Sarma, in particular chose Milton early in life for his study and research and thought long and deeply on his works. It was evidently a case of long choosing and beginning early. He seems to have made Milton a part of his life, an indispensable aspect of his emotional equipment. Or else, how would one account for six full length studies on him in a span of forty years, appearing at expected and almost predicted frequency, in addition to talks, class room lectures and periodical articles on the great poet. A rare, creditable achievement any one can justifiably feel proud about. His first book *Milton's "Paradise Lost,"* a slender volume, incorporating a portion of his doctoral dissertation, submitted to the University of Wales, appeared in 1951, brought out by a nondescript Delhi publisher. What a wealth of information in this handy compendium! All that could be said about the first English literary epic, with updated critical views, yet holding onto an authentic Indian perspective is very much in evidence in this pocket volume.

Set in seven chapters, the volume discusses some of the essential and fundamental issues in *Paradise Lost*. The book opens—and rightly so—with a discussion of epic poetry. It traces the origin of the literary epic, as different from the authentic epic, and places *Paradise Lost* historically in its native tradition. The machinery employed and the note of didacticism are both discussed with the conclusion that Adam and Eve are the prototypes of Everyman and Everywoman and the fall of Adam is a 'woe too deep for human tears.' From his early life, Milton had consciously and conscientiously trained himself in upholding a life given to virtuous living and scrupulous adherence to moral righteousness. Virtue, for him, is an active force and consists in strict obedience to God, controlling one's passion. It is in such a context that we should place Milton's great works which deal with the essential conflict between virtue and vice. The major theological problem in *Paradise Lost* is the justification of God's ways to men.

It looks as though Milton found it necessary to affirm his unswerving faith in the ways of God. The poem is the spiritual experience of Milton and his subordination to the will of the Almighty and acquiescence in God's judgment. These views are expressed in almost all the poems of Milton, as for instance in *Samson Agonistes,* where Milton affirms,

> Just are the ways of God,
> And justifiable to men,
> Unless there be who think not God at all.

Rama Sarma devotes an entire chapter to the architectonics of *Paradise Lost,* its structure, design, episodes, dramatic element and significance of the last two books. Who is the hero of *Paradise Lost?* Milton critics have entertained widely differing views on this overwhelming question. For Rama Sarma, the hero is one who excels others in piety and devotion to God. His patience and ennobling forbearance mark his heroism. Right doing and obedience to God enable Adam to get purified and hence he is the hero of *Paradise Lost.*

Finally Rama Sarma interprets the poem from an oriental point of view based on the foundations of the *Bhagvad Gita,* especially in its advocacy of Jnana Marga, signifying wisdom, Karma Marga, professing non-attachment, and Bhakti Marga, which pleads for unflinching implicit faith in God. Karma Marga is nothing but a faith in doing duty for its own sake. The poem enshrines these basic virtues preached by the perennial philosophy of *Gita.* The aesthetic appeal of the poem is seen to lie in its *Santa rasa* which is the highest of the *navarasas.* In the poem the dominant note is one of serenity and spiritual enlightenment. The emotional experience one derives is *santa.* Rama Sarma's earliest work on Milton raises all the pertinent issues associated with the poem. It serves as a reader's guide and what is of singular merit is its relation to the ethos of an Indian reader.

The subsequent critical works have been variations and further discussions at greater length on the initial study of 1951. *The Heroic Argument,* published twenty years later in 1971, is a detailed study of the four heroic poems, *Comus, Paradise Lost, Paradise Regained* and *Samson Agonistes*, supplying, as it were, a conceptual background to these great poems. The purpose is to examine how these poems illustrate and amplify Milton's concept of heroism. For Rama Sarma, "the Miltonic hero is one who resists evil, or one who exhibits remarkable powers of patience, forbearance and endurance in the face of trials and tribulations, or one who has within him the mighty potentialities for martyrdom, or finally one who can transcend earthly limitations, conquer and subdue vice triumphantly and gloriously." (24) *Comus* is the forerunner of this tetralogy of long poems and it introduces the pattern of temptation, triumph of virtue over vice—the heroic conflict, in other words—which are subjected to an extended artistic rendering in the later works. The Miltonic doctrine is that heroism does not lie in the sheer mighty deeds of daring on the battlefield, but obedience to the greater glory of God as shown in the lines in *Paradise Lost:*

> that suffering for Truth's sake.
> Is fortitude to highest victorie,
> And to the faithful Death the Gate of Life. XII, 569-71

How God reveals himself in a mysterious manner to 'just men long oppressed' is the underlying theme of *Samson Agonistes*. Samson is his own deliverer through contrition and the poem amply illustrates God's justice. In the words of Rama Sarma, "*Samson* is essentially a testament of Miltonic thought." (131) *Paradise Regained* has always suffered in comparison with *Paradise Lost*. It is neither a postscript nor a poetic footnote but a fitting conclusion to the great epic. The right response would be to understand it as a companion poem that explains Milton's concept of heroism in greater detail and with greater objectivity. In the chapter 'Milton and the Orient' Rama Sarma delves deep into Milton's poetry and seeks out evidences to prove his acquaintance with Indian geographic conditions and philosophic traditions.

The Eagle and the Phoenix (1976) is a comprehensive study of *Samson Agonistes*. After settling doubts about its date of composition and fallacies regarding its autobiographical elements, Rama Sarma examines the theme of spiritual regeneration and transcendence in the dramatic poem. Samson is ennobled and recreated through death even as the mythic bird phoenix is. The images of the dragon, the eagle and the phoenix convey with high precision the moral, spiritual strength of Samson. The play is also examined as the tragedy of the Apocalypse. The motif of martyrdom is studied in relation to *St. Joan* and *Murder in the Cathedral*. All the three plays end on a lofty note creating an abiding and deep faith in God and the saints. This full-length study on a single work of Milton enhances our understanding of *Samson Agonistes*. It freely draws out parallelisms and deft comparisons by moving out to other works.

Things Unattempted (1982) is an attempt at a close reading and local analysis of Milton's lyrics—'Lycidas,' 'L'allegro', and 'Il Penseroso.' The last section 'Epics of Righteousness and Justice' is an indication of Rama Sarma's growing interest in the Indian epic tradition. *Paradise Lost* and the *Mahabharata* are taken up for a comparative study in terms of their didactic and philosophic affiliations with the following conclusion. The chief *rasa* in both the epics is the same. The poets of both the epics seem to be moved by an inward awakening to convey the message of God. The two epics in their universality of appeal become distinct as epics of righteousness and justice. (146) The only way to account for the sublimity in Milton's poetry is by seeing him as a many-sided personality influenced by all that his age stood for. The true voice of Milton, the humanist, the scholar-statesman, the poet-priest is behind all his creations. Hence his sublimity.

Milton and the Prophetic Strain (1991) is a full-blown study of Milton's minor poems, prose pamphlets and major works. It advances the theory that "Milton's life has been 'a true poem' manifesting 'divine providence and God-realisation." The opening chapter is in the form of a bio-critical study of Milton, the poet-priest-prophet. The central argument of the book, in nine chapters, is beautifully summed up in the preface: "Prophetically he [Milton] visualises a new world, a new Heaven, a new Earth and a golden age of golden deeds when justice will prevail and peace will be established. Man attains this perfection through obedience to God, and the perfect man in a perfect world is the prophetic vision of Milton." Milton's prose pamphlets plead eloquently for a rejuvenated world. In his last years of life, due to political controversies and embroilment, his life of seclusion helped him to ponder over the mysteries of God's ways. In the final phase—as is the case with Shakespeare—the poet is able to arrive at a beatific vision of life that "suffering for Truth's sake/Is fortitude to highest victory." Milton's vision of a just world may be an unrealisable ideal; but what is of relevance to us, living in troubled times, as we are, is the timeless philosophic message, the message enshrined in the *Gita* and *Paradise Lost* that God's ways may be inscrutable but are essentially just to mankind.

Rama Sarma's work on Milton has been applauded by a large number of Milton scholars of world repute. William Hunter, Geoffrey Bullough, John T. Shawcross, the editor of *The Critical Heritage* on Milton, among others, have paid rich encomiums on Rama Sarma for his critical appraisal of Milton and the Indian sensibility he brings to bear on his study. Rama Sarma's scholarship is authentic and sound; he is able to arrive at judgments with an air of sureness and authority about them, always supported by textual evidences. He is sure of his ground and firm in his judicial criticism, never for a moment, tendencious in his argument or tentative in his observations. His major strength lies in his ability to range freely over the whole realm of Milton's poetry with a facility hardly matched by most other Milton critics.

As time goes by, one notices an increasing tendency in Rama Sarma to employ Indian aesthetic theories—particularly the *rasa* concept—for a fuller and more comprehensive understanding of Milton. This is as it should be. After all is said and done, what is expected of Rama Sarma is an Indian response to Western literature based on east-west cross cultural interaction.

To have spent a large share of one's life on a study and interpretation of Milton is in itself a much coveted reward. What can be richer than a life devoted to Milton? Rama Sarma's contribution to Milton scholarship from India is bound to be lasting.

M.V. Rama Sarma: The Miltonist in Life and Letters

K. CHELLAPPAN

Milton seems to be the guiding light or guardian angel of the life and letters of M.V. Rama Sarma, a distinguished Milton scholar, an eminent teacher and educationist, a creative writer with ideals, and above all a gentleman in whom sublimity and serenity are in perfect harmony. It was said of Milton that he 'wrote' his life and 'lived' his writings. There is a similar continuity between the life and letters of Rama Sarma, to have known whom is a kind of liberal education. Again Milton himself said once that one who writes a good poem must have something of that in himself.We may say that even a teacher of epic poetry must have some kind of sublimity in his own personality.

Though he has written on Elizabethan drama (Heywood and Shakespeare) perceptively, his major commitment and contribution has been to Milton studies, and even his creative writings are only the by-product of his critical workshop and they rearticulate and reenact the Miltonic theme of man's understanding and acceptance of the ways of God through devotion.

Rama Sarma is one of the very few Indian scholars who never changed along with changing times in his loyalty to the great master, Milton. 'Of all the faithless, faithful he stood'—and as a teacher, and critic of Milton, he combined a perceptive critical acumen with a sound scholarship, an unfailing moral sense with a sense of aesthetic delight. The core of his Milton criticism can be found in his *The Heroic Argument*, where he rightly focuses on Milton's concept of heroism in his major works.

> Thematically all the four poems, *Comus, Paradise Lost, Paradise Regained* and *Samson Agonistes* belong to the same category of 'heroic poetry.' Milton's heroic ideal of fighting the evil forces in life is well illustrated in these poems. The protagonists are exposed to temptations. The best in them can be seen only when they resist the forces of evil. Milton maintains the view that 'though God commands us temperance, justice continence, yet pours out before us, even to profusion, all desirable things and gives us minds that can

> wander beyond all limit and satiety,' man is purposely put in the midst of plenty so that he may be tempted and tested. (22)

Rama Sarma then elaborates that in *Comus* Milton presents the militant, positive and dynamic virtue actively resisting the vicious snares, whereas *Paradise Lost* glorifies the heroic qualities of patience and endurance and willing submission to God's ways: *Samson Agonistes* describes heroic martyrdom and *Paradise Regained* portrays a sublime hero. In all these heroic poems he sees a great conflict between good and evil, and the vindication of the ways of God to men, though the human interest is the centre.

While writing on *Samson Agonistes* in *The Eagle and the Phoenix* Rama Sarma gives importance to its ethical idealism and its justification of God's ways to men. He sees it as the continuation of *Paradise Lost* as it helped him "to assert eternal providence. And justify the ways of God to men." (Bk I, 25-26) Milton christianises the Classical tragedy by making Samson 'the erring human being who through resistance of temptations attains a state of heroic martyrdom.' Rama Sarma rightly emphasises the theme of martyrdom in *The Eagle and the Phoenix*. "This potentiality in men of atoning for the sins of others, as it happens in the case of martyrs, has a fascination and appeal, all its own, to Milton." (11) Samson through temptation and fall is spiritually recreated, and unlike the classical or Elizabethan tragic hero, Samson rids himself of this weakness by resisting the temptation. "He soon realises his free will in the right direction, before he can be reclaimed by God. For some time he loses faith in himself and faith in God. He has to get them through unswerving loyalty to God." (43)

Here again, we see a link between the man and the scholar. Rama Sarma's unswerving faith in God is linked with his scholarly studies of Milton's works and his moral sense, rooted in the Indian way of life as embodied in our epics, helps him to perceive this dimension in Milton more clearly than the Western scholars, and may be, this scholarly discovery in turn has helped Rama Sarma to live by the light of faith in his own life.

His Milton criticism is also comparative in this sense—he always finds affinities between Milton's epic and the Indian epics in their affirmation of good succeeding through suffering and the possibility of regeneration through the acceptance of the will of God. His latest book, *Milton and the Indian Epic Tradition* studies the parallels between the Miltonic epic and the Indian epics. Though in his earlier work, he has been more conscious of the difference between the two, in the later work he sees more affinities, though as a good comparatist, he is not blind to the differences even now. His approach to Milton is always that of an Indian rooted in his culture, but he never Indianises Milton. In his unpublished lecture 'Milton and the Indian Epic tradition' he makes perceptive comments on the heroes in *Paradise Lost*, the *Mahabharata* and the *Ramayana*.

> The Indian epics have *Dhirodatta* as their heroes. Even though Arjuna is the most valorous warrior in the *Mahabharata,* he is not the hero of the epic. Yudhistira, his elder brother, who is noble, dignified, generous and truthful becomes the hero, the central figure in the epic. He is *dhirodatta* given to lofty thinking and righteousness. Rama of the *Ramayana* by his own exemplary deeds, like the Son of God, proves himself to be sublime in his bearing and in his relationship with others. He is a dutiful son, a loving husband, an affectionate brother and a just ruler. He wants to be an ideal king and establish *Ramrajya* where justice prevails and harmony exists.

But Rama, though more idealistic than Yudhistira, never reveals himself as god. When Brahma tells him that he is an incarnation of Vishnu and that Sita is Lakshmi, Rama calmly replies, 'I am the son of King Dasaratha and consider myself a human being.' Valmiki's *Ramayana* poses the problem whether Rama is a God or a human being.

Rama Sarma also sees a parallel between the Indian epics' presentation of Gods and Milton's use of the theory of accommodation in describing the indescribable and in accommodating God's ways to the level of human understanding.

We find the synthesis of the man, Rama Sarma, as the Milton scholar and the creative writer most clearly in his recent autobiographical fiction *Height of Noon.* Here, the fiction-reality dichotomy is almost gone. This is not simply a campus novel, because its geography is only the mind of Rama Sarma. Here he tries to recapture the Miltonic pattern in his life in relation to his personal tragedy at the height of noon and in that process he connects this moment with similar moments in his life through flashback, whenever necessary. And the continuing thread of his life through Anand seems to be the Miltonic faith in the ways of God, though the final tragedy of his wife's death makes the Miltonic hero to question the ways of God, only to come back to God and Man with a clarity that can come only out of great suffering.

There is a Miltonic ring in the description of all the important moments in the life of Anand, the protagonist of the novel. For example, at the end of Chapter 3, when the writer describes Anand's commitment to work, he says,

> He [Anand] knew that God would give him what he deserved at the right time and his duty was to do his work patiently, sincerely and faithfully. His work had to be judged by God and not by human beings. So he had to do it flawlessly and to the best of his abilities. This patient waiting for God's grace and not getting unduly excited if things did not happen as he planned was developed by him through some experiences he had in life. (36)

This account of Anand, reads like the personal experience of Rama Sarma, the Miltonist. In his youth Anand, no doubt thought that it was his indomitable self effort that crowned him with success. He did not, as yet, visualise that it was God's grace that blessed him. Later, when the writer talks about the difficulty of being grateful, he simply echoes Milton that gratitude is burdensome. The way Anand visualises the marriages of his daughters as the mysterious working of God's ways again reveals the influence of Milton on Rama Sarma in creating situations of this type in the novel. The novelist comments, "It looked as if the second daughter's marriage was in a way hurried through a divine agency for only a few days later Lakshmi was ill. Anand's fortune touched the zenith and it came full circle in the declining fashion in the next few months." (122)In the sudden rise to the zenith and then coming back to a sense of reality in the shape of his wife's illness, Anand is very much like Samson though in his case, his wife brought him closer to God in a positive way. When she dies, Anand again wavers in his faith.

> He [Anand] wondered why man was discomfited and rendered helpless. He was angry with God for he never thought that he would give him a raw deal and make him miserable for the rest of his life. Like Adam he questioned why God had given him all those good things in life almost unasked for, and then had abandoned him to a life of suffering. For one moment, he could not reconcile himself with God's ways. (128)

Anand "felt that God for one moment withdrew His protective hand and he fell." (129)

As the car was bringing Anand back home from the hospital, his mind was interrogating God's ways. His faith in God's essential justice appeared to have gone but only to rebound with redoubled force through prayer. Even his quick relief from the office appears as God's response to his prayer and he thinks that he is still destined to serve Man and God. And Anand is prepared to wait for the god-given moment.

In all these intricate situations where Anand, the central figure in the novel, is exposed to trials and tribulations one finds Miltonic beliefs closely illumined. In the novel God's ways are often questioned and accepted. Anand in the last phase is like any other human being in distress. Because of the repeated references to God's ways and justice, one is inclined to think that Rama Sarma reveals himself and his Miltonic views through Anand. We see that affinity between the writer and Anand, the central character in the novel. Like Prospero in *The Tempest,* Anand seems to represent Rama Sarma, especially in adhering to and expounding Miltonic doctrines and assertions. Prospero may not be Shakespeare, just as Anand is not Rama Sarma, but the analogy in both the instances is irresistible.

Robert Kroetsch once said, 'the fiction makes us real'. Rama Sarma's fiction recreates the reality, his Milton criticism is both a product and a consequence of his personality. To him, Milton's *Paradise Lost* is not just a work of art but a way of life. And as a teacher and scholar-critic of Milton, he has converted the frozen words into a living flame. He has been able to communicate the power of Milton's poetry as a live experience. This has been possible not only because of his moral fervour but also because of aesthetic sense. He is as much alive to the poetic vigour of the god-gifted organ voice of England as his prophetic vision. In this connection, I would like to mention a scholarly lecture delivered in my department on Milton's style in which he illustrated the varieties of style in *Paradise Lost*. There is answerable style not only in Milton's works but in Rama Sarma's recreation of Milton. And this again is a reflection of his style of life. One can see a grand style in Rama Sarma's life and letters and again as in Milton, its loftiness is rooted in simplicity and humanness. That is the essence of Rama Sarma, the man and the scholar: a Miltonic sublimity in life and letters.

"Things Unattempted": Rama Sarma's Milton Criticism

G. NAGESWARA RAO

Rama Sarma's dedicated study, research and teaching of Milton for over four decades is a unique achievement and an edifying example to any student of literature, particularly in the present Indian academic scene. At present Shakespeare and Milton are not given even a fraction of the place they deserve, either in teaching or research. One of the most impressive aspects of Rama Sarma's Milton criticism is that it establishes the relevance of Milton and it gives a proper perspective of all the works of Milton. It also enables the reader to have a comprehensive view of the literary, social, political and religious conditions cherished by his age.

Further, in the course of nearly half a century of critical endeavour amply reflected in his six books—not to mention occasional contributions to such monumental critical studies like *Milton Encyclopedia* and periodical seminars of the Milton society of America—Rama Sarma's work shows how he has absorbed the best of every critical approach and enriched his own response to Milton. His first book *Milton's "Paradise Lost" (A Study)* (1951) is a part of his Ph.D. thesis, *Milton's Heroic Poetry* submitted to the university of Wales in 1949. Here he discusses in depth and detail such important aspects of *Paradise Lost* as its place in epic poetry, the conflict of good and evil in *Paradise Lost,* the theological problems embedded in it, its structural unity, its hero, its philosophical thought content and finally its aesthetic appeal. This small book which was hailed as an important contribution to Milton scholarship by critics like Bullough and Hanford contains a brief chapter of six pages entitled 'Aesthetic Appeal' which initiates and Indian aesthetic approach to Milton. Applying the critical theories of *Rasa* and *Dhvani* Rama Sarma has shown that many of the aspects of *Paradise Lost* considered by western critics as tedious narrative or unnecessary episodes are in the ultimate analysis, essential parts contributing to its emotional unity. "From a general outline we can easily see how all the *Rasas* are embodied in *Paradise Lost* though its dominant *Rasa* is *Santa.* This explains why Satan should be presented in a heroic mould, for through him the poet gives us an occasion to experience the *Vira* Rasa, heroism, though it is mock heroism. This will also explain why Milton should have indulged in the tedious description of the war in Heaven for it, in its turn, typifies the *Rasa, Bibhatsa.* The concluding books of *Paradise Lost* which are too often considered to be unnecessary intrusions into the main epic have an important role in the epic, for they provide the dominant *Rasa, Santa*, and bring it to a climax. From a purely Indian point of view *Paradise Lost* is highly artistic and it produces the nine *Rasas*, making *Santa* its essential *Rasa*."[1] Thus Rama Sarma evaluates the epic from the aesthetic angle. This book, *Paradise Lost: A Study*, serves as a pioneering effort in approaching the epic from an Indian viewpoint.

In his second book on Milton *The Heroic Argument* (1971), after convincingly arguing that the life and beliefs of Milton are inextricably interwoven with his creative activity, Rama Sarma shows how Milton's desire 'To leave something so written to after times, as they should not willingly let it die,' inspires Milton to scorn delights and live laborious days. Critics like William B. Hunter and Irene Samuel, have praised. *The Heroic Argument* in their reviews for its balanced approach and objective point of view and its restraint in dealing with very provoking attacks from such eminent critics as F.R. Leavis, Ezra Pound and T.S. Eliot. In this study Rama Sarma combines with discriminating critical insight the best results and techniques of the then existing main trends of Milton criticism: the study of Milton the man and the thinker, of his mind and art, and of his poetic achievement and prophetic appeal. By clearly defining the basic assumptions involved in Milton's concept of heroism this book provides an objective assessment stimulating critical criteria to go through the maze of the Milton controversy. Soon one realises that it is in conformity with epic traditions and conventions that Milton uses a style serious, elevated and sublime. His lofty rhyme, therefore, is not mechanical but the language of the educated classes heightened to epic grandeur and sublimity. Rama Sarma's discussion of the heroic conflict as presented in *Comus* unmistakably establishes that for the first time Milton has revealed his concept of heroism and the technique of even the righteous being tempted and tested. The same concept acquires epic depth and dimensions in *Paradise Lost*. Rama Sarma affirms that Milton is justified in giving to Satan certain redeeming features thereby making him a formidable rival to God, the Son of God and Man. Rama Sarma states, "Milton creates out of the conventioal dark devil an active, militant leader, an intriguing politician and an eloquent speaker, who on occasions expresses sentiments of universal validity."[2]

When all is said and done the final result of Milton controversy is that, far from dislodging Milton, the zeal of the anti-Miltonists has only stimulated the study of Milton's poetry, his life and ideas as nothing else has been done before. The worst attack of the anti-Miltonists has produced the best

Milton scholarship from America and other parts of the world. The last chapter of *The Heroic Argument* gives a succinct account of the oriental influence on Milton in general and of India in particular. This chapter indicates that Rama Sarma has patiently read many of the travelogues of the Englishmen who visited India in the 16th and 17th centuries, for he shows the verbal echoes from the travelogues in Books, II, III, IV, V, IX and XI. The political and historical knowledge of India enables Milton to create the effect of spaciousness of range and his family were connected with some members of the East India Company, particularly Methowold, the scholarly president of the Surat factory and later, the advisor of the East India Company. The close parallel besides verbal echoes to Sir Thomas Roe's *Embassy* in Milton's description of the coronation of Satan in the opening lines of Book II is of particular interest because it reproduces Roe's descriptive account of his first audience with Emperor Jahangir. Rama Sarma observes that Milton may not have been acquainted with the Indian epics as he is with the physical, geographical and historical conditions of India. "All the same there is a great similarity in the thought content of the Indian epic the *Mahabharata* and *Paradise Lost,* even though the former is an authentic epic and the latter a literary one. The Indian epic in its thematic content, concept of heroism, ethical idealism and insistence on implicit faith in God has affinity with *Paradise Lost.*" Whether the epic is of "the East or West, North or South, its blood and temper are the same and the true epic, wherever created will be a narrative poem, organic in structure, dealing with great actions and great characters in a style commensurate with the lordliness of its theme which tends to idealise these characters and actions and to sustain and embellish its subject by means of episode and amplification. This is true of *Paradise Lost* and the *Mahabharata* even though they come from two different ages and two different countries. Perhaps the thought content of the two epics is drawn from the same source, from perennial philosophy that is true of all ages and of all countries in the world."[3]

Rama Sarma's *The Eagle and the Phoenix* (1976) is a stimulating book length study of *Samson Agonistes* which has been hailed by Michael Lieb in *Milton Quarterly* as a substantial contribution to Milton studies. Rama Sarma shows how in *Samson Agonistes* Milton creates a unique tragedy comprising Hebraic, Hellenic and Christian thought content, projecting martyrdom and restoring the old tale for the delectable enjoyment of the 17th Century English audience. According to Rama Sarma, it is this harmonious combination of many traditions, that has contributed to the imperishable significance of the play. Its dramatic structure, autobiographical element, its artistic spirit, meaning and message have to be studied in order to do justice to the consummate artistic excellence of the poet.

Things Unattempted (1982) not only sums up lucidly Rama Sarma's important views on the life and work of Milton but also gives a well balanced account of Milton's aspirations and achievements. It reflects the growing phenomenon of oriental approach to western literature in general and to English literature in particular. Much of what the book deals with in this direction is as fresh as it is thought provoking. It is a detailed examination of Miltonic doctrines, the evolution of his concept of heroism, his interest in and knowledge of India, and the enriching cross cultural fusion of the East and the West in his poetry. The argument of *The Heroic Argument* is limited to the four major works of Milton: *Comus, Paradise Lost, Samson Agonistes* and *Paradise Regained.* In *Things Unattempted* Rama Sarma discusses how Milton began with lyric harmonies of the twin poems 'L'Allegro and II Penseroso' which reflect certain aspects of Milton's approach to life. The discussion of *Comus* emphasises the lofty theme of heroic virtue posited in terms of dramatic conflict. *Lycidas* besides presenting the tragic loss of the inheritor of unfulfilled renown Edward King, universalises the grief for the untimely death of one dedicated to the service of the heavenly Muse, poetry. A discussion of *Paradise Lost, Samson Agonistes,* and *Paradise Regained* in *Things Unattempted* reveals various dimensions of the Miltonic concept of heroism and heroic martyrdom. The concluding chapter deals with *Paradise Lost* and the *Mahabharata* as epics of righteousness and justice. The various *Rasas* evoked by the varied incidents and characters in both the epics are studies in comparison with each other and sometimes even in contrast.

Rama Sarma concludes, "To students of literary criticism it is of immense interest to find out how the two epics are mostly similar to each other in their thematic content, in their concept of heroism and in their philosophic background. The chief *Rasa* in both the epics is the same. The poets of both the epics seem to be moved by an inward awakening to convey the message of God. The two epics in their universality of appeal become distinct as epics of righteousness and justice."[4]

In *Milton and the Prophetic Strain* (1991) Rama Sarma proceeds from a much respected tradition of ancient Indian *commentators, grantha gatha samsakara,* that of elucidation of a writer's work on the basis of cherished values and ideals and the purpose of the writing all embedded in the vision verbalised in the text itself. The other tradition is, *vyakthi gatha samskara,*the individual tradition of elucidating the text based on the criteria of the commentator's varied experiences and views accumulated through his exposure to many influences. The second tradition is always given less importance than that of the first, though it is not condemned. A happy combination of the two is considered to be the achievement of the cultivated reader and critic of literature or *sahrudya.* Milton cherished the age old concept of poet as a prophet, shaped his mind and thought in accordance with that ideal and produced a body of work which reveals his prophetic vision of a perfect world governed by the principle of equity and justice.

Priest-like, Milton voices the need for man to understand God's actions and wholeheartedly surrenders himself to divine dispensation. Further Milton, like a prophet, sings of his vision of a new world, a new heaven and a new earth and of a golden age of golden deeds when justice and peace will prevail.

Apart from offering new insights along familiar lines of study, *Milton and the Prophetic Strain* opens new perspectives to Milton studies. In positing the poet-prophet ideal cherished by Milton and establishing its universal validity from Milton's own writings and the Indian epic tradition, the basis for a new direction of study is provided. Each aspect of the poet-prophet's ideal and his mission is discussed with illustrations from Milton's minor poems, major works and prose writings. The Miltonic ideals of heroism, the innovative and universal dimensions of a new kind of heroism are explained in depth and detail. And, finally it is shown how revelation has been used as a technique of epic narrative in *Paradise Lost* and the *Mahabharata.* Revelation as a technique of epic narrative is an undeniable edition of a new dimension to Milton studies. Revelation stands for 'a consolidated, coherent, encyclopedic view of human life,'[5] a phenomena, which transcends the world of ordinary reality. Rama Sarma culls together the various echoes of Milton's reference to revelation in his works in general and in *Paradise Lost* particularly and connects that to the use of revelation in classical epics of Homer and Virgil which comes from the Gods above and deftly links it with Arjuna's plea, "If you think me worthy Krishna, give me revelation" in the *Mahabharata* and thus places Milton on the highest pinnacle of poetic art.

Milton and the Prophetic Strain presents Miltonic thought content in relation to his major poems, *Comus, Paradise Lost, Samson Agonistes* and *Paradise Regained.* It also shows how revelation is common to both the epics, *Paradise Lost* and the *Mahabharata.* It emphasises the need for man to establish right relationship with God. Inner purity, dedication to duty unmindful of the reward, and surrender to the divine will both in the *Mahabharata* and *Paradise Lost* are shown as unfailing sources of ascendence in man. The ideal expressed through Michael's words,

> Nor love thy life, nor hate, but what thou livest
> Live well, how long or short permit to heaven

is almost identical with the concept of Karma Yogin of the *Mahabharata.* "The thought content of the poet-prophet, John Milton, and the philosophical message of the *Gita* remain timeless. Their immediacy to all ages is profoundly felt in their revelation of God's inscrutable, but essentially just ways to mankind, and their insistence on righteousness, *dharma,* as an ideal of the perfect world, yet to come."[6]

Milton and the Indian Epic Tradition (1995) is a culmination of Rama Sarma's lifetime study of Milton. All the work he has done so far on Milton becomes a part of the Indian approach. Rama Sarma shows that the Indian epics belong to sacred literature and the Indian epic tradition upholds loftiness of theme, historicity of plot, sublimity of heroism and delectable aesthetic appeal. *Paradise Lost* conforms to the pattern of being sacred poetry. In its thematic content, concept of heroism and historic realism it has close affinity with the Indian epics, the *Ramayana* and the *Mahabharata*. *Paradise Lost* too presents like the *Ramayana* and *Mahabharata* conjugal harmony and domestic bliss, something that one does not find in Homer or Virgil. The protagonists in these three epics Rama, Yudhistara and Adam face the temptations of life and endure the trials and tribulations as divine dispensation. The three poets Valmiki, Vyasa, and Milton project 'dreams of a golden age of golden deeds' and 'visualise a new world order,' a paradise controlled by justice and peace. *Ramarajya* of Valmiki, Vyasa's vision of a transcendent world ruled by *dharma* and Milton's millennium governed by the divine order offer humankind a new hope and a new faith and inspire humanity to strive for a life of virtue, temperance, truth and god realization. The glory of India is the glory of the *Ramayana* and the *Mahabharata*. It is the glory of Valmiki and Vyasa. The glory of England is the glory of Milton's *Paradise Lost*. The three epics form the best of the sacred literary tradition equally valid for all nations, for all races and for all ages. "The three epics *Paradise Lost*, the *Ramayana* and the *Mahabharata*, each in its own way, leads humanity to a nobler life of spiritual exaltation. These epics belong to sacred literature, mostly dependent on divine dictation. The three epic poets donning celestial robes, with their prophetic vision, give to posterity undeniable human values and glorify the ways of God to men."[7]

NOTES

1. *Milton's "Paradise Lost"* (A Study) (New Delhi: Atma Ram, 1951), p. 68.
2. *The Heroic Argument* (Madras: Macmillan, 1971), p. 90.
3. *Ibid.*, p. 164.
4. *Things Unattempted: A Study of Milton* (New Delhi: Vikas, 1982), p. 146.
5. Northrop Frye, "The Story of all Things" from *Paradise Lost*, ed. Scott Elledge, p. 422.
6. *Milton and the Prophetic Strain* (New Delhi: Sterling, 1991), p. 174.
7. *Milton and the Indian Epic Tradition* (New Delhi: Prestige, 1995).

Rama Sarma, the Milton Critic: A Perspective

C.R. VISWESWARA RAO

The Milton controversy in the twentieth century generated principally among others by Leavis and Eliot on the one hand and Waldock on the other has enthused two outstanding scholars from India to focus on aspects of Milton studies from divergent perspectives: from a standpoint that absorbs and illustrates western scholarly critical and evaluative traditions as in the case of Balachandra Rajan and from an angle that abundantly displays a spirit of synthesis of the eastern and western literary and oral traditions as in the case of M.V. Rama Sarma. With his *The Heroic Argument, The Eagle and the Phoenix, Things Unattempted, Milton and the Prophetic Strain,* Rama Sarma has a considerable body of writing on the Miltonic theme to provide adequate ground for a critical evaluation of the entire corpus of his writing on Milton complete with the publication in 1995 of what seems to be his *magnum opus, Milton and the Indian Epic Tradition.*

Milton's words in Book IX of *Paradise Lost* refer to the "answerable style" he wished to obtain from his "celestial patroness" in order to raise the heroic argument of "the better fortitude/Of patience and heroic matyr-dom/Unsung."[1] *The Heroic Argument* interrelates the four major works, *Comus, Paradise Lost, Paradise Regained* and *Samson Agonistes* in terms of an illustration of Milton's concept of heroism. If *Comus* presents the positive, militant aspect of chastity in conflict with vice, *Paradise Lost* exemplifies the heroic qualities of patience, forbearance and endurance. While *Samson Agonistes* glorifies the concept of heroic martyrdom, *Paradise Regained* presents the sublime hero who upholds the truth that in the conflict between good and evil the forces of virtue and good triumphantly assert themselves in the ultimate analysis and that evil is only partial. The four major poems of Milton form an organic unity when examined in terms of the concept of heroism. A quest for continuity is one of the scholar-critic Rama Sarma's persistent concerns. Though continuity is a concept a modern reader might tend to resist partly because modern criticism has educated him in the self- sufficiency of the individual poem, literature cannot indeed be stripped of all context, if only because the language which enters it is wrought from the context of both history and experience. This is where Rama Sarma's study of the *oeuvre* is instructive.

The Heroic Argument offers a valuable exposition and criticism of the thematic content of Milton's major poems giving an account of Milton, man and thinker. In this exploration, Rama Sarma combines the tools of historical scholarship, interpretative analysis and comparative approach. This is where the Indianness of Rama Sarma's study distinctively shows forth culminating in *Milton and the Indian Epic Tradition* (being published) where comparisons with the *Ramayana* and the *Mahabharata* abound revealing common archetypal patterns, motifs and inscriptions of patterns of orality indicating the common ground between epic poets of the East and those of the West. For Rama Sarma, a typical pattern of delineation of the Miltonic themes is possible only through an understanding of the poet's mind and his milieu. For a discovery of the growth of the poet's mind and art, Rama Sarma relies on the letters and prose pamphlets of Milton which lead him to a study of the author's intention and how it is embodied in the poem giving it encyclopaedic quality and remarkable inclusiveness. The poetry of Milton cannot be considered in isolation from the vigorously expressed Miltonic thought which generated during his lifetime both light and heat making Johnson refer to Milton's "controversial merriment." The first chapter of *The Heroic Argument,* "Milton, the Man the Poet" illustrates this mode of approach and cites extensively from *The Reason of Church Government, A Second Defence* and such other sources to point in the direction of Milton's projected aims and his carving out of a poem which shows him to be an English poet, a classical poet, and a Christian poet all in one. Hence the resonance of *Paradise Lost* as an intertext and the significance of the statement what makes the text is the intertextual. An examination of the allusive framework of the poem leads Rama Sarma to conclude that *Paradise Lost* is a typical product of the seventeenth century, even with all its prophetic element and universality. Rama Sarma redeems Milton from the charge of defamilarizing the familiar for the sake of building up an impenetrable Chinese Wall by drawing upon the seventeenth century reader's familiarity with antiquity and contemporaneity. The astonishing simile where the moon as seen through the Tuscan artist's telescope presented no problems of visualization for the reader of his time who knew the Tuscan artist's suffering at the hands of the Inquisition. Rightly, Rama Sarma does not dispute the aesthetic distancing which enabled Milton to develop a hieratic, ritual stylization necessary for the poem. But his point is that the poem was not that intractable for Milton's age.

The "truth" of an epic was not a matter of literal veracity but of verisimilitude on the one hand and of symbolic truth on the other. Yet another sense in which poems could tell the truth was their fictions could incorporate a large measure of historical fact—a thing which mattered to

Milton who wouldn't have written an epic which was merely fiction. And in the incorporation of historical fact, the Renaissance characteristic of an allegorical mode is apparent. This concern for fact also justifies Milton's use of the Biblical theme and scriptural matter, as Rama Sarma aptly remarks.

Coming to the theological background of the poem *Paradise Lost,* Rama Sarma dwells on Milton's exploitation of the medieval and Elizabethan theological picture and his use of the doctrine of free will and the Chain of Being in the poem. A seventeenth century scholar, Rama Sarma is well-acquainted with studies by Ruth Leile Anderson, Lily B. Campbell, E.M.W. Tillyard and Theodore Spencer[2] in the first half of this century which have enriched our understanding chiefly of the Renaissance world view and concept of man as also Shakespeare's intellectual background. Man occupied a central and middle status in the created order because of his protean character of sharing certain qualities with the animals and plants *below* him and certain other attributes like reason and intellect with the angels *above* him. No one has described this unique status of man better than Pico Della Mirandola whose work, *On the Dignity of Man,* was regarded as a classic illustration of the Renaissance optimistic view of man. Pico's statement, typical of the earlier Christian humanist position, laid equal emphasis on man's frailty and also on his potentialities for greatness. Well acquainted with the Renaissance views of man and society as represented in a variety of configurations in Elizabethan literature, Rama Sarma offers studies of Heywood and Shakespeare as well, apart from Milton, in his *Heywood: A Prose Shakespeare* (Glasgow: Blackie, 1962) and *Harmony Restored: Studies in Shakespeare* (New Delhi: Classical, 1991) evaluating these dramatists in the light of certain Renaissance intellectual contexts and judging them as an Elizabethan world. Hamlet's famous apostrophe to man which sums up the ethos of the whole epoch as also several passages in the play *Hamlet* are interpreted in terms of the Elizabethan world picture for which Tillyard has provided the necessary stimulus. With Renaissance literature deeply entrenched in his mind, Rama Sarma points out how Book IV of *Paradise Lost* delineates a world created perfect, bringing to mind a picture of the legendary golden world invoked by Renaissance pastoral poets. But different from the atmosphere of the pastoral, Milton wants us to believe that his Paradise really existed.

While recreating in the mind of the reader the drama of the Fall, Milton employs, as Stanley Eugene Fish notes in *Surprised by Sin* (London: Macmillan, 1967), a centre of reference that is its reader whom his purpose is to educate not so much by teaching as by an "intangling." In reply to the anti-Miltonism of A.J.A. Waldock's *Paradise Lost and Its Critics* (Cambridge, 1947), Fish, drawing upon the insights of Joseph H. Summers, *The Muse's Method* (Harvard, 1962) argues how Milton anticipated the technique of the "guilty reader" and how the coherence and psychological plausibility of the poem are to be found in the relationship between the poem's effects and the mind of its readers. Rama Sarma on the other hand is concerned with Milton's epic voice which enables the poem's material and structure to fuse to present an estimate of it as a whole work.

Satan-centred criticism postulates that either Milton approved of Satan or inadvertently made him more attractive than he had intended. Helen Gardner compares Satan to the heroes of such Elizabethan "tragedies of damnation" as *Macbeth* or *The Changeling* where during a large part of the play the audience is compelled to feel for a character who deliberately embraces evil. The peculiar emotional power of *Paradise Lost* seems to depend to some extent on the ambivalence of Milton's presentation of Satan. This idea Rama Sarma succinctly develops in his discussion of Satan by an argument based on the epic concerns of Milton and his Renaissance humanist spirit:

> Why then should Milton adopt this complicated method of glorifying and disglorifying Satan? Partly because he wants to present conventional heroism, which when applied to Satan becomes mock- heroism . . . and partly because of his humanistic belief that there is a core of goodness even in things rotten. . . . Probably he saw in the rebellion of Satan only the divine purpose of God in allowing him freedom to pursue his vain but malicious ends. *The Heroic Argument,* p. 86

The last chapter of *The Heroic Argument,* 'Milton and the Orient,' like Rawlinson's essay in the *Journal of Royal Asiastic Society* of 1947 is a comprehensive examination of the Elizabethan vastness of Milton's interests and his employing his encyclopaedic learning, especially of the orient, in a variety of contexts in the poems *Paradise Lost* and *Paradise Regained.* Rama Sarma's article in *Milton Encyclopaedia* (1978) is an elaboration of the last chapter of *The Heroic Argument* and it appears under the title, *Milton and the East.* Behind the description of the coronation in Hell of Satan is the echo of the barbaric pearl and gold sprinkled on oriental monarchs and the despotic rule they symbolise. From a deciphering of these oriental references and the recognition of the exotic appeal they make, Rama Sarma moves forward in his later works to a recognition of the *muse's method,* be it in the east or in the west, where parallel concerns, common thematic foregroundings and ideational impulsions, similarities of structural patterns, *exempla* or *topoi,* and epic devices are found. Thus his entry into the realm of comparative literature is rightly marked by a study of all literature "from an international perspective, with a consciousness of the unity of all literary creation and experience."[3] It is an attempt to study an author or a genre as a whole, that is, as a part of man's universal creativity as it manifests itself in world literature. *Paradise Lost: A Study* (1951) and the article, "*Paradise Lost* and the *Mahabharata*: The Philosophic Background" published in *Triveni*, XXI, March 1950 are a germinal approach from this perspective. Examining the similarities between the *Mahabharata* and *Paradise Lost*, Rama Sarma says "The Indian epic in its thematic content, concept of heroism, ethical idealism and insistence on implicit faith in God has affinity with *Paradise Lost*."[4] He finds further that Adam exemplifies the spirit of the Karma Yogi as depicted in the *Gita*. Though not a persistent strain, there is an illuminating use to which Rama Sarma puts the Indian aesthetic terms like *Rasa* in order to comprehend, through the subtleties and Yeatsian contrariness through which Milton presents it, the dominant emotion evoked by a poem or the predominant feature of a character as for example when he says that *Paradise Lost* is governed by the *Santa Rasa* or that Adam represents *Dhirasanta*. In *Milton and the Prophetic Strain* he works out in some detail the similarities between the Hindu concept of Trinity and the Christian concept of Trinity. The final chapter of *Milton and the Prophetic Strain*, "Revelation as Epic Narrative," introduces parallels between the *Mahabharata* and Milton's achievement in *Paradise Lost*. Describing both as epics of revelation, Rama Sarma compares the passage in Book V where Raphael reveals divine truths to Adam with Lord Krishna's enlightenment of Arjuna. Striking the keynote of obedience, he says that at the deepest level these epics produced in such different cultures show what it is to be human. The book concludes that Milton's prophetic vision of a just world offers hope for humanity, however unattainable the hope may be. What we are dealing with is a fable of the human condition. Therein lies the relevance of Milton and the timeless quality of the poet-prophet's work and the message of *Gita*.

The classical epic provides the converse of the flashback, the vision of the future. The convention of providing prophetic accounts made it possible for Milton to present the fall of man in the context of the whole of human history, from the murder of Cain to the Last Judgment. The last two books of *Paradise Lost* consist of a prophetic vision which finally obliges Adam to acknowledge the wisdom of God's ways to man.

But the most persistent quality of Rama Sarma's Milton criticism is to be found in his exploration of the intricacies of Miltonic thought content and the forging of a unity of theme in the four major poems of Milton: *Comus, Paradise Lost, Samson Agonistes,* and *Paradise Regained*. In this he follows a mode of argument which takes note of and places in its proper perspective Hanfordian bio-criticism and the autobiographical fallacy which proves a hindrance to the dating of the play *Samson Agonistes*. Analysing *Samson* in terms of its thematic content and the world of tumult, agony and frustration it creates before ending on a note of "a calm of mind, all passion spent," Rama Sarma concludes that "in its questioning and acceptance of the justness in God's ways it [*Samson*] has affinities with *Paradise Lost*. So one is tempted to question the conventional date of composition of *Samson* for it is dissimilar with *Paradise Regained* in its temper, tone and texture."[6] Though typological interpretations show Samson as a prefiguration of Chris (See K.M. Krouse, *Milton's Samson and the Christian Tradition,* Princeton, 1949), it is interesting to note that another Indian Milton critic, Balachandra Rajan in his essay, "To which is Added *Samson Agonistes?*" in *The Prison and the Pinnacle* raises a rhetorical question relating to the fulfilling of the "larger integrity" that the two pieces *Samson* and *Paradise Regained* form by extending into each other relating themselves to the poems that precede them. Declaring that *Samson Agonistes* in its dexterous interfusion of Hellenism, Hebraism and Christian idealism is essentially a testament of Miltonic religious thought content, Rama Sarma concentrates in Chapter VII of *The Eagle and the Phoenix* on the theme of martyrdom as handled by Milton, Shaw and Eliot and shows how Milton prophetically dreams of the eternal justice of God while Shaw expresses his own belief in creative evolution and Life Force in *Saint Joan* and Eliot exemplifies the idea of a twentieth century audience that Christian martyrdom is always the design of God whereby the recognition, "In His Will lies our Peace" dawns on humanity. The chapter is an example of how Rama Sarma reveals his thorough knowledge of the dramatic form from Greek times to the twentieth century. In his treatment of *Samson,* Rama Sarma invites us to contemplate *Samson* as tragedy and as more than tragedy arousing a compelling recognition of what "th' unsearchable dispose/Of highest wisdom" brings about.

There are concurrently two strains of Milton criticism: one concerned with providing a complete reading of the poem and the other with emphasizing a single aspect of it or a single tradition in which the whole can be understood better. Rama Sarma in work after work offers us a splendid overview of the Miltonic theme and doctrine projecting fine cross-illuminations. In this respect his work ranks with some of the major critical studies of Milton's *oeuvre* such as Hanford, Parker, Daiches and Rajan among others have given us. Showing how a writer is a product of his times and not its prisoner, Rama Sarma's most characteristic writing places the world of the poet or the dramatist vividly before our eyes as does *Harmony Restored,* a work on Shakespeare's major tragedies and the last plays. In this work, the chapter "Shakespeare: The Soul of the Age" succinctly analyses Shakespeare's mind and art reminding us of a *locus classicus* like A.C. Bradley's as an eminent Miltonist has observed.

NOTES

1. Edward Le Comte, ed., John Milton: *Paradise Lost, Samson Agonistes, Lycidas* (Mentor Classic; New York: The New American Library, 1961), p. 234.

2. Ruth Leila Anderson, *Elizabethan Psychology and Shakespeare's Plays* (Iowa, rpt. 1964).
   Lily B. Campbell, *Shakespeare's Tragic Heroes: Slaves of Passion* (Cambridge, 1930).
   E.M.W. Tillyard, *The Elizabethan World Picture* (London, 1943).
   Theodore Spencer, *Shakespeare and the Nature of Man* (New York, 1942).
3. Rene Wellek, "Name and Nature of Comparative Literature," *Discriminations: Further Concepts and Criticism* (New Haven, 1970), p. 19.
4. *The Heroic Argument* (Madras: Macmillan, 1971), p. 164.
5. M.V. Rama Sarma, *The Eagle and the Phoenix: A Study of Samson Agonistes* (Madras: Macmillan, 1976), p. 2.

Rama Sarma on Heywood: A Study

N. RAMA DEVI

Thomas Heywood, writing plays by about 1556 as attested by Henslowe,[1] was a prolific writer of both dramatic and non-dramatic works, though only about 20 of his plays have survived. He was a versatile playwright, "a sort of prose Shakespeare," who attempted plays of all types, chronicle play, domestic drama, romantic drama, adventure comedy, comedy of low life, and dramatized mythology, apart from pageants and masques. A well-known Milton scholar, Rama Sarma, closely following on the publication of his *Paradise Lost: A Study* based on his doctoral dissertation at the University of Wales, brought out *Heywood: A Prose Shakespeare* in 1962. Drawing his bearings from a revival of interest in the minor Elizabethans ushered in, as Rama Sarma described it, by Charles Lamb and followed up by such leading critics as Una Ellis-Fermor, Clifford Leech, F.S. Boas and T.S. Eliot, Rama Sarma analyses the work of Heywood in terms of certain of his Shakespearean attributes (for Shakespeare the "soul of the age" offers the yardstick by which the work of any dramatist of the age is measured) and by means of an examination of the genre to which certain of the plays of Heywood belong and how a study of the genre offers cross-illuminations providing an insight not only into Heywood's plays but also into Shakespeare's. Rama Sarma further delves into the Homiletic tradition of sin, repentance and forgiveness and shows how this theme is worked out in a series of creative configurations in Heywood's plays.

M.C. Bradbrook, in her *Elizabethan Comedy,* describes Heywood, Dekker and Shakespeare as three "artisans of the theatre" who practised a 'popular art,' which they modified without destroying." (137) But while Dekker and Heywood merely accepted their "opportunity," Shakespeare transformed it. Rama Sarma rightly distinguishes that though Heywood bears comparison with Shakespeare in fecundity of imagination, popular appeal and rich humanity, it goes without saying that his work lacks the poetic genius, not to mention the breadth and intensity, of his great contemporary. Rama Sarma cities from the Prologues and Prefaces of Heywood, especially from the "Preface" to *The English Traveller* to point in the direction of the moralistic strain in Heywood's plays. This is important from the point of view of showing Heywood and Shakespeare in a comparative (contrastive as well) light. Rama Sarma quotes from a valuable source—the "Preface" to *The Rape of Lucrece*—wherein Heywood refers to the badly mangled and corrupted plays of his which, he says, "I have been as unable to know them as ashamed to challenge them."[2] This raises questions associated with textual scholarship of the kind R.W. Van Fossen takes up in his Revels plays edition of *A Woman Killed with Kindness* (London: Methuen, 1961). This is an area of scholarship where sometimes a whole issue is clouded by a hypothetical second edition. The critical debate on solving the textual problems remained elusive, with A. Brown's definitive edition of Heywood's plays expected around the 1960s. Rama Sarma touches upon the theme of family honour in Heywood's plays and thus guides his readers into the realm of domestic drama to which he gives an elaborate introduction followed by an illustration of the themes of individual plays such as *A Woman Killed with Kindness* (an acknowledged masterpiece which best exemplified this theme) and *The English Traveller, The Wise Woman of Hogsdon.* At the opposite end of *A Yorkshire Tragedy* where with a fierce intensity the central figure of the play, the husband, destroys his family in a wild fit of passion, there is *The Honest Whore* by Dekker anticipating the modern "domestic drama." This domestic drama, we may say with Allardyce Nicoll, creates for contemporaries a "Progressive theatre," a "kitchen-sink" kind of play.[3]

A Woman Killed with Kindness belongs to the group of plays which can be described as examples of realistic tragedy. Akin to *Arden of Feversham* and *A Warning for Fair Women,* the play does not simply exhibit a domestic murder but mingles a story of death with the presentation of a problem, enriching the treatment of the problem by a deliberate avoidance of violent, sensational incident. The romantic and courtly Italian stories borrowed from Painter have been domesticated and transformed into something inherently English by Heywood and he imbues the material with the spirit of contemporary country life. Domesticity pervades the play from Sir Charles' encomium of Anne in Scene i to Frankford's final speech of forgiveness. Rama Sarma's critical account of *A Woman Killed with Kindness* is based on an exploration of the play's relationship with earlier middle-class tragedies, out of which genre-wise the play is a natural outgrowth, and with the didactic tradition on which it relies. While the most useful book on the subject, H.H. Adams' *English Domestic or Homiletic Tragedy* (Columbia University Studies in English and Comparative Literature, No. 159, 1943), somewhat exaggerates the importance of the homiletic tradition at the expense of artistic considerations, Rama Sarma strikes a balance between the two and points attention to Heywood's 'Apology for Actors' and shows how like a man destined for the Church Heywood moralizes but stresses the domestic tragedy aspects in the presentation of which "he exhibits his intimate knowledge of and abundant sympathies for the middle class."[4] (In the more recent explorations of varied interconnections between the verbal and visual, especially in Shakespeare's theatre language, it has been recognised that Heywood's "Apology for Actors" exalts the visual appeal of drama and stresses the interaction of poesy and picture).

H.H. Adams defines domestic tragedy as "a tragedy of the common people, ordinarily set in the domestic scene, dealing with personal and family relationships rather than with the large affairs of state, presented in a realistic fashion, and ending in a tragic or otherwise serious manner."[5] Rama Sarma further rightly recognizes that this group of plays owes something in subject matter and in tone to the medieval morality plays in which, apart from an explicit didacticism, there is the plain citizen, like Everyman, who is an apt character suitable for serious drama.

But far more important from Rama Sarma's point of view is not to consider Heywood's drama in isolation but to see the entire Elizeabethan drama in a perspective, with Shakespeare providing the artistic backdrop against which the polarities of religious didacticism and Elizabethan psychology are clearly visualized. Placed side by side with the stark realism of Heywood is Shakespeare's artistic rendering of the theme of sin, repentance and regeneration in his last plays. Taking the cue from his illustrious teacher S.L. Bethell's interpretation of *The Winter's Tale*, Rama Sarma concentrates on the restoration—spiritual and actual—of Hermione and suggests thus: "The simple homiletic tradition of the morality play acquires for itself mysticism and symbolism in Shakespeare's tragi-comedies" (101) He thus offers cross-illuminations revealing how artistic considerations are subordinated to tendencies of moralizing in Heywood whereas in Shakespeare there is a consummate artistry which holds the mirror up to nature even while offering something "rich and strange." This is an idea best illustrated in the Chapter on 'Scenes of Recognition' where the canvas is rather broad and makes the author dwell at length on scenes of recognition in Shakespeare's *The Winter's Tale*, *Pericles* and *Cymbeline* and similar scenes in Heywood's *The Fair Maid of the West* and *The Captives*. While tracing these patterns of similarity, Rama Sarma nevertheless strikes a note of caution. He raises the question of who borrowed from whom, cites Ernest Schanzer's " Heywood's *Ages* and Shakespeare," published in *The Review of English Studies* in February 1960 and concludes thus:

> These parallelisms show that Heywood has some idea of *Pericles* when he is writing *The Captives*, or perhaps some scenes of *Pericles* may have been written by him. The brothel scenes and the incorruptible purity of the maidens smack of a Puritan bias, which Heywood has indicated in almost all his plays. Similarly Heywood's *Golden*

> *Age* and *Silver Age* are connected with *The Winter's Tale* and *The Tempest.*

An obstacle to our getting a clear view of Shakespeare's Romances is our uncertainty about *Pericles, Prince of Tyre* which has come down to us in a maimed text. Perhaps, as Philip Edwards conjectures, there once existed an entire Pericles-play of Shakespeare's invention. Again, perhaps with differing degrees of infidelity it was reconstructed in order to provide a text for a rival company.[6] Whatever the attempts at an archaeologist's inferring of the nature of *Pericles* from its ruins, Rama Sarma draws on one of the strongest themes in the play—the clash between virgin innocence and the worst of the slaves of Venus together with the reunion of father and daughter—for offering a comparison between Shakespeare's more mature handling of the theme of recognition and renewal and Heywood's treatment of it. He concludes thus:

> In all these scenes of recognition Heywood is nearer Shakespeare. As craftsmen they employ the same tricks of the trade. But one is a poet with a mystic vision and a rich imagination. Especially in the tragicomedies Shakespeare writes with a certain religious awakening and conviction. Therefore, the scenes of recognition vibrate with a rich, spiritual enlightenment. . . . Heywood's scenes have a gentle, persuasive force. They are not deeply religious, yet they too move us with their essential appeal to our human emotions. (134)

But more useful from the point of view of understanding the dramaturgy of Heywood is the chapter on *Othello* and *A Woman Killed with Kindness* in which Rama Sarma treats both these plays as belonging to the genre of domestic tragedy, though *Othello* is no doubt in the heroic tradition. It was Moody E. Prior who drew a contrast between *Othello* and *A Woman* by observing that Frankford's basic qualities remain in large part unthreatened by the action. While *Othello* is tragic, he says, *A Woman* is "sad and pathetic."[7] Added to this is T.S. Eliot's perceptive comment on a specific passage in Heywood and the generalization from that about "Heywood's versification is never on a high poetic level, but at its best is often on a high dramatic level."[8] Heywood's verse which fills its dramatic function effectively and his sense of dramatic structure redeems his plays from too ready submission to sentimentality, though the sentimental strain is occasionally evident. While he is aware of the Shakespearean expansiveness, Rama Sarma, like Moody Prior, takes cognizance of the "verisimilitude" of Heywood's diction to the extent that it prevails. However, his comments on *A Woman* in comparison with *Othello* have a scholarly, scintillating quality about them in the close parallels they draw and in the cautious negotiation of the respective terrains of the heroic tradition and the middle class tradition they present. Rymer's observation that *Othello* is a tragedy of the handkerchief and the moral he draws from it come in handy for Rama Sarma in this consideration.

In conclusion, in the judicious account of Heywood's drama which Rama Sarma offers, he expresses his agreement with a profound observation L.C. Knights has made: "In Heywood's general dramatic technique statement takes the place of evocation . . . in other words, Heywood's drama is sentimental rather than ethical."[9] Rama Sarma refers to the "enactment" of moral judgment in Heywood and maintains that Heywood's drama, in its emphasis on the ethical basis of life, tends to be sentimental. But nevertheless Heywood drives home the moral that "to err is human, but to forgive is divine." More than a mere study of Heywood and an examination of his work from a historical and interpretative perspective, "Heywood: A Prose Shakespeare" offers fruitful parallels between the works of Heywood and those of Shakespeare, Dekker, and Ford.

NOTES

1. W.W. Greg, ed., *Henslowe's Diary* (1904-8), I, 45.
2. W.W. Greg, *A Bibliography of the English Printed Drama to the Restoration*, III, 1207.
3. Allardyce Nicoll, *British Drama* (Rep. New Delhi: Doaba, 1973), p. 113.
4. M.V. Rama Sarma, *Heywood: A Prose Shakespeare* (Glasgow: Blackie, 1962), p. 47.
5. H.H. Adams, *English Domestic or Homiletic Tragedy*, 1943, 1-2.
6. Philip Edwards, "An Approach to the Problem of *Pericles*," *Shakespeare Survey*, V, 1952, pp. 25-49.
7. Moody E. Prior, *The Language of Tragedy* (New York: Columbia University Press, 1947), p. 96.
8. T.S. Eliot, *Selected Essays* (1932: London: Faber & Faber, 1972), p. 75.
9. L.C. Knights, *Drama and Society in the Age of Jonson* (London: Chatto & Windus, 1937), p. 249.

Rama Sarma: A Shakespearean

P. HANNAH PADMA

As we approach the end of the century, two facts seem to be very significant in literary theory and criticism: the geometrical progression of various theories of literature and the support they receive from the establishment. The later half of the century has seen the emergence of "alternative Shakespeares."[1] The moment we open any book on Shakespearean criticism, we confront a bewildering variety of Shakespeares: the Elizabethan, the Jacobean, the Renaissance Shakespeares; and the Romantic, the Symbolist, the Metaphysical, the Chicago, the New Critical, the Structuralist, the Post Structuralist, the Foucaultian, and the Feminist Shakespeares. It is not easy for a student of Shakespeare to place Rama Sarma's *Harmony Restored*[2] in this daunting catalogue of Shakespeares. The preceding schools of Shakespearean criticism have made Shakespeare inaccessible to those who think that it is delightful to read a Shakespearean play and it is a pleasure to see it enacted on the stage. Moreover, in the Anglo-American critical circles, theoretical ingenuity is slowly giving place to critical honesty in the sense of an intelligent and controlled response to the plays, as exemplified in the criticism of Dr. Johnson, Arnold, Edmund Wilson, Leavis, and Trilling. Given the present critical climate of opinion, it is very refreshing to turn to the pages of Rama Sarma's *Harmony Restored* for acquiring the sort of knowledge and critical intelligence essential to appreciate Shakespeare.

One gathers from the blurb of *Harmony Restored* that Rama Sarma taught Shakespeare for over three decades. A well known Milton scholar, he also specialized in the pre- and post-Shakespearean drama. The insights he does acquire have led to the writing of *Heywood: A Prose Shakespeare*. In *Heywood*[3] we have a scholarly discussion of the link between *A Woman Killed with Kindness* and *Othello*. In this way Rama Sarma's versatile scholarship and teaching experience have impelled him to write *Harmony Restored*. The insights he acquired as a teacher have percolated into his criticism. In this sense Rama Sarma's *Harmony Restored* has immense value for the students and scholars of Shakespeare. In the Preface to *Harmony Restored* he says, "Harmony is disrupted in the tragedies, but harmony is restored in the tragi-comedies" (vi). The later part of the statement is a familiar idea but the first part of the statement is significant because it provides a thematic continuity in the canon.

The individual chapters on tragedies and tragi-comedies offer an incisive analysis of the plays which are the fruits of long and rewarding teaching career. As an accomplished scholar of the Elizabethan drama, Rama Sarma accounts for the success of Shakespeare as a dramatist. Shakespeare's predecessors and his contemporaries provided him with enough creative material so that his powerful imagination could turn it into a magnificent dramatic discourse. The response of a critic to a given play may be assessed by the perspective he establishes in analysing it. Influenced by Shaw, Rama Sarma thinks that *Hamlet* is a play of ideas. He is also aware that Tillyard called *Hamlet* a problem play and discussed it as a problem in his book *Shakespeare's Problem Plays.*[4] But in a later chapter, "The Existential Predicament in Shakespeare's Tragedies" in *Harmony Restored,* he tries to place it in the category of an existential play. But as a sound humanist Sarma is not prepared to go the whole hog with the existential argument. He seems to remember Isabella's words in *Measure for Measure*:

> . . . man, proud man,
> Dress'd in a little brief authority,
> Most ignorant of what he's most assur'd,
> His glassy essence, like an angry ape,
> Plays such fantastic tricks before high heaven
> As makes the angels weep: who, with our spleens,
> Would all themselves laugh mortal. (II.2: 117-23)

Concluding his argument, Rama Sarma says,

> Existentialism as a philosophy has its own limitations. It is considered to be a doctrine impregnated with pessimism. Even though literary works in recent times have been existential in their bearing, yet existentialism has not received the acclaim and the acceptance of many writers. But we cannot reject existentialist doctrines as absurdities for 'they merely reveal the fact that life on the planet is on the point of becoming absurd.' This is one way of looking at life. Shakespeare's tragedies can profitably be studied from an existentialist point of view. Presumably this is another approach to Shakespeare criticism. (109)

His critique of *Othello, King Lear* and *Macbeth* is lucid and incisive. A redoubtable Heywood scholar that he is, Rama Sarma thinks of the corresponding domestic situations in *Othello* and *A Woman Killed with Kindness.* It would have been more useful if Rama Sarma had established a thematic link between the continental and the English drama of Shakespeare's time. The most significant essay in this volume appears to be his essay on *King Lear.* According to Rama Sarma *King Lear* "poses the most fundamental questions of humanity" (59) in its presentation of human suffering. His analysis of *Macbeth* is interesting and persuasive, in that Rama Sarma is able to establish that the play, full of sound and fury, ends on "a note of 'God's benison' that would make 'good of bad, and friends of foes'" (92).

Discussing Shakespeare's last plays, Rama Sarma dwells on the various dramatic devices that Shakespeare employed to restore harmony. He seems to credit the popular idea that Shakespeare's last plays were the result of the cumulative influence of Sydney, Spenser, and Beaumont and Fletcher. The central thesis of Rama Sarma's criticism of the last plays is lucidly summed up in the following passage:

> Despite all the strange machinery of myths and miracles that Shakespeare and Kalidasa use in these plays, there is a sense of fruition and harmony for each play ends on domestic peace and royalty. Even Prospero, the Superman, goes back to a worldly life abjuring magic. In the late romances, and in *Sakuntala* we find a world far off and remote from the world we live in, but it is a rewarding experience to enter that utopia where justice prevails and divine Providence establishes eternal harmony. These plays give us the impression that God is in his heaven and all is right with the world. (127)

The citation may not be to the satisfaction of ingenious theorists of Shakespearean drama. Making Shakespeare our contemporary, there are critics who notice in *The Tempest* themes of colonisation and decolonisation.[5] The critics, if we were to invoke the distinction made by E.D. Hirsh Jr., are talking not about the meaning of *The Tempest* but its significance. A great virtue of Rama Sarma's criticism is that he talks more about the meaning of the plays than their significance. As a sound scholar of the Elizabethan and Jacobean drama Rama Sarma scaffolds his Shakespearean criticism with the Elizabethan cultural milieu. Shakespeare's contemporaries seemed to have believed that in the visible universe there are certain priorities the violation of which would lead to a disaster. Shakespeare called this 'degree' and placed it in the speech of Ulysses in *Troilus and Cressida.*

> O when degree is shaked
> Which is the ladder of all high designs,
> The enterprise is sick. How could communities,
> Degrees in schools, and brotherhoods in cities,
> Peaceful commerce from dividable shores,
> The primogenitive and due of birth,
> Prerogative of age, crowns, sceptres, laurels
> But by degree, stand in authentic place?
>
> (I.3: 101-8)

The violation of 'degree' seems to operate in the dramatic framework of the great tragedies. In the last plays the degree is restored to its original place. Although this is a simple formula to explain the reversals and restorations in the plays, it is an unmistakable observation that ideas like these have made the plays understandable to Shakespeare's audience. By and large Rama Sarma's criticism drives home the point that modern and contemporary theories have used Shakespeare's texts to endorse theories but not to bring to the core the sweetness and light that the plays themselves offer. Rama Sarma, with his Arnoldian view of the function of literature and with his Johnsonian response to the plays themselves, has made the plays accessible to the student and the scholar alike.

NOTES

1. John Drakakis, ed., *Alternative Shakespeares* (New York: Methuen, 1985).
2. M.V.Rama Sarma, *Harmony Restored: Studies in Shakespeare* (New Delhi: Classical, 1991).
3. M.V.Rama Sarma, *Heywood: A Prose Shakespeare* (Bombay: Blackie & Son, 1962).
4. E.M.W.Tillyard, *Shakespeare's Problem Plays* (London: Chatto & Windus, 1965).
5. Francis Barker and Peter Hulme, "Nymphs and reapers heavily vanish: the discursive contexts of *The Tempest*," *Alternative Shakespeares*, pp. 191-205.

Bibliography

A. Primary Sources

(*i*) *Novels*

The Stream. Madras: Triveni, 1956.
The Farewell Party. 1971.
Look Homeward. New Delhi: Blackie, 1976.
The Bliss of Life. New Delhi: Chand, 1979.
Pastures New. Madras: Emerald, 1985.
Height of Noon. Guntur: Maruti, 1994.

(*ii*) *Plays*

Collected Plays. Ed. G.Nageswara Rao. Madras: Pearl, 1982.

(*a*) Before Going Abroad
1. *Youth and Crabbed Age*
2. *Like to Like*
3. *Marpessa*
4. *This Busy World*
5. *Ignorance and Idiocy*
6. *Sakuntala* (A Play in Three Acts)

(*b*) While in U.K. (1946-1949)
7. *Urvasi*
8. *Towards Marriage* (A Play in Three Acts)

(*c*) Between 1950 and 1980
9. *The Carnival* (A Play in Three Acts)
10. *Inspector Raghavan*
11. *The Mahatma*

(*iii*) *Books of Criticism*

"Paradise Lost": A Study. 1951, Reprinted 1969.
Heywood (A Prose Shakespeare). New Delhi: Blackie, 1962. Reprinted 1981.
The Heroic Argument (A Study of Milton's Heroic Poetry). Macmillan, 1971.
Tne Eagle and the Phoenix (A Study of *Samson Agonistes*). Macmillan, 1976.
Things Unattempted (A Study of Milton). Vikas, 1982.
Milton and the Prophetic Strain. Sterling, 1991.
Harmony Restored. (Studies in Shakespeare) Classical, 1982.
Milton and the Indian Epic Tradition. New Delhi: Prestige, 1995.

(*iv*) *Critical Editions*

Milton's Minor Poems. Madras: Macmillan, 1973.
Milton's *Samson Agonistes*. Madras: Macmillan, 1980
Heywood's *A Woman Killed with Kindness*. Madras: Macmillan, 1980.
Milton's *Paradise Lost*, Bk. IX. Madras: Macmillan, 1981.
Milton's *Paradise Lost*. Books I, II and IV. Madras: Emerald, 1986, 1987, 1991.

B. Secondary Sources

G. Nageswara Rao, "The Inescapable Odyssey of the Self: A Study of Professor Rama Sarma's Novels," *Studies in Arts and Sciences*.

———. "Evolution of Being: A Study of the Novels of Professor Rama Sarma." *The Journal of Indian Writing in English*, Vol. 6, No. 2. (1978).

———. "The Perennial Predicament" in *Studies in Indo Anglian Fiction*, ed. Madhusudan Prasad.

———. "The Bliss of Life: A Study," *Journal of English Studies*, Vol. 10, No. 2 (April 1979).

———. Review of *The Farewell Party*. *Journal of the Karnatak University: Humanities*, Vol. XVI (1972).

———. Review of *Look Homeward*. *Journal of the Karnatak University: Humanities*, Vol. XXI (1977).

Review of *Look Homeward* by V. Sachithanandan, *The Journal of Indian Writing in English* (Jan. 1977).

Review of *The Farewell Party* by G.B. Gupta, *The Journal of Indian Writing in English* (Jan. 1975).

Review of *Look Homeward*, by A.G.K. Murthy, *Triveni* (Oct.-Dec.1977).

"The Bliss that is in Surrender," a Review of *The Bliss of Life*, *The Mail*, June 16, 1979.

"Recapturing Vanished Life," a Review of *The Bliss of Life*, by Anniah Gowda, *The Literary Half-Yearly*, Vol. XX, No. 2 (July 1979).

The Heroic Argument: A Study of Milton's Heroic Poetry, Review by William B. Hunter, *Seventeenth Century News*, Vol. XXX, No. 1 (Spring 1972).

———. Review by Geoffrey Bullough, *English* (Spring 1972).

———. Review by John T. Shawcross, *Studies in English Literature*, Vol. XIII (Winter 1973), No. 1.

———. Review by Irene Samuel, *English Studies* (August 1972).

———. Review by S.P. Appasamy, *Triveni*, Vol. XLII (July-Sept. 1973), No. 2.

———. Review by G. Nageswara Rao, *The Karnatak University Journal: Humanities*, Vol. XV (1971).

The Eagle and the Phoenix. Review by Michael Lieb, *Milton Quarterly*, Vol. XI, No. 3 (1977).

N. Parvathi Devi, "Milton Criticism of Professor Rama Sarma," *The Laurel Bough*, ed. G. Nageswara Rao. Madras: Blackie, 1980, pp. 107-12.

H.G.S. Arulandram & S. Raman. "M.V.Rama Sarma's *Look Homeward:* The Novelist as Myth Maker." *The Laurel Bough*, pp. 203-10.

M.R. Ashok. "From Protest to Acceptance: A Study of the Plays of Rama Sarma," *The Laurel Bough*, pp. 211-18.

Syed Mukharam. "*Bliss of Life* and the Concept of Devotional Love," *The Laurel Bough*, pp. 219-26.

Index